Rachel Bowlby – Unexpected Items

The Feminist Library: Essays in Cultural Criticism
Series Editor(s): Jackie Jones, Alison Light, Gill Plain

Published
Alison Light – Inside History: From Popular Fiction to Life-Writing
Alison Light

Rachel Bowlby – Unexpected Items: Shopping, Parenthood, Changing Feminist Stories
Rachel Bowlby

Forthcoming
Cora Kaplan – Double Crossings: Feminism, Race, the Popular
Cora Kaplan

www.edinburghuniversitypress.com/series-the-feminist-library-essays-in-cultural-criticism

Rachel Bowlby – Unexpected Items
Shopping, Parenthood, Changing Feminist Stories

Rachel Bowlby

EDINBURGH
University Press

Edinburgh University Press is one of the leading university presses in the UK. We publish academic books and journals in our selected subject areas across the humanities and social sciences, combining cutting-edge scholarship with high editorial and production values to produce academic works of lasting importance. For more information visit our website: edinburghuniversitypress.com

© Rachel Bowlby 2024, 2025

Edinburgh University Press Ltd
13 Infirmary Street
Edinburgh EH1 1LT

First published in hardback by Edinburgh University Press 2024

Typeset in 10.5/13 Bembo by
IDSUK (DataConnection) Ltd

A CIP record for this book is available from the British Library

ISBN 978 1 3995 2840 5 (hardback)
ISBN 978 1 3995 2841 2 (paperback)
ISBN 978 1 3995 2842 9 (webready PDF)
ISBN 978 1 3995 2843 6 (epub)

The right of Rachel Bowlby to be identified as the author of this work has been asserted in accordance with the Copyright, Designs and Patents Act 1988, and the Copyright and Related Rights Regulations 2003 (SI No. 2498).

Contents

Series Editors' Preface vii
Acknowledgements ix
List of Abbreviations x

Introduction: Unexpected Items 1

Part I Parenthood

1. Generations 15
2. A Tale of Two Parents: Dickens's *Great Expectations* 31
3. Finding a Life: George Eliot's *Silas Marner* 45
4. How Not to Be Parented: Speech Creatures in *Pamela* and *Pride and Prejudice* 60

Part II Consumer Culture

5. Soft Sell: Marketing Rhetoric in Feminist Criticism 73
6. Make Up Your Mind: Scenes from the Psychology of Selling and Shopping 79
7. The Uses of Shopping: Richard Hoggart Goes to Woolworth's 102
8. Scenes of Shopping 120
9. Buying the Baby, Growing Your Own 131

Part III Feminist Directions

10. Fifty Fifty: Female Subjectivity and the Danaids	143
11. Domestication	168
12. 'We're Getting There': Woolf and Feminist Criticism	188
13. Untold Stories in *Mrs Dalloway*	203
14. 'I Had Barbara': Women's Ties and Wharton's 'Roman Fever'	224
Index	237

The Feminist Library: Classic Essays in Literary and Cultural Criticism

Series Editors' Preface

Libraries are a vital part of culture and community. They celebrate the written word, safeguard its history and make knowledge available to all. This series aims to be just such a library, building an archive of recent feminist scholarship and making it newly accessible in lasting print and digital form. The Feminist Library will publish incisive and thought-provoking essays by influential contemporary critics working across the intersections of gender, class, race and sexuality; it will illustrate feminism's complex encounters with history, popular culture and the canon; and it will offer to readers, new and old, exemplary instances of what it means to read and write as a feminist.

Each volume of essays will be selected and introduced by its author, permitting personal and critical reflection on the value of thinking as a feminist. The collections will range from challenging think-pieces to classic yet often out-of-reach articles to new work and new directions, reflecting the suppleness of feminist thought and its capacity to engage across radically different contexts and forms. In this sense, the volumes in this library are also handbooks or, perhaps, intellectual autobiographies. They dissolve the distinction between the academic and the activist, the personal and the political, to demonstrate what a life of feminist enquiry might look like and the diverse, protean forms it might take.

Feminism is, of necessity, always a work in progress. The ideas, questions and debates explored in the volumes of The Feminist Library will mean new things to a new generation of readers, and will be put to new purposes, but they will also act to remind us of our history.

The social, political and intellectual challenges of the recent past have not gone away, and earlier feminist interventions can enrich our engagement with those of the present. The Feminist Library brings into focus twentieth-century questions that the twenty-first century cannot afford to ignore; but it also has another purpose. Libraries do not just inform, they seduce, liberating the imagination and generating pleasure. To that end, The Feminist Library collects eloquent, incisive, provocative writing with the simple aim of enabling rich, rewarding reading.

Jackie Jones
Alison Light
Gill Plain

Acknowledgements

My warmest thanks to the three editors of the Feminist Library series – Jackie Jones, Alison Light and Gill Plain – both for inviting me to be part of it and then for all your invaluable suggestions and reflections along the way, as I put the collection together.

Somehow, Edinburgh manages to make the process of producing a book seem straightforward for the author at every stage—as if nothing is too much trouble. I would like to thank everyone in the team, especially Fiona Conn, Elizabeth Fraser and (once again) Jackie Jones. It has been such a pleasure to work with you.

Abbreviations

GW Sigmund Freud, *Gesammelte Werke* (1951–87; Frankfurt am Main: Fischer Taschenbuch Verlag, 1999), 18 vols.
SE *The Standard Edition of the Complete Psychological Works of Sigmund Freud*, trans. James Strachey, 24 vols (London: Hogarth Press, 1953–74).

Introduction

Unexpected Items

One summer in the middle of the 1980s, I couldn't stop reading Freud. I had a mission in mind, which was to find the place – if it existed – where Freud referred to the topic of femininity as being like a dark continent. That sounds odder now than it did at the time – or at least than it did in the corner of the university world where, by that time, I had found my place. I was working at the University of Sussex, well known as a coolbed of new kinds of cultural thinking; there was for instance an undergraduate course called Studies in Feminism, while feminist questions were at the heart of the Masters programme in Critical Theory. Endlessly argued over at that time was the issue of whether Freudian psychoanalysis, with its theory of the structural priority of masculinity, was inherently anti-feminist; or whether, on the contrary, its analysis of patriarchal structures was a prerequisite to dismantling them. Much of the impetus for the pro-psychoanalytic version of feminism – the version which said that you couldn't do feminism without knowing something about psychoanalysis – had come from recent French interpretations of Freud: by the controversial psychoanalyst Jacques Lacan, and by women analysts and philosophers who followed and also took issue with him and who came to be known elsewhere, collectively, as 'French feminists' (even though some weren't French, and some didn't think of themselves as feminists).

The primary texts in this development almost all came out within a very short period of time in the mid-1970s.[1] Some of these writings – especially those by Hélène Cixous and Luce Irigaray (the first Algerian, the second Belgian) had begun, by the 1980s, to be translated into English, and it was this, along with – in the UK – the ongoing production of the brightly coloured volumes of the Penguin Freud collection, that made it possible for university courses to engage directly with the theories that were up for debate. This was also a time when detailed rhetorical analysis was in favour, a practice akin to literary criticism and attracting many trained in that mode, though its exemplary models in French – in the work of Jacques Derrida and Michel Foucault – were formed in philosophy. In this context the close reading of Freud (even translated Freud) seemed as natural as the close reading of Shakespeare or Wordsworth. It also seemed self-evidently political, and vital for feminist thinking.

Towards the end of his life, Freud had written a number of texts that directly engaged with the question of women's psychology. Like a miniature canon, these few short essays (including one 'lecture', never delivered as such, entitled – in its English translation – 'Femininity') were fundamental to the later French and Anglophone discussions of Freud's views about the different development of women's subjectivity.[2] Again and again, the same suggestive analogies were repeated in references to these texts. Freud had likened new findings about female sexuality in his time to the then just happening archaeological discoveries about the Minoan–Mycenaean civilisation of ancient Greece. As a whole other world now found to lie before and beneath that of the 'golden age' of fifth-century BCE Athens, this was a 'new' old culture whose differences could shake up the way that the classical world was understood. That was how momentous the hitherto unimagined difference of women might be.

That comparison in Freud was easy enough to locate: it was there, quite simply and quite directly, in an essay of 1931 called 'Female Sexuality': 'Our insight into this early, pre-Oedipus phase in girls comes to us as a surprise, like the discovery, in another field, of the Minoan-Mycenaean civilization behind the civilization of Greece.'[3] But there was another Freudian analogy to which the new feminist-psychoanalytical writers in both French and English repeatedly referred, usually in the same summarising breath as their mention of the Minoan–Mycenaean civilisation. This second reference was to the 'dark continent' of femininity, with its connotations – unlike those of the ancient Greek analogy – at once more modern and more politically charged. The archaeological finds on Crete had caused scholarly stirs of curiosity and excitement; the late nineteenth-century imperialist 'scramble for Africa' was a live matter of European colonial power. By making this comparison, Freud was likening the study of female subjectivity to the European conquest of much of the African continent in the recent past.

But where *did* he say this? For all my reading of Freud I couldn't find it anywhere, and when I asked others they found, with some surprise, that they didn't know either. Then I came across a footnote in a book by the American critic Jane Gallop, admitting that she too had been at a loss to locate this famous passage. That was the clue or cue I needed, and so I set off, intrepid and hopeful, to seek out the missing words.

The search extended over many weeks and many Penguin volumes; I can't now recall how many of either, and as it went on I stopped caring anyway. When the dark continent did turn up, round the bend of one more as yet unventured page, I realised that I had stopped expecting it ever would. I couldn't believe my eyes. But there it was, clear as black on white. 'The sexual life of adult women', says Freud, 'is a "dark continent" for psychology.'[4] It was in the middle of a short book of 1926 called *The Question of Lay Analysis*, a mock-Socratic dialogue in which Freud stages a conversation with a sceptical interlocutor and sets out to persuade this personage to reconsider their view of psychoanalysis.

But there was more to come. When I looked up the original text, I found not some equivalent German phrase but instead the exact same thing. Which is to say that the dark continent, in English, was a dark continent, in English, within Freud's own text as well: 'ist doch auch das Geschlechtsleben des erwachsenen Weibes ein *dark continent* für die Psychologie.'[5] The inverted commas of the 'dark continent' in James Strachey's translation may be meant as a rendering of Freud's italics; but framing as it does an English formula in a sentence itself in English, it cannot convey the same strangeness as Freud's attribution which, in its German setting, starkly stands out and points directly to the dominant British part in the European colonisation of Africa.[6]

I had been looking for what I had heard of as Freud's dark continent, strangely lost – and what I found was exactly that, *exactly* that: in such a way as to complicate the recovery or discovery in any number of ways. Already, initially, that image for femininity had drawn together the general feminist question of sexual difference with the history of colonisation, in a gesture that then opened up the issue of the connections and divergences between the two, both theoretically and politically. With its approach as if to a primitive land awaiting both exploration and enlightenment, the famous metaphor deprives the investigation of neutrality and objectivity from the outset.[7]

And then, in addition, the dark continent discovered in its uniquely English form may also have an effect of a different kind. It is just a formula – just a sequence of letters; the looming grandiosity of the phrase then just dissipates into thin linguistic air. This doesn't imply that the powers of patriarchy or imperialism might be no more than a matter of words, but it indicates in plain printed sight that the emperor's power is a fragile construction.

What happens at the start of Toni Morrison's first novel, *The Bluest Eye*, is a comparable kind of visible verbal dissolution. In those first paragraphs we see before our eyes the smug sentences about Mother, Father, Dick and Jane in the children's reading primer collapse into meaninglessness. First the punctuation falls away and then the spaces between the words drop out. The unravelling is purely formal, messing up the connections that make the meanings, but it breaks up the sentence semblance of white perfection just like that.[8] It is not immutable; it falls apart.

Forty years on from that deferred encounter with Freud's dark continent, almost the same time has passed as the distance, then, from the first Freudian flourish of writing about femininity in the interwar years. In the 1980s, the 1920s and early 1930s, long before my time, were like ancient history, unimaginably long ago. But decades later, the1980s now seem to me not much further back than the year before last. That discrepancy must be the delusion of individual ageing time. And it does not prevent a recognition that much, in the meantime, has changed in the evolving world of what's no longer often called by that abstract and French-derived name of sexual difference.

Rereading a fragment of Freud, once again, may offer an indication of what has occurred. In the 'Femininity' lecture, Freud makes an almost casual remark, behind which lies a whole theory of the fundamental and formative significance of the sexual divide. 'When you meet a human being', he says, 'the first distinction you make is "male or female?" and you are accustomed to make the distinction with unhesitating certainty.'[9] This remark is preliminary to saying straight after that 'you', in that case, are mistaken to be so sure, since there is much that is uncertain, scientifically, in the difference of the sexes. But underlying the abstract frame is the experiential suggestion that there is something about that alternative of male and female, or masculine and feminine, which is unlike any other kind of human classification. When you meet a person, the *first* distinction you make is that one. You do make it; it's not just a given, and it comes, implicitly, before any number of other possible assessments, which Freud does not name but which would presumably, then as now, be to do with age or social class or race or ethnicity or size – for instance. The implication is that the 'male or female?' judgement occurs as if automatically: you barely notice you're making it. You need to get that straight first.

But the sentence also seemed to suggest that if sexual difference is obvious – it goes without saying, you don't even notice you're noticing – it is also, potentially, a source of disturbance. If hesitation enters the scene in place of that easy either/or call, then nothing is sure, everything is in doubt; again, the whole construction might fall apart. Ordinary language depends on the same priority, with pronouns that make the distinction, all the time, unavoidably. In order to take their place in someone else's sentences, a person does not get far (or used not to) without being gendered one way or the other, as him or her.

Against this fixity of designation, Freud's writings open out onto the contingency and fluidity of sexual identity, away from the strictly binary form in which it is set, as one or the other of two. Many strands of feminism have also done this, in different ways; in the domain of literature, the sheer variety and mutability of sex is almost a commonplace, from Ovid to *Orlando*. Until very recently that mobility was largely a theoretical proposition; not many people were living their lives beyond or elsewhere than the sex assigned them at birth. Today, though – and this is the change – the non-binary is more than a matter of critical recognition or transgressive enjoyment, with the increasing possibility, in some cultures, for real, lived identities outside the binary norm. So that now when you meet a person you may no longer immediately and automatically make the distinction 'male or female?', or expect to do so with unhesitating certainty; nor are you necessarily troubled when you can't. Which suggests that if change there is, ongoing or achieved, it is not only to be found and embodied in large identifiable acts of legislation and reform, essential as those are. It also happens – and this has been axiomatic for feminist argument too – in the least regarded movements and gestures of daily life – of each exchange of words or each time you meet a new person. The largest changes are also a matter of the smallest elements, moment by moment and word by word: revolution in the pronouns!

If the essays in this book have something in common it may be their searching for seemingly insignificant things that sometimes speak feminist volumes. The analysis of language, pronouns and all, is part of this. Close reading can be a mode of historical critique and it can be used for looking not only at literature and philosophy but also at forms of writing not valued in that way. Many different types of text are quoted and discussed in these pages, reflecting changing and continuing feminist interests over the past several decades, as I will try to explain.

First, the book's title, which is lifted from a minor frustration of modern shopping. It is that moment in the supermarket when the programmed voice of the self-scanner pipes up with its stalling admonition: 'Unexpected item in the bagging area!' This unanswerable utterance belongs with the latest phase of a long-term process of retail automation. It is quite different from the scenarios of earlier settings, when assistance was offered – if not imposed – at every stage of the choosing and buying process, and 'Just looking, thanks' was the customer's standard phrase for politely refusing it. With its sense of slow time and leisure, 'Just looking' suggests a quite different relationship to shopping than the practical operation at the checkout. For this type of shopping – typically in a larger store – the unexpected item is not a system-stopping problem but just the opposite, a surprise of the sort that the customer might vaguely be hoping for and the store will surely want them to find. The unexpected item is the very definition of novelty, the search and desire for which is the driving force of shopping and fashion which keeps the customer looking and buying, more and more.

The autobiographical way of starting off this capsule shopping history would be to say that my first book, published in 1985, was called *Just Looking*. It was mainly concerned with nineteenth-century novels about department stores – quintessentially, women's domain – and it was undertaken in the early years of what has since become an extensive academic field devoted to the history of consumer culture, largely ignored before. For a PhD student, as I was when I wrote it, there was a rare freedom in coming in near the start of what was not yet a developed area of specialisation. There was no established bibliography for the history of shopping or for women as consumers; instead, the field was wide open for digging out and freshly planting where no researcher might ever have gone before. In the process, I got to spend a year of afternoons in the attic archives of a Paris department store, the one that Zola had studied for his 1883 novel *Au Bonheur des Dames* [*The Ladies' Paradise*], and the one that had been the subject, also, of a recently published book that had set me on this consuming trail.

Michael Miller's study of the first decades of the Bon Marché department store had been the spark – initially via the chance reading of a review when it came out, a century after Zola's novel, in 1981.[10] Women and shops – of course! I had gone to Yale as a graduate student because I wanted to study French theory, including deconstruction and psychoanalysis, and to be able to do that there, at that time, was a wonderful change – beyond even the hopes I had had – for someone who had never been comfortable with the specialisation of the traditional English academic education. Comparative Literature – a subject that didn't really exist at that time in Britain – was associated in the US with all things French and philosophical, as against the more national and historical emphasis of single-language literature departments. There were two years of seminar courses mainly in that theoretical vein, and I was also able to take, for instance, a sociology module and another on African-American literature. When I saw that review of the Miller book, I was seeking a dissertation topic that would engage not just with literature and theory but also with cultural history and especially with women's history.

Department stores were based, at that nineteenth-century time, on the fast sale of affordable fashion in a beautiful environment open to all. You didn't have to make a purchase; you could simply enjoy the spectacle and the atmosphere ('just looking') – so that going shopping, with no particular object in mind, became a new way of spending leisurely time. Thus these stores were aimed at the conscious creation of a new kind of shopping femininity, made for the madness of endless buying. And they came into being at precisely the same historical time as Freud was beginning his work. What does a woman want? It would be Freud's famous question, and it was also, from then on, a primary question for advertising and marketing in all their persuasive forms and settings.

There were other sides to shopping – and to woman, and to psychology – than the glamorous, novelistic worlds of the first palatial department stores. With supermarkets, the great retailing invention of the twentieth century, shopping is more basically 'doing the shopping' rather than 'going shopping': a matter of regular household provisions rather than a special outing and a change of scene. A later book, *Carried Away*, explored the then uncharted twentieth-century history of supermarkets and self-service: uncharted, I think, because back in that time of their out-of-town ubiquity,[11] no one really imagined them having a history at all. It's not such intrinsically attractive territory. The coming of online delivery, along with the return of small high street branches of national supermarket chains, was to change the view, putting the megastores of the late twentieth century firmly into the past.[12]

The middle section of *Unexpected Items* has some of this work on consumer culture – both in relation to retail history, and as its marketing languages have infiltrated into broader cultural discourses, including feminism. On the ethics of consumption today there is much to be gleaned, for instance, from a comparison with William Cobbett's rants against shops two hundred years ago; and more, in another mode, and at the same time, from Jane Austen's gentle appreciation of small-town shopping culture (Chapters 9 and 8). Richard Hoggart, the subject of Chapter 7, is a rare case of a twentieth-century cultural critic who wrote, as a man, about shops and shopping. The other two chapters in this section uncover some permutations of marketing modes of thinking: in twentieth-century selling guidelines that draw on long-standing literary scenarios (Chapter 6) and, conversely, in discourses like some versions of feminist theory, which take up the language of marketing as if it were natural (Chapter 5).

Arguments about consumer subjectivity have often dwelt on different types of choice: the manipulated or the rational, the forced and the free, the feminine and the neutral. At the height of the later twentieth-century rise and critique of a 'mass' or 'consumer' society, that passive and powerless side was systematically linked to women's exploitation and sometimes to a supposedly natural female stupidity finding its housewifely destiny in the zombie aisles of the supermarket. The protest against it took the form of asserting the rights of a rational consumer, a neutral him or her who, rather than being seduced by the machinations of marketing, was capable of making a buying choice based on solid information. This was the sensible consumer of *Which?* magazine, which goes back to 1957, two years after the first TV ads in Britain, taken as signs or portents of a newly rampant commercialism. This rationally choosing consumer is also a precursor of the 1980s citizen-consumer and (in general) of the overtly male consumer who came into his own in that same later period, just in time for 'the consumer' to acquire a newly neutral status – neither necessarily female nor necessarily dumb. Today, when men really do shop more than they did, that positive, or at least not negative image of the calculating consumer who knows what they want and gets the best deal – Go Compare! – is the gender-neutral norm, at least in the flattering representations of marketing. There is no need to mourn the passing of the crude either/or mid-century phase of manipulation-speak, with 'the housewife' always on the blunt end of it; but for my money the professional language of present-day marketing comms can't hold a candle, not even an iPhone torch, to the well-wrought prose of the first generation of advertising psychologists in the early twentieth century – some of whom make an appearance in Chapter 6.

An equally contested notion of choice, but in a different register entirely, has been at the forefront of feminist engagements with questions of parenthood – the topic of the opening section of the book. The very word, when linked to feminism, immediately conjures up arguments about abortion, as in 'a woman's right to choose'. From this point of view the legalisation of abortion takes its place alongside other quite different twentieth-century innovations, from contraception to IVF, that have made physical maternity more an active decision than simply a likely marital event (or an unlucky event outside marriage). But questions of parental choice – to stop or prevent or seek a pregnancy – potentially carry an emotional charge of another order from the relative banality of buying. It is inherently difficult to find a usable language for thinking about parental or pre-parental wants and fears and longings: all the many ways and degrees of expecting or not expecting a baby. In these contexts, the language of rational choice has limitations that it may be necessary, for strategic reasons, to ignore; but this has also led to strange asymmetrical polarisations in which a right 'to choose' is improbably set against a right to life.

A woman's choice in the field of the slogan is implicitly negative ('termination'), refusing an otherwise ongoing bodily process; a natural course of events is stopped midway. For no area of human experience is more closely tied, whether temporally or existentially, to a predictable outcome: all pregnancies end. To be 'expecting', without more linguistic ado, is to be pregnant; the object or item expected can somehow be left unsaid. As with the fraught field of 'choice', there is more going on than the words can say or the ultrasound can show (or the persons concerned may know themselves). But the bland modern language of 'planned' parenthood promotes the sense of a simple continuity between a rational project and an expected result. Like an item ordered online, a baby goes through quality controls, with scans and measurements, prior to delivery – to the point that the almost always unexpected experience of becoming a parent can itself come to look like one of the predictable features of the event: unprecedented every time.

My interest in feminist takes on parenthood – or motherhood – developed in part from a fascination with stories of the new reproductive technologies (as they used to be called): *in vitro* fertilisation most of all, starting with the first IVF baby, Louise Brown, born (in Oldham) to the accompaniment of massive media hype, in 1978. This was just over a decade after the contraceptive pill had become available on free prescription to unmarried (as well as married) women. Despite their diametrical contrast in other respects – to prevent or to create a pregnancy – these two new medical technologies both consolidated a separation of reproduction from sexuality. Contraception is sex without the possibility of pregnancy; IVF is pregnancy without sex having taken place. From this point on, the 'choice' of pregnancy, to have or not have, became an active one in entirely new ways; the very facts of life are changed.

Beginning with 'Generations' (Chapter 1), the essays in this section consider the changing modern conditions and terms of parenthood, women's and men's, 'biological' and adoptive, dual and individual – and more. Some of the complex situations invoked in literary texts from Victorian novels to Sophocles' *Oedipus* now speak to the pro-parental preoccupations of today in which the active wish to become a parent may be a valid and achievable personal ambition unyoked from the historically expected setting of (heterosexual) marriage. Dickens's *Great Expectations* (Chapter 2) features two single people determined to have children on and of their own; while George Eliot's *Silas Marner* (Chapter 3) portrays the happy difference made to a lone person's life through becoming an adoptive parent almost by chance. Among other things, such novels suggest how family forms have in practice rarely conformed to the small and stable nuclear norm that is taken as the measure of late twentieth-century disintegration. Earlier times included all the complexities of step-parents and step- and half-siblings – with subsequent marriages the likely reason, as today. The difference is that the cause was not divorce but death, as widowed parents found new spouses.

Parental stories are rarely the obvious focus of literary narratives. In *Great Expectations*, they are revealed – if you look – as the driving expectations (of Magwitch and Miss Havisham), tucked away behind the apparently primary story of Pip and his childhood terrors and grand hopes. In other novels, they may be found in the wings of a romantic love story that is centre stage. Another kind of historical continuity appears in two famous novels not known for their parental focus: Samuel Richardson's *Pamela* and Austen's *Pride and Prejudice* (Chapter 4); in both, abject (but successful) suitors – ultimately, Mr Right – berate their own self-centred behaviour up to the time of their recent reform under the influence of their wonderful future wives. And both men, drawing on a thoroughly modern version of child psychology, attribute the character they now reject to the fact that they were spoiled in childhood: bad parenting made the (bad) man they used to be.

The book's third section, 'Feminist Directions', concentrates on questions of narrative: what kinds of past and future story are blocked or enabled in different kinds of feminist argument or demand? With the theme of domestication (Chapter 11), I was interested in some common deployments of this curious word. A concept with clear material connections to women's lives and history is taken up as if as a neutral term in theoretical arguments, including feminist ones, to indicate the simplification or dumbing down of an initial originality. That gesture – as well as creating an over-simple narrative sequence of its own – ignores the complex history and meanings of the word as well as its obvious relevance for feminism. Domesticity is the classic situation and space that the woman is meant, in the feminist story of liberation, to leave.

Stars of this section, the mythical female figures of the Danaids (Chapter 10) stand out as a spectacular case of female suppression; if you haven't heard of them, that proves the point. The Danaids, a family set of fifty (yes, *fifty*) sisters, are at the centre of a tragedy by Aeschylus, *The Suppliant Women*, which tells the story of their protest against the marriages – to fifty brothers, of course! – that are being forced upon them. Not only that, but their punishment for the upshot of that protest – they murder their bridegrooms on the wedding night – is to perform, eternally, the quintessential act of domestic drudgery: forever refilling containers that have holes in them. For present-day feminist purposes, the Danaids' fate epitomises the downgrading of women's work and women's grievances as well. As if taking place behind closed doors, their useless labour is unregarded; whereas Sisyphus, that better known underworld inmate, with his equally fruitless endeavour, is regarded as almost heroic as he endlessly pushes his boulder up to the not quite top of the hill. Stretching it beyond the limit, Sisyphus even gets to replace the Danaids at one point in the English translation of Freud – who never even mentioned him.

Over the long time that I was finding out about them, I grew attached to my Danaids; it was as if they had become the key to all feminist mythologies. Of the many features that made them appear as emblematic, it was the repeated forgetting of them over thousands of years that was most striking of all, as if each time they came back into view in one text or another, they were doomed to vanish again. I felt that I wanted to rescue them, bring them out in all their forgotten manifestations. And they were not the only ones. With the little remarked character of Milly Brush in Virginia Woolf's *Mrs Dalloway*, there was a similar work of retrieval, though on an infinitely reduced scale: unlike the Danaids, Miss Brush is a recently made character, and one with just a sentence or two to her name. 'Untold Stories' (Chapter 13) looks in detail – what little detail there is – at this most minor of minor characters, whose very elision may suggest what occurs in real-life narrative ways with a person (assumed to be) of no importance.

Chapter 12, '"We're Getting There"', considers another of Woolf's sidelined characters. She is an old lady sitting in the corner of a train carriage who was invented by Woolf in the 1920s to illustrate the predicament of every misrepresented woman in mainstream novels of the time. Woolf wants to do right by her, to rescue her from the distorting attentions of the men. From the later reading perspective of the 1980s, this then leads to a new possibility that Woolf, by then in effect the queen of feminist literary studies, has herself been cast in a comparable role: constantly having her identity challenged and corrected in line with the moods and movements of changing feminist times.

The final chapter, on Edith Wharton's 1930s short story 'Roman Fever' (Chapter 14), takes up directly this capacity for meanings to change, in the light of new questions and new frames of historical or personal reference. That is what happens within its narrative, as two middle-aged women, both widowed and waiting for daughters, go back over a distant episode of their shared past, only to find that they have both got it radically wrong. It is also what may happen when any story is reread or heard again at a new cultural time or for a different, later reader. In this case, what comes out, in a present-day rereading, amounts to an age-old tragedy of female feuding – and a contest of feminist interpretations.

Any story sets up a temporal dimension in relation to which its events are said to unfold. Different types of story and different circumstances of narration produce their own expectations for the sort of event that will seem plausible or normal. The kind that does not seem so – that doesn't fit the established categories – might be one indication of a genuine change in the order of things, their relative weight and their likely sequence. One indication, that is, of a really unexpected item. Looking back and looking forward, that is perhaps what all the new things of feminism will have been.

NOTES

1. Lacan's year-long lecture series of the year 1972–3 was published in 1975 under the title *Encore*. Among the books by women were Hélène Cixous and Catherine Clément, *La jeune née* [The Newly Born Woman] (1975); Luce Irigaray, *Speculum: de l'autre femme* [Speculum: Of the Other Woman] (1974); Annie Leclerc, *Parole de femme* [Woman's Word] (1974); and Michèle Montrelay, *L'ombre et le nom: sur la féminité* (The Shadow and the Name: On Femininity] 1977). *New French Feminisms*, edited by Elaine Marks and Isabelle de Courtivron, a selection of short translated extracts from these and many other texts, was published in the US in 1981.

2. I say 'feminine' subjectivity, but the gendering adjectives do not smoothly align between French and German and English, which led and leads to problems of translation. The English 'female' sounds biological, more appropriate for labs than persons; while 'feminine' and 'femininity' sound cultural in an almost decorous way. Attempts to get round this difficulty, such as the long-winded and little-used Anglo-Saxon word 'womanliness', didn't work well either, if only because of the rarity of such words and the equally obstructive cultural baggage they carry.
3. Freud, 'Female Sexuality' (1931), SE XXI, 226.
4. Freud, *The Question of Lay Analysis* (1926), SE XX, 212; in the Penguin Freud collection, where I found the reference at last, this text is in volume 15, *Historical and Expository Works*, which had just been published, in 1986.
5. Freud, GW XIV, 241. The Standard Edition has a translator's footnote in square brackets to point out that the words are 'In English in the original'; this information is omitted from the Penguin.
6. The woman turns out a bit different too, for what that's worth: modified in translation from the grown-up female – literally – of the original text to the simplified 'women' in English (with the reasonable avoidance, on Strachey's part, of that less human and more scientific suggestion of the word 'female' in English). Different languages have different ways of parsing their people; even for so basic a division as this, there is no direct mapping of one onto the other. The differences are cultural, not natural.
7. By the time of Ranjana Khanna's *Dark Continents: Psychoanalysis and Colonialism* (Durham: Duke University Press, 2003) the path to the textual location of the phrase *The Question of Lay Analysis* is well trodden, its earlier obscurity unmentioned.
8. See Toni Morrison, *The Bluest Eye* (1970; London: Granada, 1983), 7–8.
9. Freud, 'Femininity' (1933), SE XXII, 113.
10. See Michael B. Miller, *The Bon Marché: Bourgeois Culture and the Department Store, 1860–1920* (London: Allen & Unwin, 1981).
11. Living in rural East Sussex, I worked out then that there were no fewer than twelve 'superstores' that were each about half an hour's drive away, like points on the circumference of a circle. Thus the same spot was both remote and (literally, equally) central.
12. See Rachel Bowlby, *Carried Away: The Invention of Modern Shopping* (London: Faber & Faber, 2000), and *Back to the Shops: The High Street in History and the Future* (Oxford: Oxford University Press, 2022).

PART I
PARENTHOOD

1
Generations*

THE LAST GENERATION

It was when I was asked to present a paper for a conference panel on 'Feminism, sexuality and gender' that something about generations and changing stories started to intrigue me.[1] This, as it happened, was a psychoanalytic conference in 2006, marking the 150th anniversary of the birth of Freud. But it struck me that the rubric could have been exactly the same for a conference twenty or twenty-five years before that – a generation ago, let's say – in a number of different fields, from literature to film studies to sociology. Fifty years before, on the other hand, it would have made no sense. Feminism, sexuality and gender in the 1950s? I don't think so. It is unlikely that any of these words would have been up for discussion then, unless possibly sexuality in some specialised contexts – such as psychoanalysis. Gender did not even exist; it was a purely grammatical term, which had yet to be extended to suggest the socially sexed being of every human him and her.

By the 1980s, though, gender and sexuality had become common terms of academic and political argument – as had feminism, which had a long, intermittent history of its own. There was some suspicion of 'gender' as falsely equalising and neutralising, especially in comparison with the older term 'sex' – as in 'Sex: male or female?'. Twenty or twenty-five years before you might also, or instead, have had the more exotic and psychoanalytical-sounding term 'sexual difference' in place of the 'gender and sexuality' combination.[2] 'Sexual difference' does have the advantage that it can or should keep open questions that that odd couple of gender and sexuality tends to treat as settled, as if

---

* First published in *Textual Practice* 21:1 (March 2007).

gender's social issues of masculine and feminine are in a category that can be clearly separated from another, more bodily category of sexuality.

But even if the type of conference and the panel title could have been identical in say the late 1970s or early 1980s, the issues those words addressed, I think, would have been very different from those that interest us now. A generation ago feminism was a strong force politically, and especially within universities, where courses in women's studies were being set up in all sorts of disciplines within the humanities; in many ways, feminism appeared as *the* interdisciplinary subject, and the history and theory of women and womanhood – always 'femininity' in the French-inspired theoretical language – was increasingly visible and prominent as a question across every field. Psychoanalysis had a crucial cross-disciplinary place of its own in these initiatives and debates, because of its special relationship with feminism – frequently if not usually an antagonistic one.

This theoretical focus on women did not mean that feminism was indifferent to other categories or commitments: class and, to a lesser extent, race, were also, at times, brought into the frame.[3] As in previous moments of women's history, 1960s feminism had partly developed out of an existing radical political movement which, to begin with, took no account of sex (sex that was not yet gender). Psychoanalysis was particularly useful here because it offered a theory of the structural primacy of sexual difference as preceding any and every other kind of difference. But the characteristic form taken by political demands, both those that were and those that were not influenced by psychoanalysis, was a refusal of everything that tied women to the place allotted to them by an overarching patriarchal (or 'phallocentric') order. This included an idea of sexual freedom that had much to do with the availability of contraception. The emphasis was on the right for women *not* to have children – on pregnancy and motherhood as burdens, if not the key to all female oppression. This in turn implied the longer-standing feminist claim to the right to a life in some other sphere than the family. Motherhood, at this time, was really not much of an issue in feminist debate – at least the debates I remember, from my neck of the feminist forests – other than negatively, as what not to do or to be. Theoretically, it was either the reproduction of patriarchy (just as, in Marxist theory, it had been the reproduction of the proletariat for capitalism);[4] or else, in Freudian terms, it was a compensation for not being a man (and what kind of a 'choice' was that?).[5]

THE PRESENT

So gender, sexuality and feminism were all conceptually alive and argued over, in relation to one another, twenty-five years ago. But if the *terms* of debate appear to have mutated very little in the past generation, then what they talk about, the personal or collective issues that they evoke, or might evoke, have altered out of almost all recognition, and far more than they changed over the previous quarter-century. The social and also the biological conditions for thinking about sexual identities have undergone radical changes in just a single generation – probably far more so than across the previous two or three, back to Freud's own time. To say 'a single generation' in this context is ambiguous, of course, since the length of a generation is one of those seemingly semi-natural categories that is actually subject to huge variations in history and culture – and even from one generation to the next, as we might question-beggingly say. While differences in generational length are necessarily constrained by the limits of biology and mortality, they also involve a combination of both personal and social factors.[6] Even in modern societies in which, to an increasing extent, having a child is a choosable option, not a social and familial expectation, the currently typical ages for having children are never a matter of indifference to women's decisions (or couples' decisions) about when to seek to have a child. But that decision or choice is also, at another level, a personal one, just as the arrival or not of the child that is 'planned' or wished for is also a matter, at least in part, of biological (and sometimes technological) chance.

'Generations' have themselves changed quite a lot since say thirty years ago, with a significant rise in the average age of first maternity, and this is not unrelated to many other changes in Western family forms and norms and in reproductive possibilities and desires. For the sake of description, I'll separate these changes into the social and the biological, but the overlaps and mutual influences between them will be obvious.

First, then, social changes. The kinds of parenting regarded as possible or ordinary have gone forth and multiplied, to the point that the previously normative and usual unit of a married heterosexual couple, both first-time partnered, who raise two or three children to adulthood may now seem not just not assumed but not even particularly common. Parents may be single by choice, or gay, or cohabiting but not married. The stigma of illegitimacy has all but gone, with the term 'single parent' – a man or a woman, and often post-married – bearing almost no ideological relation to the now obsolete and culturally meaningless 'unmarried mother'. And where previously the new cultural focus was on the right not to have babies, it is now, and not only for women, much more on the right and the positive wish to be a parent. The question of where that wish might come from, or how it might differ between women, or between men and women, is rarely mentioned in any kind of discourse: where before it might have been seen by many as a normative ideological imposition on women, now it is almost always presented as a natural desire, sometimes bordering on a right, and not only for women. More broadly, in place of the old sexual division of labour – men as breadwinners, women as homemakers – the assumption has been shifting towards regarding all men and women as both workers and parents, potentially, whose needs in performing both of these roles should be met as far as possible with the help of various kinds of enabling legislation, from longer maternity (and paternity) leave to flexible work-time.[7] All these developments are related to another equally prominent social change, which is the dramatic rise in serial families (when a parent starts a new family with a subsequent partner) and, concomitantly, in the break-up of parents' relationships. No permanence in the parental couple is to be assumed – as it was before, when marriage was the parenting norm, and divorce was unusual.

On the biological side, the changes are equally striking. Alongside the proliferation of new family forms are the new reproductive technologies. There could be no more spectacular illustration of the difference of emphasis from a few decades ago, when the technological and medical news was all about reliable birth control, about how you didn't have to have children, as opposed to now, when it is about how you might be helped to do so. In general, the new reproductive technologies have the effect of separating sex from reproduction, just as contraception did in a different way: in IVF, as with artificial insemination, there is no two-body sexual act prior to conception. Conception outside the female body also undermines one essential difference between the two sexes as parents, bringing the contribution of each down to a neutrally named 'gamete'.

In other ways too, that difference between mothers and fathers is seen to diminish. Previously, it rested upon a fundamental dissymmetry, mentioned by Freud in his 'Family Romances' paper and elsewhere, whereby the identity of the father is always open to doubt – *pater semper incertus est*, in the Latin legal tag, which Freud quotes – whereas the mother visibly and palpably isn't 'uncertain' in this way: from her the baby is seen to be born.[8] Now, DNA testing has made it possible for the first time in human history to know a biological father with scientifically proven certainty. Yet at the same time, biological motherhood has taken on an equally unprecedented degree of potential doubtfulness. A child now may have two 'biological' mothers, the one who provides the egg and the one who is pregnant and gives birth. This is true of some cases of surrogacy (where the future mother supplies the egg for a child gestated in another woman's womb) and in all cases of egg donation.

In a recent case that was front-paged in the *Daily Mail* in November 2005, a baby girl was born to a woman in her fifties who was thereby both her (surrogate) mother and her (biological) grandmother. She had been implanted with an embryo produced from the gametes of her son-in-law and her adult daughter (who was unable, because of a medical condition, to sustain a pregnancy herself), and the baby had been given the (middle) name Trinity. Intra-familial scenarios of this kind, blurring identities either within or between generations and sometimes involving quasi-incestuous combinations, are not uncommon in surrogacy arrangements or egg or sperm donation. The oddities of the situation tend to be unspoken even though the printing of the story in the first place suggests otherwise.[9] For such stories seem to verge on the fantastic, as if coming from the realm of myth, monstrosity or science fiction – which is why they feature in the *Daily Mail*.[10] 'Still' seem, I was going to say – they probably won't seem sensational for long. We should remember that IVF, at its inception in the late 1970s, was regarded in just the same way: the extraordinary sci-fi case of the 'test-tube baby'. But in the space of, yes, a generation, IVF has come to be seen as a routine medical procedure.

Such rapid transformations in the norms and possibilities of chosen reproduction may take us back to the strangeness of all and any process of conception and birth – a tale of secret seedings and metamorphoses whose astonishing improbability fades away in the light of grown-up and responsible familiarity with 'the facts of life'. The mutability, at present, of those supposedly given conditions or 'facts' of reproduction also reveals the contingency in a part of the old reproductive story so well engrained as rarely to be spelled out: that a child is assumed to be the child of two parents and two only, one of each of two sexes. Here technological invention is amplifying and reinforcing the changes that are going on in the social forms of parenting. Now, biologically as well as socially, it is possible to have two parents of the same sex; socially, it is also common to have three or more active parents – when the first parental couple has split up and one or both of them has a new partner. In 1897 Henry James's character Maisie, the child of divorced and remarried parents, was 'vaguely puzzled to suppose herself now with two fathers at once. Her researches had hitherto indicated that to incur a second parent of the same sex you had usually to lose the first.'[11] Today, it is probable that she would not be puzzled at all.

The multiplication of parents and family forms is inseparable from other changes, of incalculable significance: the loosening of social constraints on acceptable forms of sexual relationship, and a lessening of the social divisions between the sexes such that women, who may well positively choose to have children, are no longer seen as primarily meant for a maternal and domestic role (so that that's no longer the argument that feminism needs to be having). Looking positively at these changes, it might seem that now, it is possible to live out and choose identities and behaviours that the first Freudian patients could only dream of. At one level, that's true. At another, of course, there's no evidence to suggest that the limits and conflicts in people's lives, in their identities as parents or offspring or lovers or anything else, have diminished – or that the surrounding ideologies of sexual and family identities are progressive in some absolute sense.

Consider this recent statement on the part of a well-meaning fertility consultant, speaking in relation to the legal change that from 2005 deprives sperm donors in Britain of the right to anonymity; this has led to a dramatic fall in the number of volunteers. He is concerned that the facility should be available, because of the cases when women have no male partner; if necessary, women will have to turn to the internet, which bypasses the constraints on anonymity. 'Using these services', he said, 'has got to be a step better than asking some half-drunk man to have unprotected sex, which is presumably what happens otherwise'.[12] Poor women! In order to have a baby, they might actually have to have sex – caricatured here in its most binge-unappealing form of the 'half-drunk' pick-up. (Why *half*-drunk, by the way? Perhaps this is no casually vulgarising adjective, but rather a precisely measured calculation on the part of the unfortunate maiden, because fully drunk he would be unable to deliver, and without a glass or two he might be unwilling to.) And poor men too! – now to find themselves pursued by women who are literally only interested in them for one thing.

The ideological shifts and continuities are fascinating here. First, the attitude on the consultant's part is one of the chivalrous protection of girls and ladies that would formerly have been offered to those in danger from the unwelcome and pregnancy-risking onslaughts of crude male lusts. Male and female sexuality are still what they always were, and why should women have to resort to bodily involvement with a live and present man, rather than one who can arrive hygienically in a sober brown envelope? Second – and this is the crucial change, to which the old idea of protecting the lady has been readjusted – the woman without a partner, whether straight or gay, is deemed not just not unsuitable for motherhood, but having a positive right to choose and achieve it.

A HUNDRED YEARS AGO

Freud's 'nuclear' complex, concentrating on the basic trio of mother, father and son, may now seem questionable in its focus, at a time when that particular arrangement has lost its normative moral force as well as its predominance in reality.[13] Yet in terms of demographic history, the curious thing is that Freud's minimalist family of father, mother and child projected a social reality that, in his own time – at least in his youth and middle life – was yet to be. The theory anticipates a specifically twentieth-century historical moment in which for a few decades, for the first and perhaps the last time in history, the typical reproductive pattern in Western industrialised societies involved a lifelong parental couple with a limited number of children, and no additional family members living with them. In this mid-twentieth-century world, 'family planning' was acceptable and available; divorce had not yet become ordinary; life expectancy was rapidly increasing.

The tendency today is to think of second marriages and serial families as characteristically contemporary phenomena. But prior to this twentieth-century nuclear moment of both marital and spousal longevity, the frequency of early death, resulting particularly from childbirth, meant that more than one marriage, and more than one family, were commonplace, as they are now. There were the accompanying complexities, again as today, of step-parents and half- and step-sibling relationships. The one crucial difference between the periods before and after the heyday of the nuclear family is that children then acquired step-parents only, or almost always, after the death of a birth parent (which is why James's Maisie would have been puzzled then, but wouldn't be puzzled today).

Freud's theories involved another prescient projection of a future lived reality. His separation of sexuality from reproduction, in the *Three Essays on the Theory of Sexuality* (1905), became a social norm with the increasing use of contraception in the twentieth century; and this development is bound up, of course, with the changing possibilities in women's lives and identities over the same period. And as I've already suggested, reproductive technologies go one stage further: here not only is sex separated from procreation, but procreation can happen without sex.

Freud's isolation of the 'starter unit' nuclear family is interesting in another way from the point of view of his own family history. He was the son of his father's second wife, the first having died in childbirth, and had two older half-brothers who were around twenty years his senior; his mother, twenty-one when he was born, was the same age as the half-brothers, her stepsons. When Freud was born, the first son of his younger half-brother was a year old: the two generations were thereby on a level, horizontalised. And this was a lived actuality for little Sigmund: the other child, technically his own nephew (or rather half-nephew), was a near neighbour and a regular playmate in the first years of his life. This means that the generational conflation was not just some piece of family knowledge he might only have acquired at a later stage; it was there as his own given world from the very beginning. In Freud's own case the core intergenerational Oedipal unit is bordered at home by the evidence of other possibilities which, like the presence or arrival of siblings, challenge its stability and complicate the identity of the child. Generational blurring makes it impossible to separate out the siblings from the parents as the 'vertical' from the 'horizontal': the two can no longer be set either alongside or at different levels from one another, as clearly distinguishable levels or categories.

Yet as so often in Freudian connections, it is the extreme cases which show up the confusions that may exist within the apparently normal. Even without the pluralisation of parents, whether from death or divorce, the division between the generations is often not simple. Parents may be widely separate in age even without there being previous marriages on either side – though almost invariably, for both reproductive and social reasons, the father is the older one. Siblings may be widely separated in age for reasons other than parents' new partners: not just when there are a large number of them, but often through the phenomenon of the late baby, the 'surprise' born some time after the rest, who may be 'mothered' by older siblings more than by its real mother, and for whom these big brothers and sisters may figure very differently from siblings of a nearby age. By the same token – and Freud's female homosexuality case history is an example of this – the age-gap baby may have the effect of confusing the older children's ongoing arrival at the next, would-be adult and potentially procreative stage of their own lives.[14]

OEDIPUS AGAIN

I have been stressing how much has changed since Freud's time, and especially in the shorter term since a few decades ago, but also suggesting how these changes can point us towards hitherto unnoticed aspects of earlier or continuing family formations. Taking this in another direction, I'd like now to go right back to Sophocles' *Oedipus the King* using Freud's source-text for the Oedipus complex, which, read in the light of recent changes in the social and biological conditions of identity, can I think seem surprisingly contemporary – and surprisingly un-Oedipal.

At the surface level of the story – before the revelations of incest and parricide – the play involves a second family, a problem of infertility and an adoption – and a transnational adoption at that. None of these features is mentioned by Freud. Baby Oedipus, born in Thebes to Jocasta and Laius and abandoned to die because of the oracle saying he will kill his father, is adopted across the borders to parents in Corinth, Polybus and Merope; linked to this is their situation of childlessness. The second family is Jocasta's four children with Oedipus, following the death of the husband with whom she had had one child (Oedipus himself as it later turns out). In addition to these open data of the legend, the buried story also concerns more than the classic Oedipal – Freudian Oedipal – double parental violations of incest and parricide. A further point, and also unspecified by Freud though it is close to his concerns, is that the incestuous children bring about a blurring of the generations and of relational categories. Sophocles, though not Freud, lays stress on the intolerable confusion of identity that this entails, and he makes the point like a structural anthropologist, by way of the impossibility of naming that ensues when incompatible relational terms overlay one another, mixing fathers, brothers and children, and brides, wives and mothers.[15]

It has often been said that Oedipus cannot himself be thought to have had an Oedipus complex, for the simple reason that the Jocasta he married and the Laius he killed meant nothing to him emotionally; they were not the parents with whom he grew up, and he had no idea, when he murdered one and married the other, that these were his birth parents. That Freud never mentions the fact of Oedipus' adoption is all the more bizarre in the light of his own claim, in another context (the 'Family Romances' paper, again), that every child at some point fantasises that they were adopted, thereby 'replacing' their existing or present parents with better ones, and perhaps also displacing a sibling or two along the way – if they alone derive from the superior source. What happens to Sophocles' Oedipus in fact involves a transfer between two royal households, like a sort of double jackpot: no need for upwardly mobile adoption fantasies in the first place if your parents are the king and queen; but ironically enough, in this case there really was an adoption from equally superior parents.

Looking from another angle, the fortunes of the infant Oedipus bear a striking resemblance to some contemporary practices of transnational adoption that may involve an interim period of fostering after a baby's abandonment; in Britain, 'local' adoptions too are regularly preceded by a period of fostering. The baby is cared for initially by two shepherds, the first of whom, Laius' servant, does not leave him to die as instructed, but gives him to a second one, who then in turn gives him to the childless Corinthian royal couple. The 'giving' is highlighted in both cases, and defended by the first shepherd against the adult Oedipus' angry accusation that he might have 'sold' the baby.

The legendary Oedipus does in one way exemplify the Freudian Oedipal scenario, since he grows up as the only child of two parents. But there the comparison ends, and in any case those adoptive parents are not the ones in relation to whom Oedipus commits his 'Oedipal' crimes. Another significant feature of the Freudian interpretation is that it ignores those aspects of Sophocles' tragedy that concern not the son's emotions but those of the parents – all four of them, plus the shepherd foster-fathers who take the baby from Thebes to Corinth. In Freud's account, the Oedipus complex is generated as if by nature; it comes from the child. To have let the parents have a hand in it (as Freud does occasionally allow, only to pull back and reassert the other perspective) would have let in too much scope for the intervention of contingent historical factors: only infancy guarantees (or at any rate suggests) innateness and inevitability. But in Sophocles' *Oedipus*, the baby's parents, or at least Laius (it is not clear what part Jocasta played) had determined to have their baby boy killed: the violence began with them, if not just with him.

The adoptive parents, on the other hand, give their son love that is said, at least in Polybus' case (Merope, the adopting mother, remains in shadow in the same way that Jocasta does) to be all the stronger because of the childlessness they had endured until they had him. 'Did he still love him a lot even though he had received him from someone else?' asks Oedipus. 'He was convinced by his former childlessness [*apaidia*]', says the Corinthian shepherd, directly (lines 1023–4). Infertility and childlessness are significant issues in the play. Polybus and Merope are childless before they gain Oedipus, and childless once again after he abruptly leaves home; Laius and Jocasta have understood the oracle to mean that they should remain without children.

Childlessness is also a theme in many other Greek tragedies, but is not one explored by Freud in this connection, and rarely in others. In terms of tragedy, there is a brief, unelaborated mention of childlessness in relation to *Macbeth*, right after the crucial passage on *Oedipus* and *Hamlet* in *The Interpretation of Dreams*.[16] Generally, Freud stays with the hypothetical fantasies of the child, or the childhood-derived fantasies of the adult. A woman's wish to be a mother is a secondary formation; it is the normal way of finding something to make up her deprivation of masculinity, which is her lifelong unconscious preoccupation. As for men, Freud never analyses their wish (or not) to be fathers; it does not figure in his discussions of masculine development.

Yet on the other hand, it can be seen as radical on Freud's part, in his time, to have seen maternity as a problem for women, not something to be taken as a natural instinct, and this is the positive reading of his myth of maternal desire as a secondary formation, and a compensation for non-masculinity. It could be argued that fatherhood in Freud's time impinged much less on men in its psychical and practical demands and pleasures than it usually does today, whereas for mothers, even more than now, it was at the centre of their lives. But it is still intriguing that Freud did not turn his attention to the meanings of fatherhood for men; here, it is as if he did take the socially normal masculine-paternal development for granted, if not for natural.

Sophocles' *Oedipus*, then, is much concerned with parental, or pre-parental, desires and fears in relation to possible children; it is not at all about the desires or hatreds of a small child in relation to its parents. It is, however, about an older or grown child's need to know his origins. It is often pointed out that Oedipus fulfils the oracle's warnings only as a result of the evasive action taken against them – first by his birth parents, who try to kill him, and later by Oedipus himself, at the point when he leaves his home in Corinth, or rather fails to return there, after he has himself heard the oracle's bad news: he decides he must stay away from his mother and father in case he should accidentally murder one and have sex – and children – with the other.

But behind Oedipus' departure lies a story of parental withholding, which has nothing to do with avoiding the oracle. A drunken – or maybe half-drunk – man had insulted young Oedipus at a dinner by saying that Polybus was not his real father. This gets to Oedipus, who then goes and questions his parents; they are angry at what has been said; Oedipus is relieved, but then still, he finds, disturbed. It is at that point, in his later retelling of this turning point in his life, that he goes off to consult the oracle – crucially, without telling his parents, *lathrai* (line 787), 'in secret', as if picking up on the parents' own secretiveness as well as, overtly, feeling the need to get information for himself. The oracle's extreme and seemingly unrelated response relating to a destiny of incest, incestuous children and parricide then implicitly does away with the earlier doubt about who his father is; in fear of the future foretold, he runs away from those he knows as his parents.

But if those parents had communicated what they knew of his origins from the beginning, and all the more at the point when Oedipus questions them, then once again, as with the acts that were meant to evade the oracle, the 'Oedipal' events would never have come about. From this point of view, Oedipus' downfall arises from what we could perhaps call, in a currently popular understatement, a parental 'error of judgement'. And the parents' denial of there being anything to tell – their failure to say that Oedipus' origins are not only the ones he knows – then has its counterpart in Oedipus' own secrecy and his clinging to a fantasy of knowing, without any possible doubt, where he comes from: his country and his parents.

Oedipus' birth parents do what they do, in abandoning him, out of fear (of the oracle); no motive is given for Polybus and Merope's failure to tell Oedipus that he is adopted. But the episode now speaks to discussions about the disclosure of origins in relation not so much to adoption – where that is usually now taken for granted – as in cases of sperm or egg donation, where it is a highly contested issue. In most cases, a donor parent will never have known that they engendered this particular child, who may well, in addition, have unknown biological half-siblings, perhaps many of them, all raised by different parents. What we might call the proto-parent is a different kind of parent for the child to know of or come to terms with, and all the more so when the eventual postnatal parents wish to forget this other origin, as used to happen in most cases of adoption.

The donor parent is someone who, again in most cases, has never had a sexual or other relationship with the eventual parent of the other sex (the one with whose second gamete the baby is conceived) and who may, as in the so-called 'reproductive tourism' of those who seek IVF treatment abroad, have a different cultural origin from the future parents. Or else, at the other extreme, the donor may be confusingly close to home, a friend or someone who is already part of the family, but whose position in relation to the new baby is to be understood as other than that of a parent. The peculiar status of donors also raises the question of just how many parents a child can imagine or seek, now that both biologically and socially the old assumption has broken down that in the beginning there must have been two, who once had sex, and to whom the baby was born.

In the wake of the radical changes to the social and scientific modes of reproduction, a further question arises about what differences remain between mothers and fathers. I mentioned as shadowy the figures of Jocasta and Merope. Jocasta's account of the exposure of her baby is icily controlled, and ostensibly designed only to prove the uselessness of oracles rather than to express any feelings of hers about having, or losing, let alone killing babies – and in her case for a reason that, she believes, turned out to be mistaken. She assumes that that baby did die, and that it was not he who murdered Laius; she doesn't mention a prophecy of mother-marrying and incestuous children. On the Corinthian side, Merope is only represented as an obstacle to peace of mind: when the shepherd reports that Polybus is dead, Oedipus points out that even if the father-murdering issue is out of the way, what he crudely calls 'the one alive' or 'the living woman' ('*tês zôsês*', l. 988) is still a source of fear. It is Polybus who is given some psychological interest: in the shepherd's report, he loved his son to bits because that was the lesson of his childlessness. And Oedipus wonders, when told of his death, whether the oracle might not have been fulfilled after all, if Polybus died from grief at his son's departure, out of 'longing for me' ('*tômôi pothôi*', line 969). For Sophocles, it is the fathers' emotions that are marked.

In our own time, perhaps the seeming neutralisation of parental difference as the contribution of two separate but equal gametes, together with the new ascertainability of paternity and vagueness of biological maternity, have taken attention away from the dissymmetries that remain or that now appear in new forms. At the basic biological level, women have a limited store of eggs, men an infinity of sperm; egg donation is a complicated and protracted process, while sperm donation, comparatively, is not. Pregnancy, whichever mother is doing it, is quite different from biological fathering – 'It only takes ten seconds, Dad', I was told of a six-year-old pleading, who very much wanted a sibling (and got one). It is perfectly possible for a man to be unaware of being a father (and until DNA, arguably, it was impossible for him to be sure that he *was* one); it is virtually impossible for a woman not to know that she has given birth.

Sophocles' *Oedipus* touches on yet another issue in relation to the new ways of begetting, and getting, children in which, once again, some given differences between the sexes appear to be reaffirmed. I mentioned Oedipus' rush to surmise that the discarded baby must have been used for profit. After the Corinthian messenger has spoken of the baby as a 'gift' to the childless Polybus (line 1022), Oedipus suspiciously asks whether he had paid for him (line 1025). Indignantly, the shepherd denies this and points out that he was 'your rescuer, child, at that time' (line 1030).

The new forms of transnational adoption and the new reproductive technologies almost always involve issues of money: babies, or the ingredients to make them, or the means of gestating them, can be bought. Private IVF clinics, as Sarah Franklin has argued, trade on the purchasability of an indefinite 'hope' that in reality is not usually fulfilled.[17] In the past ten years, the internet has greatly facilitated processes of personal selection and research; surrogacy services, eggs and sperm, as well as ready-made babies, can be sought and found and paid for. Sophocles' dialogue between the shepherd and Oedipus is on the same ideological side as the standard modern revulsion against the mixing of babies with profit, but the (equally traditional) image of the woman or couple 'desperate' for a baby tends to override the monetary issue: the internet has had the effect of bringing down moral as well as national boundaries in this connection. Apart from the specifically financial aspect, some of the new practices, some of the time, involve new forms of the exploitation of women's labour (in both senses).[18] As in sexual tourism, so-called, so in reproductive tourism, so-called: here the differences of women's bodies from men's determine what they can be used for or paid for; the technologisation and depersonalisation of baby production at one (scientific) level is matched at another by an age-old reliance on the bodily contributions of individual women's often painful work.[19]

Payment for reproductive services also makes them into an area of consumer choice. Potential parents can shop online for possible donors or surrogates, with different qualities emphasised or visible in each case: the donor's education and attractiveness, the surrogate's health and sturdiness. Here two newly separable bits of the mothering process may be divided not just between two individuals, but along class lines too (professional, educated women are not normally the ones who do surrogacy). While the argument about 'designer babies' has focused on the selection of embryos in IVF and the kinds of preference or requirement that should or should not be considered, such selection is seen as quite natural for the purpose of choosing donor parents, part of the process of 'sourcing' suitable proto-parents for your future child.

Oedipus' situation as one who was adopted from one country to another has the further effect of blurring his origins geographically, as well as parentally. The two are given equal weight in the characteristic ancient Greek identity question, put to every new arrival, every stranger who turns up, in tragedy or epic: '*tis kai pothen?*' – 'Who are you and where do you come from?' With four parents and two countries of origin, this is another aspect of the confusions and multiplications of identity to which Oedipus is involuntarily subject. Today, the growth of transnational adoption has made this once unusual situation seem characteristically modern and even ordinary. It occurs in another form when IVF babies are conceived abroad using sperm and eggs from local donors, and then born in the mother's home country; in this case the place of birth is set apart from the place of genetic origins.

Yet we should also remember that origin has always been – at least – double: two parents, and sometimes two places of origin. When Oedipus gives his own life-story – as he knows it – he begins: 'My father was a Corinthian, Polybus; my mother Merope, a Dorian': no single origin even in the simple story. Similarly, a baby's parents always have two separate lives prior to their becoming that unit that 'had' him or her.

As I hope to have shown, Sophocles' *Oedipus* continues to speak to issues of contemporary identity, just as it did for Freud. The play, like Freud's own theories, becomes like a buried source or origin, but one whose meanings change all the time, in each generation, as it is unearthed and reinterpreted in the light of our new day – so like and so unlike the old days.[20]

NOTES

1. This essay is an extended version of that talk; references to 'twenty-five years ago' and the like start from that perspective of the early 2000s. The conference 'Freud Yesterday, Freud Today', organised by the Freud Museum and the British Psychoanalytical Society, took place on 28–9 January 2006. Juliet Mitchell was the other speaker for the session on 'Feminism, sexuality and gender', which was chaired by Felicity Dirmeik.
2. A big conference on the topic of Sexual Difference, under the aegis of the theory journal *Oxford Literary Review*, was held at the University of Southampton in 1985. 'Sexual difference' was still flourishing, just about, in 2006, though the term 'gender' was coming to supersede it.
3. I am speaking here of the British context; in the United States, for instance, race and class in this formulation would be the other way around.
4. Nancy Chodorow's book *The Reproduction of Mothering* (1978) made mothers essential to this process in their (unconscious) inculcation of the

gender-differentiated dispositions that would then, in turn, produce the next generation of mothers and men.
5. Freud's argument for the roundabout route to female normality in the form of heterosexuality and motherhood was useful to anti-maternal feminists at the time, not only because it emphasised the difficulties of getting to this seemingly obvious point, but also because it denaturalised female reproductive desire. Feminism was thus not against nature, but simply against patriarchal values and conditions in which motherhood was the best substitute for women's lack of any other kind of life.
6. These 'natural limits' are themselves subject to wide variation, through cultural differences in health and life expectancy, and depending on whether the generation is measured from the maternal or paternal point of view. Menopause, not death, puts an end to women's natural reproductive capacities, so that maternally measured generations are on average shorter. But new reproductive technologies may well abolish this difference, as post-menopausal women are enabled to become pregnant via IVF with donor or frozen eggs. In July 2006, a British woman aged sixty-two who had had treatment abroad gave birth to a child.
7. In the United States, while the dual-income couple has become the norm as elsewhere, there has been a marked absence of the parent-friendly legislation, starting with state-supported maternity leave, that has been enacted to varying degrees in most other Western countries.
8. See Freud, 'Family Romances' (1909), SE IX, 239.
9. 'I'm not a smoker', the newly delivered granny was quoted as saying, or prompted to stress – as if that was the issue.
10. The story also featured positively in the *Guardian*, in the context of an article about the donation of body parts (such as kidneys) between family members: see Emma Cook, 'Our Flesh and Blood', *Guardian* 'Family' section, 25 March 2006, 1–2. Incidentally, the fact that the *Guardian* now [in 2006] has a 'Family' section rather than a women's page is symptomatic of the ideological and social changes I have been invoking: the new assumption that parenting is not an exclusively female concern; and concomitantly, an end to the assumption that an interest in family matters detracts from 'broader' social or political interests.
11. Henry James, *What Maisie Knew* (1897; Harmondsworth: Penguin, 1982), 46.
12. Bill Ledger, quoted in Ian Sample, '"Severe shortage" of sperm donors', *Guardian*, Monday, 15 August 2005, 10.
13. Juliet Mitchell's work has drawn attention to the way that the inter-generational Oedipal model obscures the significance of siblings – always assumed in Freud, in fact often assumed to make up a virtually endless succession;

sometimes given quite big parts in the case histories, but always, at the end, subordinated to the parent-child stories that are seen as the primary ones. See Mitchell, *Siblings* (Cambridge: Polity Press, 2003).

14. See Freud, 'The Psychogenesis of a Case of Homosexuality in a Woman' (1920), SE XVIII, 147–72. The eighteen-year-old girl who is the subject of the study has a young brother who was born when she was sixteen.
15. See Sophocles, *Oedipus the King*, lines 1405–6. Oedipus is both father and (half-) brother to his four children, and son of their mother; Jocasta is bride, wife and mother – all three – to Oedipus. Oedipus speaks of the *haima emphulion*, intra-family or incestuous 'blood' or kinship, produced by these crossed relationships, which represent 'the most shameful things for people' (line 1408). Throughout the play, the horror of producing incestuous children is the most prominent fear in Oedipus' utterances about the oracle pronouncing his incestuous and parricidal future.
16. 'Just as *Hamlet* deals with the relation of a son to his parents, so *Macbeth* (written at approximately the same period) is concerned with the subject of childlessness [*auf dem Thema der Kinderlosigkeit*]', Freud, *The Interpretation of Dreams*, SE IV, 266, GW II-III, 272.
17. See Sarah Franklin, *Embodied Progress: A Cultural Account of Assisted Conception* (London: Routledge, 1997).
18. I say 'women' because in sperm donation, the oldest and simplest reproductive technology, which occurs in another form in IVF, there is no long-term labour involved. Egg donation, on the other hand, requires disruptive hormone injections and a potentially painful process of extraction; while surrogacy takes pregnancy's full nine months and involves the woman in all its risks but few of its pleasures: she must consciously avoid the emotional bonding of a mother-to-be with the growing baby. In this regard, it is striking that many women are willing to offer their services as egg donors or surrogates as a gift; in the UK, surrogacy, for instance, is not permitted other than on an 'expenses only' basis.
19. Wet-nursing – whereby babies were given to lower-class women to be breast-fed – is an earlier, postnatal version of surrogate mothering; but in that case the practice occurred not because the mother's own body could not do the job, but for social reasons. For ladies, the too bodily job was not appropriate; while working women such as servants had to 'farm out' their mothering because of their own jobs.
20. The topics of this article are further discussed in Rachel Bowlby, *Freudian Mythologies: Greek Tragedy and Modern Identities* (Oxford: Oxford University Press, 2007) and *A Child of One's Own: Parental Stories* (Oxford: Oxford University Press, 2013).

2

A Tale of Two Parents

Dickens's *Great Expectations**

Great Expectations is not known for its parental stories. But they are very much there, they are very odd, and they involve some curious precursors to the present-day possibilities of single people seeking parenthood. That these stories do not, as a rule, get noticed in Dickens's novel is indicative of the tendency for parental perspectives and presences to be missed or disregarded in relation to other stories that more readily summon attention.[1] We have all been children; perhaps, where there is a strong story of childhood emotions, it is to this and not to other facets of a work that our interest is drawn, and parenthood, as in the real order of things, comes subsequent (in later life; on second reading).

On the surface, the enigmatic developments of *Great Expectations* are centred on Pip, the narrator of the story. He is the one whose childhood is marked by his encounter with the convict Magwitch, his involvement with the fabulous Miss Havisham and her daughter Estella, and then by his removal to London to be formed for the fulfilment of grand 'expectations' of undisclosed origin. Dickens evokes the feelings of a child who is powerless in the face of an assortment of tyrannical adults, from Magwitch, who appears in the opening chapter, to the frightening Miss Havisham who orders him to 'Play', to the affectionless much older sister who is bringing him up, along with her gentle husband, Joe. The novel's world is seen through the eyes of this boy, as remembered by the somewhat chastened man of middle years who now recounts what has been his misdirected life (the unrelinquished aspiration for the love of the cold Estella who cannot love him back, the assumption that the benefactor who moved him to London was Miss Havisham, when really it was Magwitch). As such, *Great Expectations* has rightly been seen as a brilliant study of the emotions of

---

* First published in *A Child of One's Own*, Oxford University Press, 2013.

childhood – for Dickens, involving more terror and impotence than Romantic wonder – in keeping with the nineteenth century's relatively newfound attention to that state and time of life (the novel was published in 1861).

But underneath and alongside the story of Pip's awaitings, greater and lesser, his childhood, and his ill-fated love, there are stories in this novel that are concerned with other kinds of expectation: not children's but parents'. (As if to acknowledge this, there is currently a British company called Great Expectations that chirps on its homepage: 'Hello, welcome to Great Expectations and congratulations if you are newly pregnant'; it sells maternity wear.) These parental stories are not at the forefront of *Great Expectations*, but they are there, and they stand out more now, I think, in relation to the changed circumstances and norms of parental seeking in the twenty-first century.

It would seem reasonable to suggest that before our own time, parenthood was not much of a plot-pusher, in literature or in life: it happened or it didn't, and parents took back seats in relation to the driving force of the child and subsequent adult's story, leaving the parents behind him. The child appeared as unique and central, charged with any number of possible and fascinating futures; whereas parental characters flatly fulfilled a pre-scripted part, fixed and secondary, their role being simply to enable (or else to inhibit) the young person's development. But now parenthood has moved from being a back-story, a necessary but unspectacular prequel before and behind the child's story, to becoming, potentially, a foregrounded, front-of-house story in its own right. Previously, parenthood might figure in the child or the adult's search for identity – Who are my parents? Who was the father? – but now there is a forward direction, as parenthood comes to be commonly imagined as a significant life choice or life ambition, bound up with the identity and desires of the prospective parent or parents; one element, and perhaps at a given stage the major one, in a personal *Bildungsroman*. A parent is something to be! And crucially, whereas in its classically uneventful mode, parenthood was almost always bound up with the initial existence of a couple – some kind of attachment, whether lifelong or night-long, to a co-parent – the new parental stories need have no such mooring or starting point. A child of one's own can be, quite simply, a child that is just my child and no one else's.

Great Expectations offers a nineteenth-century fictional version of what is nowadays a frequent, not an exceptional story of the child as a 'seekling' for the parent. It features two separate instances of unmarried, unattached adults, acting on their own behalf, who go out of their way to become parents, with huge and idiosyncratic emotional and financial investment in their adopted children.[2] The first of these is Miss Havisham, the woman whose life came to a stop when she was jilted on the morning of her wedding. Miss Havisham gets herself a girl 'to rear and love' – Estella.[3] The second seeking parent is Magwitch, the transported convict, who uses the money he has made and inherited in Australia to transform the life of the boy who helped him on the marshes – Pip.

Nor are these the only adoption stories in the book. Adoption is actively sought by Miss Havisham and Magwitch for their own purposes; but (and this is a regular feature of Dickens's novels) there are many other scenarios of adoption – so many, in fact, that the unusual situation is rather the one in which a child lives with both its birth parents. This is just about true in the case of the Pocket family; though the parents, if present, are not strong on parenting: 'I saw that Mr and Mrs Pocket's children were not growing up or being brought up, but were tumbling up' (184). And it is only fully actualised at the very end, with the two-child family of Biddy and Joe Gargery – in effect a second family for Joe, who has earlier been the most loving of stepfathers to Pip. At the start of the novel the primary family is this nucleus of Pip, Joe, and Joe's wife, sister turned adoptive mother: she has taken on the upbringing of her small brother on the death of the parents of both of them. In the same village is Biddy, the 'girl next door' figure whom Pip will spurn, and who will end up, happily, with Joe. Biddy lives with her great-aunt: 'she was an orphan like myself; like me, too, had been brought up by hand' (43). In addition to these informal kinship adoptions, in which a child is raised by other members of their family than the parents because the parents have died, several households consist of an adult child and a widowed parent: Clara Barley and her father; the clerk Wemmick and his 'Aged P.'; Mrs Brandley and her unnamed daughter – 'The mother looked young, and the daughter looked old' (296) – who are joined by Estella as a kind of paying guest. Like Biddy before her great-aunt's death, Wemmick and Clara Barley are in effect carers for their very old fathers (delightful in one case, a drunken control freak in the other).

Amid this general population of disparate types of family, Miss Havisham's famous household arrangements are already so peculiar that their inclusion of an adopted child may escape notice as being perhaps one of its less eccentric features. This is yet another of the adoptive family set-ups in the novel – and one of the two extraordinary sought adoptions on the part of wealthy adults. Both Miss Havisham and Magwitch have or had personal expectations in their adopting, and both are led to articulate these at a much later stage, in the presence of their grown adoptive children.

In a characteristically Dickensian way, the two adoptions turn out to be intimately entangled in ways unknown to either parent or, for most of the novel, to either child: eventually, Pip discovers that Estella's father was Magwitch. This closeness makes Miss Havisham and Magwitch something like secret co-parents

– a mother and a father who are unaware that they have a child in common. Or even two: it is not just that Miss Havisham becomes the mother of Magwitch's daughter, but also that Magwitch adopts the boy who has grown up alongside Estella, regularly going round to her house. The ironies are compounded by Pip's assumption, over many years, that it is Miss Havisham who is secretly his own adopting parent, funding his change of social status – 'She had adopted Estella, she had as good as adopted me' (229) – when in fact it is Magwitch, the man who is really Estella's father, although she never knows it. Overseeing both adoption narratives, to the point that Pip knows him as 'my guardian', a further parental figure is Mr Jaggers, the consummately successful criminal lawyer.

Magwitch and Miss Havisham have certain perversities, parental and otherwise, in common. Both are over-hungry, in relation to their children or their food almost interchangeably; in both cases they want too much, or can't get enough. Miss Havisham has a 'greedy look' (232) – or worse, 'a ravenous intensity that was of its kind quite dreadful' (237). After Magwitch's arrival at Pip's lodgings in London, 'He ate in a ravenous way that was very disagreeable, and all his actions were uncouth, noisy, and greedy' (327). Miss Havisham wildly feeds as she roams the house at night; the first meetings with Magwitch, when Pip is a small boy, involve his frantic consumption of all the 'wittles' that Pip can provide and procure. Both these unsociable eaters have also undertaken their adoption projects in part as a kind of revenge. By creating a gentleman, Magwitch will outdo his nemesis, the higher-class Compeyson; Miss Havisham – according to Herbert Pocket – has 'brought up' Estella 'to wreak revenge on all the male sex' (175), no less. (The man who jilted her turns out – of course, this being a Dickens novel – to have been none other than this same Compeyson.) Pip then interprets the behaviour he witnesses in the same way: 'I saw in this, that Estella was set to wreak Miss Havisham's revenge on men' (298). Estella has been trained as a sort of professional man-eater, a centre of men-wrecking excellence.

Leaving aside these idiosyncrasies of attitude and behaviour, both Magwitch and Miss Havisham have actively sought (and, for that matter, bought) their children, rather than finding themselves parents in more passive or ordinary ways; and both of them at different points articulate their sense of their parenthood and their reasons for seeking out a child – a particular individual in one case (Magwitch's Pip), and a general 'girl' in the other. Magwitch, who has illegally returned from Australia specifically to see him, shows up late one night at the adult Pip's London address, and the man of expectations is confronted with the most unexpected and unwanted of declarations: 'Look'ee here, Pip. I'm your second father. You're my son – more to me nor any son' (315). However far along in the series of possible Pip-fathers Magwitch might be – it could be said that he is the third, not the second, following his stepfather Joe as well as the actual father who is dead – Pip does, against his own first 'aversion' (338), come to accept or recognise, in relation to him, the place of a son, responsible for the welfare of a parent. In his turn, he adopts as his father this man who has unilaterally made him a more-than-son.

Magwitch's claim is to the achievement of a quite specific parental project: 'Yes, Pip, dear boy, I've made a gentleman on you! It's me wot has done it!' (315). In part Magwitch sees his 'son' as a piece of property, to the extent that the gentleman state is purchasable (with clothes, with appropriate living quarters, with the personal mentoring of Matthew Pocket and his son Herbert). Magwitch describes to Pip how he would say to himself, to parry the imagined taunts of 'them colonists', 'If I ain't a gentleman, nor yet ain't got no learning, I'm the owner of such. All on you owns stock and land; which on you owns a brought-up London gentleman?' (317). But at the same time as he lays stress on Pip as a paid-for possession, there is an altogether different dynamic at work. His saying he owns him seems to be a way of asserting his rapture at what he believes his money has been able to do for both of them: Pip has become a gentleman, and he has become a father to one. And beyond even the pleasures of gentleman-making, Magwitch is also almost in love with his image of Pip, who thereby becomes a sort of perfect virtual child: 'When I was a hired-out shepherd in a solitary hut, not seeing no faces but faces of sheep till I half forgot wot men's and women's faces wos like, I see yourn' (315). Between the 'solitary' shepherd and the unique face in an unpeopled continent, Pip represents a very particular kind of only child: he is in effect the only boy in the world.

But Magwitch fervently needs not only to own, and to love, at a distance, but to 'make myself known to him, on his own ground': hence the life-risking (and in the end, life-forfeiting) illegal return from Australia. The own and the known go together. Magwitch is compelled to get Pip to recognise him for the father he wants to have been to him. To make himself known in this way is a vital, a life-and-death part of the project: bodily co-presence involving the communication of his identity as father (or second father). He needs Pip to acknowledge him for what he has done, what he has made of him: 'Well, you see it *was* me, and single-handed' (316), the one and only parent to match the one and only child.

Miss Havisham's parental story is told very differently, even though she, even more than Magwitch, has brought about a dramatic change of social place for her adopted child: Pip comes from a respectable village family, but Estella's background is the criminal underclass. In Miss Havisham's case, the money she may have put into Estella's elevation is not at issue. As a wealthy brewer's daughter, Miss Havisham has never lacked, still less earned, financial means; the sense of what newly made money can do, so primary to Magwitch's conception of his project, plays no part for her. Her adoption of Estella as her future heir is also partly to spite the assortment of sycophantic relatives who hang about waiting for her to die. There seems to be no mystery or ambiguity attached to Estella's position, either for herself or for anyone else. Her adopted status is known to all; more than once she addresses or refers to Miss Havisham as 'Mother by adoption' (300, 359). Her surname is Havisham, as Pip verifies by questioning Jaggers on precisely this point (239); she appears to have all the normal expectations of a daughter of the family, and is even sent off to a finishing school abroad.

Late in the novel's time, Miss Havisham, now full of regrets at the miserable results of Estella's emotional formation ('What have I done?' she keeps repeating), gives a compressed narrative of how and why she came to adopt her, with the help of the lawyer Jaggers:

> I had been shut up in these rooms a long time (I don't know how long; you know what time the clocks keep here), when I told him that I wanted a little girl to rear and love, and save from my fate. (396)

The three very different objectives are precisely stated: rearing, loving and saving from having the same story as herself. Implicitly, a girl is specified because only a girl is comparable enough to Miss Havisham herself to have a different 'fate'. There is no mention of making (or not making) her a lady, which happens as though as a matter of course.

Magwitch boasts of having 'made' Pip a gentleman; Miss Havisham is less concerned with making Estella a lady than with cultivating a particular kind of love-proof personality. Estella subsequently complains that she has been shaped according to a perverse agenda of emotional education, whose effects she is now powerless to undo: '"You must know," said Estella, condescending to me as a brilliant and beautiful woman might, "that I have no heart"' (235). This programmed heartlessness was meant, however, to have one exception. Miss Havisham reproaches her daughter with being unfeeling to her – 'You cold, cold heart!' Estella retorts that 'I am what you have made me' (300). Much later, when Pip's and Estella's lives have both gone wrong, Miss Havisham will come to blame herself, at the novel's last minute acquiring 'an earnest womanly compassion' and declaring to Pip that 'I stole her heart away and put ice in its place' (395). There is no disagreement about the psychological mechanism, one that recurs in other Dickens novels.[4] A heart is there at the outset, but it can be removed by experience or negative training. Estella comes out with a clear analysis of, and protest at, her own formation by Miss Havisham who, like Magwitch with Pip, has 'made' her according to a definite plan.

The two adoptions can be compared in several other ways. To begin with, they are almost poles apart in geographical terms: Magwitch adopts at an Antipodean distance, while Miss Havisham never budges from her English home. During their children's growing up, the two of them are like caricatural versions of the absent father and the constantly present mother. Magwitch is never anywhere near Pip, and indeed his identity is unknown to his 'son'; but Miss Havisham is like a grotesque embodiment of a literally 24/7/365 stay-at-home mother: she never ever goes out of the house. In other respects, of course, she is not quite the model of maternal domesticity, and it is perhaps doubtful whether her establishment, with its drapings of dust, and food decades past its decay-by date, would have passed the home visit reports of twentieth-century social workers checking her out as a prospective adopter. A client assessment is evidently not something that Jaggers considers to be part of his remit, omniscient as he is. It is he who lets slip at one point that curious detail of Miss Havisham's nocturnal eating: 'She wanders about in the night, and then lays hands on such food as she takes' (239).

There are also some similarities between the adoptions. Both parents have a clear idea of the sort of adult they want their child to become, and see a need to form him or her specifically for that end. Miss Havisham's rearing is personal: she herself has made the heartless Estella, or made Estella heartless. We never see exactly how she does it, although there are some very slight indications of her parenting practices. She tells Pip that initially she only wanted to 'save her from misery like my own', but that when Estella

> promised to be very beautiful, I gradually did worse, and with my praises, and with my jewels, and with my teachings, and with this figure of myself always before her a warning to back and point my lessons, I stole her heart away and put ice in its place. (395)

It is as if the words and the things – 'with my praises . . . with my jewels . . . with my teachings' – can be virtually interchangeable as forms of relentlessly repeated persuasion.

Magwitch's rearing, while equally directed towards a specific outcome, equally designed to produce an offspring whose story will be the opposite of the parent's, is delegated. A gentleman's education is something he is unable to provide in any other way: he isn't qualified and he isn't there. In both cases, the child is meant to be for the parent what the parent has not been able to be, and these are obviously gender-differentiated goals: in Miss Havisham's case it is about avoiding a particular kind of love-destiny, and in Magwitch's it is about achieving a worldly status. But Miss Havisham's 'save from my fate' suggests a timeless female doom; whereas Magwitch's gentleman is cast into a modern narrative of social aspiration and upward mobility.

A further connection between the two adoptions is that both have recourse to an intermediary to do the business – and it is the same individual in both cases. After the sentences in which she speaks of what she sought in a child – 'I told him that I wanted a little girl to rear and love, and save from my fate' – Miss Havisham provides the background to her approach to Jaggers:

> I had first seen him when I sent for him to lay this place waste for me; having read of him in the newspapers, before I and the world parted. He told me that he would look about him for such an orphan child. One night he brought her here asleep, and I called her Estella. (396)

Jaggers appears to have taken on each of Miss Havisham's two unusual commissions, first to wreck and then to rescue, with an agent's impartiality. But his delivery of the baby is almost magical in Miss Havisham's telling: 'One night he brought her here asleep.' This transitional sentence metamorphoses the indefinite type, 'such an orphan child', into the real 'her' who then becomes Estella through her naming by the woman who now becomes her parent. Jaggers's role in both this adoption and Pip's is pivotal, not to say miraculous. The man is famous. Magwitch says that the case involving his own wife established Jaggers's name, and Miss Havisham had read about him (incidentally, this casual mention of newspaper-reading is a tantalising glimpse, the only one, of a Miss Havisham before her catastrophe, engaged with the outside world). Jaggers is invested with infallible powers: for both parents, he appears as the man who can get them their girl or boy – and he does. 'Well, you see it *was* me, and single-handed', as Magwitch says; but he immediately adds: 'Never a soul in it but my own self and Mr Jaggers' (316).

Yet for all his professional neutrality and distance, Jaggers is not, it turns out, without views about the job he is asked to do for Miss Havisham: he gives a lengthy statement of his private opinion on the matter, something he is not heard to do with regard to any other case. This comes up when Pip has been letting him know what he has discovered (and Jaggers himself is unaware of), that Magwitch is Estella's father; Jaggers refers to himself hypothetically and in the third person:

> 'Put the case that at the same time he held a trust to find a child for an eccentric rich lady to adopt and bring up.'

'I follow you, sir.'

'Put the case that he lived in an atmosphere of evil, and that all he saw of children, was, their being generated in great numbers for certain destruction. Put the case that he often saw children solemnly tried at a criminal bar, where they were held up to be seen; put the case that he habitually knew of their being imprisoned, whipped, transported, neglected, cast out, qualified in all ways for the hangman, and growing up to be hanged. Put the case that pretty nigh all the children he saw in his daily business life, he had reason to look upon as so much spawn, to develop into the fish that were to come to his net – to be prosecuted, defended, forsworn, made orphans, be-devilled somehow.'

'I follow you, sir.'

'Put the case, Pip, that here was one pretty little child out of the heap, who could be saved.' (408)

This is a theory of almost statistically packed non-expectations, or negative expectations; the 'saving' of one from 'the heap' is an act of human redemption in the face of the dire effects of overpopulation ('their being generated in great numbers'). A single symbolic gesture comes to the rescue, against the odds of biology and criminality, and 'one pretty little child' is plucked from the swarming mass, the 'spawn', to be given a chance as against all the numbers whose lifespan is merely a passage from bare and brutal existence to 'certain destruction'. By comparison, Miss Havisham's wish to 'save' her girl from 'my fate' appears to come from a different universe entirely. In some aspects Jaggers's picture resembles the modern biology textbook, in which reproduction is represented as the one-in-a-million chance success of the single sperm that gets to make a life. The difference here is that the lucky one is actively helped on its way, is 'saved' by deliberate and miracle-working intervention. The scenario is similar to contemporary techniques in which a doctor will indeed select and pick out a single, hopefully viable sperm with which to fertilise the precious egg.[5] Jaggers goes on to give the pragmatic reasons for why, in the particular case of the girl not yet Estella (her original name is never stated), the parents would be likely to consent: 'Give the child into my hands', as he says he would have said to the mother (408). He becomes the recipient and bearer of the little girl, taking her from the first to the second mother. Carrying out Miss Havisham's instructions becomes a matter of physically carrying and delivering the child, according to the commission.

By his own account, then, Jaggers is endowed with almost divine powers. He can give a different life to one single chosen child. At the same time this action is situated against the background of a violently anti-social picture of the human world, in which life for the 'vast numbers' aimlessly 'generated' has only the end of 'destruction'. Jaggers is not himself a parent. Nor, for that matter, is he a son (or a brother, or a husband): he is one of a very few characters in the novel – the villain Orlick is another – for whom there is no information given about their early history or any family they might have been part of. Such isolation, splendid in Jaggers's case, has the effect of enhancing his assumed powers to make or break. In this connection the provision of an ethical rationale of his own for the saving of a single child is very striking.

I have described Magwitch and Miss Havisham as two consciously choosing adoptive parents, each of them using the same lawyer to achieve their aim, and each with a sure sense of what they want for the child they have so deliberately taken to be their own. But the opening setting already involves Pip's first, *de facto* adopting parents, the gentle Joe and the punitive sister (her first name, Georgiana, the same as her and Pip's mother's, is given only at the very end of the novel). Technically a brother-in-law, Joe figures for Pip as a loving, companionable father; they are also buddies and allies against the arbitrary rages of 'Mrs Joe'. Towards the end, after the death of Magwitch, whom Pip has taken care of, it is Joe who nurses Pip through a long illness, and despite Pip's earlier abandonment of him in the period when he still had his expectations and was turning his back on what Estella had mocked as his 'coarse' and 'common' identity (64). Joe is in many ways the moral centre of the book, a paragon of selfless devotion to others and honest pride in his work. He is both good father and good mother, 'strength with gentleness' (139), and he is also Pip's friend and confidant. When Pip's 'expectations' and thereby his imminent removal from home are first announced, Joe spurns the money offered by Jaggers as Magwitch's agent: 'But if you think as Money – can make compensation to me – for the loss of the little child – what come to the forge – and ever the best of friends . . .' (139). Pip is Joe's irreplaceable 'little child'; and though no mention is made of the fact, it is significant that he and Mrs Joe have no children.

The goodness of Joe, unlike the fierceness of his wife, is given a specific aetiology when he tells Pip the story of his own upbringing, with a mother who was always escaping from and then being forced to return to a violent and drunken husband. Pip is to understand that Joe's own father's failures as a father and husband have shaped his own conscious forbearance in the face of the shortcomings of his wife, and also reinforced his wish and willingness to do right by 'the little child'. In a proto-twentieth-century way, Dickens explores the influence of patterns of family behaviour on the next generation. Joe becomes Joe through seeking not to repeat the behaviour of his own father; but that behaviour is the determining cause of what makes Joe Joe as a parent (and husband). In general, *Great Expectations* tends to explain its characters, when it does explain them, by their rearing and their life experience, not by their birth. There is no sense of hereditary taint or virtue, and nor does the original social milieu determine what the baby born into it will later become if transferred to a different one. There is no suggestion, beyond the social stigma that the revelation would entail, that Estella might be negatively affected by being her violent birth mother's daughter; instead, she has been formed by Miss Havisham in the way that Miss Havisham intended, and she herself sees her character as being entirely the wrongful making of her adoptive mother. Pip says of Miss Havisham 'That she had done a grievous thing in taking an impressionable child to mould into the form that her wild resentment, spurned affection, and wounded pride, found vengeance in' (394). An entire theory is implied in this: both the power of parenting to form a child, and of what makes a parent parent in a particular way or to a particular end. Rearing, in this theory, is what moulds a child, through the 'impressions' from its outside environment that mark its mind; and in that sense all children are adopted. They become what they become because of how they are shaped emotionally, consciously or not, by those who raise them, who may or may not have been also their natural parents.

Apart from Magwitch, who emerges as having been Estella's father, and actively – he is said to have been 'extremely fond' of her (401) – none of Estella's and Pip's birth parents are fleshed out with feelings for their children. Pip's family before his parents' death is not a subject of local story or of the novel's interest; instead Joe emphasises how 'When I got acquainted with your sister, it were the talk how she was bringing you up by hand' (47).[6] It is almost as though, in marrying his wife, Joe's first motive was to cherish the child: to give him a loving parent. Estella's mother is the only birth parent to be in any way party to the adoption of her child, 'whom the father believed dead, and dared make no stir about' (408). Her relinquishment of the toddler who will become Estella is in effect forced upon her by Jaggers, in exchange for his defending her in court for the murder he knows she committed. Nothing is said of Estella's mother's response, in words or gesture, or of her thoughts (was she, as Magwitch is said to have been, 'extremely fond' of their daughter?). Molly's giving, or giving up, of her small child is passed over silently. Similarly we never hear anything of Magwitch's feelings about the loss – as he supposes – of his daughter, let alone about the possible relationship of that loss to his wish to attach himself to Pip as a second child of his own.

Miss Havisham's moulding to 'save her from my fate' has not succeeded in bringing Estella happiness (she goes through a loveless and abusive marriage), and that, together with Pip's own unhappiness, is the source of the eventual self-reproach for what she has actually and unintentionally 'done'. By contrast Magwitch, whose own adoption has almost equally unhappy consequences for his 'son', never has to confront the failure of the project to which he, like Miss Havisham, has devoted himself to gratify a fantasy of his own. Instead, Pip carefully keeps from the dying convict the knowledge that all the money he has saved to assure Pip's affluent future will necessarily revert to the Crown on his death, because of his return from Australia. Nor does Pip ever protest – as Estella does to Miss Havisham – against the gentlemanly education that Magwitch has given him, or thrust upon him. But in proudly rather than penitently proclaiming his influence, Magwitch uses the same language of 'doing' and 'making' that Miss Havisham and Estella apply to her formation. On the night when he comes to Pip's lodgings and reveals his part in his history, Magwitch recalls how he used to say to himself, ' "but wot, if I gets liberty and money, I'll make that boy a gentleman!" And I done it' (315).[7]

There is an even deeper failure that the two determined adoption projects have in common. Miss Havisham unwittingly causes Estella to live another ill-fated story of abusive love, with Bentley Drummle. Magwitch's raising of Pip is meant to give him a life far removed from his adoptive father's, but it also, uncannily, re-enacts what was done to Magwitch. Pip's transfer from one sphere of life to another, and away from the place where he was born, comes about without any agency on his part. For the young Pip it represents the fulfilment of the vague expectations set in motion by his frequenting of Miss Havisham and Estella, but it occurs with the same irresistible fatefulness as Magwitch's own capture and subsequent transportation. First, a companion of Magwitch's comes to check out Pip's origins, and then some time later Jaggers himself comes to inform Pip of his expectations and arrange for his removal to London and his new mode of life. Thus agents seek out Pip and take him away, just as they do with Magwitch. For all that he longs to give Pip what he himself has never had, what Magwitch actually does, from this point of view, is to give him a life sentence in a new world, just as had happened with himself. No different from the unquestionable absent authority of 'His Majesty's service' (30), which commands that blacksmiths must help in arresting convicts on Christmas Day, and sends its agents to capture them, Magwitch becomes the anonymous personage on whose behalf Jaggers is sent from London to track Pip down; Jaggers 'come arter you, agreeable to my letter', as Magwitch precisely puts it (317). Meaning to do the opposite, both Magwitch and Miss Havisham inflict an aggressive repetition of their own stories upon the children whom they adopt for a different life.

When I began to think about the proactive parents, the self-made parents, in *Great Expectations*, my idea was that this aspect of the novel was a small but significant sub-story (or rather two), behind the principal plotline. As I continued to think about it, I found that this double parental story kept growing to the point that it seemed to have pushed everything else in *Great Expectations* to one side: all I could now see was Miss Havisham and Magwitch and Jaggers beside them, driving the action, driving the whole of Pip's and Estella's lives. (I apologise, but not too much, for this monomania.) In Pip's case, both the actual expectations, the ones derived from Magwitch, and the delusional expectations, the ones he imagines to come from Miss Havisham, are derived from the two parenthood projects: the real expectations directly, and the mistaken ones because Miss Havisham wants to use Pip as part of her malign experiment in negative emotional training for Estella. Pip's narrative begins with the encounter on the marsh from which, ultimately, Magwitch's gratitude and gentleman-making scheme will emerge. And the day of Pip's first visit to Miss Havisham's house is singled out as having been, in biographical terms, the day without which his whole life would have been different (71).

Miss Havisham's adoption is worth attention, I have suggested, because of the peculiarity of its aims and the special method used to get hold of a daughter in the first place. But there is also the fact that the parenthood initiative is a move beyond the static, stalled world in which she has encased herself. We see the picture of Miss Havisham stuck there with her clock at twenty to nine, her mouldy ever after wedding feast, and her journeys that go nowhere, round and round the room; and this image of life stopped and suspended is what we remember. But sending for an Estella was actually a definite break in that cycle, taking Miss Havisham back out into the 'world' from which she was 'parted', and henceforth requiring various kinds of organisation – from the days of Pip and Estella's dreadful playdates to the timing and planning of schooling and boarding elsewhere. The adoption and raising of Estella undermine the general spectacle of Miss Havisham herself as living in a time-warp of her own: in this respect she has in fact re-entered the world. By getting herself a child, she has started a new story beyond the fatal wedding day, setting out to do something with another life. Like Magwitch, she has treated parenthood as a reason for living in this world and a compensation for her own disappointments. For both of them, parenthood has been a second chance: or a means of getting their 'own' back.

NOTES

1. For other examples of overlooked odd family scenarios in Dickens's novels see e.g. Holly Furneaux, *Queer Dickens: Erotics, Families, Masculinities* (Oxford: Oxford University Press, 2009), especially ch. 1.

2. For a reading of the novel in relation to adoption that concentrates on the experience of Pip and Estella, rather than on their parents, see Marianne Novy, *Reading Adoption: Family and Difference in Fiction and Drama* (Ann Arbor: University of Michigan Press, 2005), 109–14. Adoptions by single people in England and Wales in fact constituted a significant proportion of the total in the years that followed the Adoption Act of 1926: 'unmarried women, and men, generally middle-class, could and did adopt children, with legal sanction after 1926, setting themselves up publicly as unmarried parents'; but after further legislation in 1949, 'Adoption by single people became difficult and rare'; Pat Thane and Tanya Evans, *Sinners? Scroungers? Saints? Unmarried Motherhood in Twentieth-Century England* (Oxford: Oxford University Press, 2012), 42, 99. Sometimes the adopting parent was in fact the birth mother or (more rarely) father, which gave both child and parent a legal status, instead of the child being officially nobody's (*filius nullius*), for purposes of inheritance.
3. Charles Dickens, *Great Expectations* (1861), ed. Margaret Cardwell (Oxford: Oxford University Press, 1994), 396. Further page references will be given within the main text.
4. Another Dickens woman who is aware of no longer having a heart and knows what happened to it is Dombey's second wife, Edith Granger: 'Oh mother, mother, if you had but left me to my natural heart when I too was a girl . . . how different I might have been!'; *Dombey and Son* (1848), ed. Peter Fairclough (1970; London: Penguin, 1985), 514. The remark is prefaced by Edith recalling to her mother how she has 'more than once'sat at the window when 'something in the faded likeness of my sex has wandered past outside'.
5. Intra-cytoplasmic sperm injection (ICSI) began to be used in the early 1990s as a remedy for generally low sperm quantity or quality.
6. Joe goes on:

> 'As to you . . . if you could have been aware how small and flabby and mean you was, dear me, you'd have formed the most contemptible opinions of yourself!'
> Not exactly relishing this, I said, 'Never mind me, Joe.'
> 'But I did mind you, Pip,' he returned, with tender simplicity.

7. A comical counterpart to Magwitch in loudly asserting his role in Pip's social rise is Mr Pumblechook, the local corn merchant and uncle of some sort to Pip's family. He puts it about that he is Pip's 'earliest benefactor and the founder of my [Pip's] fortunes' (470), and declares, upon Pip's humbled return, that 'I would do it again' (471).

3

Finding a Life

George Eliot's *Silas Marner*★

Great Expectations has a multiplicity of adoption scenarios that appear beneath the surface of the primary narrative of a boy who was himself adopted not once but twice: first by his older sister and then, in effect, by a transported convict whose money transforms his life. But these parental stories are not the obvious focus of Dickens's novel. In George Eliot's *Silas Marner*, on the other hand, which was published in the same year, adoption is clearly at the centre. And although, implicitly, her adoption does change the life of the toddler who is taken in, the novel is much more concerned with its effects on the man who becomes her father. Parenthood is the beginning of Silas Marner's 'new self', a rebirth for someone who had been up till then almost totally withdrawn from his local world and who had suffered the loss of the one thing to which he was attached, his accumulated 'gold'.[1] More than anything, this is a novel that morally urges the power of parenthood to give meaning to an individual life; it does this not only in showing what happens with Silas Marner himself, but also by the contrast with another father – the original father of the adopted girl – whose own life, after he has failed to 'claim' her – either to acknowledge her or to bring her up – is marred by childlessness with his wife. As in *Great Expectations*, there is no promotion of the superiority of 'natural' parenthood.[2] Sometimes natural family ties are offered as happy and functional, but this is not the novel's norm, and Silas Marner's unusual story serves as a kind of parable of what the unexpected and unconditionally accepted child – the 'found' child *par excellence* – can mean to the parent.

The two-year-old girl who comes into Silas Marner's cottage on New Year's night is in effect a foundling. Out of the dark she appears, lighting up

---

★ First published in *A Child of One's Own*, Oxford University Press, 2013.

the life of a man who, at the point when the novel begins, has been living for some time as a semi-recluse near the village of Raveloe; he is 'not yet forty' (19), but old before his time. Silas has cut himself off from human connection since leaving his home town as the result of a false accusation that led to his fiancée breaking off their engagement. Working as a weaver, he has stored up a large amount of gold, which has become the only object of his devotion, lovingly counted and handled every evening. Its disappearance one night while he is out is a catastrophe that wrenches away what has been his only consolation and companion:

> To any one who had observed him before he lost his gold, it might have seemed that so withered and shrunken a life as his could hardly be susceptible of a bruise, could hardly endure any subtraction but such as would put an end to it altogether. But in reality it had been an eager life, filled with immediate purpose, which fenced him in from the wide, cheerless unknown. It had been a clinging life; and though the object round which its fibres had clung was a dead disrupted thing, it satisfied the need for clinging. But now the fence was broken down – the support was snatched away. (73–4)

Into this now purposeless void there enters the child who will be called Eppie, her arrival as magically unexplained as the departure of the supporting gold.

Silas repeatedly represents the relation between the gold and the girl as an equivalence. In a minimal sense, she takes its place as an object of devotion. But much more than that, she offers a prospect of life that is incommensurable with the gold-acquiring concentration of his previous existence. She gives him a future, and a present that is sensually enjoyable:

> The gold had asked that he should sit weaving longer and longer, deafened and blinded more and more to all things except the monotony of his loom and the repetition of his web, but Eppie called him away from his weaving, and made him think all its pauses a holiday. (124)

Through his daughter, Silas is able to live or relive an experience of awakening to life: 'As the child's mind was growing into knowledge, his mind was growing into memory; as her life unfolded, his soul, long stupefied in a cold narrow prison, was unfolding too, and trembling gradually into full consciousness' (124). Eliot's language brings out a Wordsworthian world of childlike wonder. But here, instead of a countervailing encroachment as 'Shades of the prison-house begin to close',[3] there is now, in later life, an opening out into freedom. The growth of the child is the growth and flourishing of the parent – the parent's second life.

Many times Silas describes the girl as having been 'sent' to him, a deliverance and a destiny. His adoption of her comes about without any premeditation, as a refusal of the proposal that she should be taken off his hands:

> 'No – no – I can't part with it, I can't let it go,' said Silas, abruptly. 'It's come to me – I've a right to keep it.'
>
> The proposition to take the child from him had come to Silas quite unexpectedly, and his speech, uttered under a strong sudden impulse, was almost like a revelation to himself: a minute before, he had no distinct intention about the child. (113)

From this point on, Silas holds fast to the sense of himself as the rightful and single parent of the girl he calls Eppie. More than anything, this involves a commitment to all the tasks of childcare (something that Dickens's Miss Havisham, who sought a little girl 'to rear and love', is never seen to engage in with Estella), and this goes together with a demand for exclusivity. He rejects Dolly Winthrop's offer of help: 'I want to do things for myself, else it may get fond o' somebody else, and not fond o' me. I've been used to fending for myself in the house – I can learn, I can learn' (120). His reasons combine, without welding, the practical and the emotionally demanding. 'I can learn' – but also, I want her to love just me.

Learn he does – and the reader too, from a passage several pages long that gives details of Mrs Winthrop's many parenting tips. But Silas is adamant from the very beginning that the parent of Eppie is him, and him only. In a practical sense, becoming the child's father entails him adopting the role that would normally be a woman's. His first gesture, after he finds her lying on the hearth in his cottage, is to feed her with some of his porridge. He rejects the assumption that 'an old bachelor, like you' (116) could not possibly be thinking of looking after a small child. In fact Silas's occupation as a weaver becomes a kind of special qualification for his unusual role, as Dolly says:

> 'Why, there isn't many lone men 'ud ha' been wishing to take up with a little un like that: but I reckon the weaving makes you handier than men as do out-door work – you're partly as handy as a woman, for weaving comes next to spinning.' (128–9)

Silas is more an old spinster than an old bachelor. But if he sets out to be all things, both parents, to Eppie – 'I want to do everything as can be done for the child' (122) – there is also a movement of identification: 'it's a lone thing – and I'm a lone thing' (116). His very first response, when he finds the golden creature, is to see her as being conceivably 'his little sister come back to him in a dream – his little sister, whom he had carried about in his arms for a year before she died, when he was a small boy without shoes or stockings' (109). This phantom memory of love and loss bears with it the physical closeness that will come to be Silas's life with his daughter, to whom he gives his sister's name.

Like Joe Gargery in *Great Expectations*, Silas becomes both a nurturing parent and a brother to his adopted child; as well as being 'ever the best of friends, Pip!' as he often reiterates. Joe is technically Pip's brother-in-law. But the significance of the companionate parenthood that both Joe and Silas undertake is quite different. Joe from the start is fully integrated into his community, and remains so until the end amid all the vicissitudes of Pip's own separate life. Silas is on the outside: he has come from elsewhere, and other than through his work he has never sought to make himself part of the local world in which he has settled. For him, the new child comes to make him part of the village life from which he had previously been detached. Eppie enables his own growth, alongside hers; there is even a 'double baptism' (123) as though Silas, too, had only just arrived in this world; 'the child created fresh and fresh links between his life and the lives from which he had hitherto shrunk continually into narrow isolation' (123).

Eliot presents the arrival of Eppie in Silas Marner's life as unambiguously positive; it is the making of him, an unequivocally happy event. At the end of the novel, Eppie's wedding to Dolly's son Aaron Winthrop – with whom, in effect, she grew up – is marked carefully as more a continuation than a break with the perfect harmonious domestic life that Silas and Eppie have led: Aaron will come to live with them, and Silas will not lose his daughter. But throughout the novel, Eliot reinforces the joyous, quasi-magical tone of the tale of Silas and Eppie by counterpointing the story of the man who, unknown to anyone in the village, was Eppie's first father.

At the beginning Godfrey Cass, the eldest son of the village squire, is in love with the suitable Nancy Lammeter, but has blighted his life by contracting a secret marriage to the mother of the baby who will later be Eppie. Of this Molly, little is ever said. She lives at a distance from Raveloe; she is addicted to opium (which eventually causes her death, the night she falls asleep outside Silas Marner's cottage); she apparently worked in a pub, since her mind is a 'poisoned chamber, inhabited by no higher memories than those of a barmaid's paradise of pink ribbons and gentlemen's jokes' (106). Molly is represented as the lowest of the low, the antithesis of the now unattainable Nancy:

Instead of keeping fast hold of the strong silken rope by which Nancy would have drawn him safe to the green banks, where it was easy to step firmly, he had let himself be dragged back into mud and slime, in which it was useless to struggle. He had made ties for himself which robbed him of all wholesome motive, and were a constant exasperation. (30)

Before the death of Molly (and the arrival of Eppie), Godfrey bore marriage and fatherhood not only as the impediment to his marrying the woman he loves, but as the guilty secret he is sometimes on the point of confessing, but never does. Eliot then brings the moral issue to a head through the crisis engendered by Molly dying on the way to declare to Godfrey's father her situation as the wife of his son and mother of his child. This releases Godfrey from the state of marriage, but confronts him with the more focused and immediate dilemma of whether to admit his relationship to 'the "tramp's child"' (118).

Eliot carefully presents all Godfrey's impulses as tending in the opposite direction from Silas's; the actual father resists and rejects what comes naturally to the man who has no connection with the child. The contrast is made more starkly as Godfrey, like Silas, experiences the toddler's arrival as something supernatural. For him, though, it has the effect of breaking in upon the courtship of Nancy in which he has been indulging at the New Year's party:

But when Godfrey was lifting his eyes from one of those long glances, they encountered an object as startling to him at that moment as if it had been an apparition from the dead. It *was* an apparition from that hidden life which lies, like a dark by-street, behind the goodly ornamented façade that meets the sunlight and the gaze of respectable admirers. It was his own child carried in Silas Marner's arms. That was his instantaneous impression, unaccompanied by doubt, though he had not seen the child for months past. (112)

Godfrey recognises 'his own child', his back-street child – as her mother's social class is merged into a metaphor of the dark and 'hidden' quarters of Godfrey's mind. The narrator states, indirectly, that he has been, in modern terms, an absent father, and the lapse of time adds to the shock of what is so indisputably a recognition. But this absence is put the other way round, as the child's non-existence in Godfrey's world.

There are two subsequent scenes, one the same night and one years later, when Eppie is grown up, in which Godfrey and Silas are set against one another as the two fathers of a now motherless child. In the first of these scenes, Godfrey sees in Molly's death 'the sudden prospect of his own deliverance from his long bondage' (115). The child is an encumbrance for which he will make some minimum of provision: 'As for the child he would see that it was cared for; he would never forsake it; he would do everything but own it' (117). Godfrey refuses to 'own' his child in the confessional sense; Silas subsequently lays claim to her with an owning that verges on the proprietorial: 'she'll be *my* little un . . . She'll be nobody else's' (121).

Much later, the question of the father's 'owned' child is raised once again, after Godfrey has belatedly told Nancy, now his wife for many years, that he is the original father of 'the weaver's child'. This is the day when Godfrey eventually comes home to tell her that the remains of his long-vanished brother have been found, along with the long-missing gold that had disappeared from Silas Marner's cottage – and also, at last, reveals the suppressed story of his early marriage and fatherhood. In the meantime Nancy is reflective. She is thinking about the history of her life and marriage, including a baby who died; Eliot gently generalises her preoccupation as the result of a life that has been denied the outlet of motherhood:

> This excessive rumination and self-questioning is perhaps a morbid habit inevitable to a mind of much moral sensibility when shut out from its due share of outward activity and of practical claims on its affections – inevitable to a noble-hearted, childless woman, when her lot is narrow. (149)

Despite Godfrey's sense of 'deliverance' through Molly's death, and the wedding to Nancy he wished for, the further sequel of children has failed to occur – or occurred only in the form of loss: 'Was there not a drawer lined with the neat work of her hands, all unworn and untouched, just as she had arranged it there fourteen years ago – just, but for one little dress, which had been made the burial-dress?' (150).

Yet Nancy sees their childlessness as having been more her husband's loss than hers; her 'deepest wounds had all come from the perception that the absence of children from their hearth was dwelt on in her husband's mind as a privation to which he could not reconcile himself' (150). For women, in Nancy's theory, a husband can partly take the place of children in a way that is not symmetrically true for a man: 'a woman could always be satisfied with devoting herself to her husband, but a man wanted something that would make him look forward more' (150). This accords with what Eliot has emphasised as being the newfound future perspective given to Silas by his own fatherhood of Eppie; it also extends the pragmatic attitude to domestic happiness put forward in the first phase of the novel by Nancy's older sister Priscilla, who is uninterested in marriage and intends to spend her life living with their father: 'thank God! My father's a sober man and likely to live; and if you've got a man by the chimney-corner, it doesn't matter if he's childish – the business needn't be broken up' (92).

Nancy's meditations partly turn on the two moments, precisely dated as four and six years before now, when Godfrey had mooted the possibility of their adopting a child. It is here that Eliot draws the narrative towards a broader discussion of adoption. In passing, there is a general authorial statement about changing social attitudes: 'Adoption was more remote from the ideas and habits of that time than of our own' (151).[4] The novel implicitly contrasts the situations of Nancy and Godfrey, a childless couple who might have sought to adopt, with that of Silas, who is made a father by the wholly unanticipated arrival of a child. Nancy's objection to adoption centres on what she regards as the wrongness of actively seeking to go against what has been ordained:

> To adopt a child, because children of your own had been denied you, was to try and choose your lot in spite of Providence: the adopted child, she was convinced, would never turn out well, and would be a curse to those who had wilfully and rebelliously sought what it was clear that, for some high reason, they were better without. (151)

This rationale is striking in the way that it speaks of trying, of choice, of seeking, of the desire for children 'of your own' – all the elements that are present in the formulation today of the predicament of the childless person or couple. Yet here they are raised in order to refuse their legitimacy, to the point of imagining a punishment in the 'curse' of the child who 'would never turn out well'. Even the rituals of remembrance for the baby who died must be deliberately abandoned, in case they should represent a protest against what has happened: 'she had suddenly renounced the habit of visiting this drawer, lest she should in this way be cherishing a longing for what was not given' (150).

In the conversation that Nancy recalls, Godfrey counters her argument about an adopted child turning out badly with the local case of Eppie: 'She has thriven as well as child can do with the weaver; and *he* adopted her' (152). The irony of Godfrey knowingly but unconfessedly referring to the child who is actually his is followed by the comedy of casual argument from hearsay. Like Godfrey, Nancy makes an inference about adoption in general from a single case, but hers is at two removes, and placed under the rubric of social chitchat: 'Don't you remember what that lady we met at the Royston Baths told us about the child her sister adopted? That was the only adopting I ever heard of: and the child was transported when it was twenty-three' (152).

Godfrey's perspectives on his childlessness are very different from Nancy's. It is not just that he favours adoption – favours the seeking of a possible solution – nor even just that he harbours the secret he has so far still failed to communicate to Nancy, that he was Eppie's father. His guilt in relation to this, both the fathering and the failure to confess it, does cause him to imagine the present situation as something like Nancy's own sense of a punishment: 'His conscience, never thoroughly easy about Eppie, now gave his childless home the aspect of a retribution' (154). But more generally his attitude is contrasted with Nancy's supreme resignation to her losses. 'Meanwhile, why could he not make up his mind to the absence of children from a hearth brightened by such a wife?' (154). As for her, the good marriage is raised as a possible compensation, a different source for domestic fulfilment; but raised in the form of Godfrey's own impatience with his inability to take the children out of the picture, to cease to see and feel an 'absence'.

Eliot pursues this theme with a passage of extensive moral generalisation, linking Godfrey's mental state to the stage of his life:

> I suppose it is the way with all men and women who reach middle age without the clear perception that life never *can* be thoroughly joyous: under the vague dullness of the grey hours, dissatisfaction seeks a definite object, and finds it in the privation of an untried good. Dissatisfaction, seated musingly on a childless hearth, thinks with envy of the father whose return is greeted by young voices – seated at the meal where the little heads rise one above another like nursery plants, it sees a black care hovering behind every one of them, and thinks the impulses by which men abandon freedom, and seek for ties, are surely nothing but a brief madness. (154)

Like an unwanted lodger, the awkwardly personified 'dissatisfaction' is brought into the house to be given its own place at the hearth and then round the family table. In the first case, like Godfrey, dissatisfaction imagines what the 'childless hearth' excludes, enviously fleshing out the counter-scene of a returning father. But in the second instance, surprising the sentence after a dash, without any kind of contrasting connective, it jumps into a very different household, reversing rather than supplying an image of parental fulfilment. First the dissatisfaction of the childless hearth adds what is seen as missing; then the ostensibly happy scene is viewed as just a façade. Initially cute, with their 'little heads' and their natural growth, the picture of the children suddenly goes into the negative, without exception – 'a black care hovering behind every one of them', so that the number of children now becomes simply the multiplication of troubles. Parenthood, finally, becomes not the long anticipated goal, nor even the monochrome dailiness of the 'grey hours' of middle age, but a prison sentence – 'men abandon freedom' – brought about by a moment of madness. And this fatal passing folly is not, as might have been expected, a yielding to love or lust; much more disconcertingly, and in full conformity with social propriety, it is what happens when men settle down to 'seek for ties'.

Eliot's moral reflections at this point seem to take children or their absence, an excess or a scarcity, as one trigger among any number of others for the dissatisfaction that is an age-related probability – at least for those who have not yet acquired a capacity for compromise in the form of 'the clear perception that life never *can* be thoroughly joyous'. But this passage is more like a moment of impatient aberration in a novel which otherwise quite intently examines many kinds of both large and small change that parenthood, or the denial of it, may bring. There is no question but that Silas Marner's adoptive fatherhood is the making of him, the happy turning point in his life; and it is also made clear that the different distresses experienced by Godfrey and Nancy Cass in their not having children in practice take far more complex forms than a simple excuse for some general sense of middle-aged unhappiness.

The second exchange between Eppie's two fathers occurs in quite different circumstances from the first, even though notionally there is still the same discrepancy between the natural and the adoptive father. On the first occasion, Silas was taking, and taking in, the child not yet named Eppie, and Godfrey was failing to 'own' his relationship to her. On the subsequent occasion, many years later, Silas is the man whom Eppie has known as her father for almost all her life, and Godfrey is the alternative father come to take her away, and presenting his claims to her first as part of a would-be adopting couple, then for himself as the natural father.

Godfrey and Nancy go together to the cottage where Silas and Eppie live on the same Sunday that Silas's gold has turned up again, and with it the evidence that shows it was Godfrey's younger brother who stole it all those years ago. These buried secrets, now come to light, have prompted Godfrey at long last to tell his wife the now ancient story of his clandestine marriage – and how Eppie is really his child. The belated confession does not just bring out what had been suppressed. It is now a story about a girl who is eighteen years old, and it is told to a Nancy who has lived without being a mother throughout her married life (and with the grief of the baby she lost), not to a younger, not yet married Nancy likely to be turned away by the news of a prospective husband's failings.

To Godfrey's surprise, Nancy's response now – though she then admits that it might have been different at the earlier time – is to pledge herself retrospectively as the mother to Eppie she has not been able to be:

> 'And – O, Godfrey – if we'd had her from the first, if you'd taken to her as you ought, she'd have loved me for her mother – and you'd have been happier with me: I could better have bore my little baby dying, and our life might have been more like what we used to think it 'ud be.' (158)

The child whom Godfrey always saw as an obstacle to his life with Nancy might after all have been the compensatory gift that would have made parents of them – the role that she did fulfil for Silas. Nancy estimates what would have been Eppie's value, in making her a mother and supplying the nearest possible version of the happy future that she and Godfrey had imagined. Her quick enumeration of the lost compensations fits with the novel's careful computation of parental satisfactions and deprivations, with the primary example being the golden child 'sent' to take the place of the gold that has gone from Silas's cottage. Eliot spells out the equation one more time: it is on the very day that the gold has suddenly come back that Godfrey and Nancy go to the cottage to take Eppie away again.

Godfrey first makes his request in the form of an offer of adoption, implicitly connected to the new discovery that it was his brother who stole Silas's hoard. Eppie will be given a better life:

> 'You've done a good part by Eppie, Marner, for sixteen years. It 'ud be a great comfort to you to see her well provided for, wouldn't it? She looks blooming and healthy, but not fit for any hardships: she doesn't look like a strapping girl, come of working parents. You'd like to see her taken care of by those who can leave her well off, and make a lady of her: she's more fit for it than for a rough life, such as she might come to have in a few years' time.' (162)

Addressed to the potentially relinquishing parent, the argument is the same one that would be relentlessly used to persuade unmarried mothers in the middle decades of the twentieth century that they should give up their babies for adoption. A parent who wants the best for their child would be selfish in refusing to place it in a higher social setting. The first parent is quickly cast in the role of a depriver, in relation to the superior provisions that their child could enjoy elsewhere; and 'It would be a great comfort to you in your old age, I hope, to see her fortune made in that way' (163).

Godfrey then proceeds to a second strand of what is still an adoption argument, dwelling on a different kind of deprivation – not in the current prospects for Eppie, but in the lives of himself and his wife. Material surplus is urged, along with a personal lack that Eppie could come to supply:

'Mrs Cass and I, you know, have no children – nobody to benefit by our good home and everything else we have – more than enough for ourselves. And we should like to have somebody in the place of a daughter to us – we should like to have Eppie, and treat her in every way as our own child.' (163)

Eppie, not Silas, replies, on both counts: 'I can't leave my father, nor own anybody nearer than him. And I don't want to be a lady. I couldn't give up the folks I've been used to' (163). Eppie – in reality the daughter of a gentleman – refuses the social elevation offered with as much assurance as Pip's acceptance of the equivalent offer in *Great Expectations*; both novels firmly endorse the desirability of staying in the (lowly) position you grew up in.

Having failed so far, Godfrey now moves on to make his case quite differently, by declaring himself as Eppie's real father:

'But I have a claim on you, Eppie – the strongest of all claims. It is my duty, Marner, to own Eppie as my child, and provide for her. She is my own child – her mother was my wife. I have a natural claim on her that must stand before every other.' (164)

After a little while, the 'natural' claim on Eppie becomes Eppie's duty to 'your lawful father' (167), but the gap between nature and law is already half elided in this first declaration by the gloss on 'my own child' that justifies the father legally as the husband of her mother. Still, the stress on the lawful father accompanies a shift of emphasis away from positive suggestion – what Godfrey and Nancy can offer – to almost threatening demand. What Godfrey calls his 'natural claim' sets him, individually, against both Silas and Eppie (Nancy is no longer in the picture). The force of the claim is that it can put itself forward as primordial: it is natural and therefore it 'must stand before every other'. Godfrey presents himself now as the one and only parent (in comparison with Silas) and also as the only person, parent or prospective parent or child, with a valid 'claim'.

The question of claims had entered into Godfrey's arguments with himself at the distant first stage of this parental debate, all the years ago when Eppie was found by Silas and recognised by Godfrey as his daughter. Then, he had reflected 'that he ought to accept the consequences of his deeds, own the miserable wife, and fulfil the claims of the helpless child' (115): the claims were the child's, not the parent's. The later insistence on 'the strongest of all claims', as a father, still includes the two elements of public recognition ('to own Eppie as my child') and an obligation to 'provide for her'. Both these disparate functions are placed under the head of 'duty', which is thus inextricable from the overarching 'claim'.

Godfrey's demands are rejected by both Silas and Eppie with argument and feeling. The 'natural claim', if it ever was one, has in effect been invalidated by Godfrey's failure to make it from the outset: 'then, sir, why didn't you say so sixteen year ago, and claim her before I'd come to love her, I'stead o' coming to take her from me now, when you might as well take the heart out o' my body?' (164). Without him spelling it out, Silas's image gives a different meaning to the 'natural' claim. Eppie has grown into being the vital part of his own self; with these two, there can be no differentiation between the claims of the child and the parent, since they are as one. Taking her from him, 'You'd cut us i' two' (165): they have no existence apart from one another. And Silas returns to the image of the child as a gift, while acknowledging that as the original father, Godfrey would have had the prior claim:

> 'God gave her to me because you turned your back upon her, and He looks upon her as mine: you've no right to her! When a man turns a blessing from his door, it falls to them as take it in.' (164)

Godfrey had first refusal – and refused.

Beyond his impassioned appeal to the double self that he and Eppie have become, Silas also recasts Godfrey's rhetoric about his paternal duty to provide for a daughter. He rejects Godfrey's idea that in living elsewhere, down the road, 'She'll feel just the same towards you':

> 'Just the same?' said Marner, more bitterly than ever. 'How'll she feel just the same for me as she does now, when we eat o' the same bit, and drink o' the same cup, and think o' the same things from one day's end to another? Just the same? That's idle talk. You'd cut us i' two.' (165)

Silas does not present his fatherhood as the transfer or provision of means from himself to his child; instead, food and drink are a part of a fully mutual daily life, in which the two are merged in their thinkings and doings.

In the final stage of the tense discussion between the four people, Nancy comes back into view. Her opinion, unspoken, is given: 'She felt that it was a very hard trial for the poor weaver, but her code allowed no question that a father by blood must have a claim above that of any foster-father' (166). It is a simple reiteration of the argument of a natural claim over any other – one real father, above 'any' number of others; no mention of a marriage or a mother that might dilute or complicate the primary case. Silas's own assertion of the difference made by a lifetime of being, in practice, the father is reduced to the secondary status of 'foster-father'. But Godfrey then modifies his own line by adding in Nancy as a positive persuasion: 'And you'll have the best of mothers in my wife – that'll be a blessing you haven't known since you were old enough to know it' (166). Here Godfrey makes no distinction between the natural and the adoptive or foster-mother: for the purposes of asserting Nancy's future merits, there must be no distinction. Nor does motherhood lead to claims and rights for either mothers or children; having a mother is a contingent 'blessing', a gift to a child, just as the child, in Silas's account, can be gift to the parent.

In many ways, the confrontation in Silas's cottage situates the four people present as two symmetrical couples, both of whom have lived and developed together over the past fifteen or sixteen years; Nancy and Godfrey were married the year after Eppie's arrival (and Molly's death). These two emerge more, not less, united than before from the effects of Godfrey's confession and their joint attempt to persuade Eppie to live with them. When they have gone back to their house there is a pause, after which:

> At last Godfrey turned his head towards her, and their eyes met, dwelling in that meeting without any movement on either side. That quiet mutual gaze of a trusting husband and wife is like the first moment of rest or refuge from a great weariness or a great danger. (168)

Eliot's image of the gestures of love, the peaceful return home, reinforces the symmetry between this married relationship and the bond between Silas and Eppie which is also, on her side, 'till death us do part', and without any possible putting asunder: 'I'll cleave to him as long as he lives, and nobody shall ever come between him and me' (167).

Having settled Eppie so finally and forever with her father, Eliot perhaps has a little difficulty in playing the final scene. Eppie's connection to Aaron is not presented as having the passionate unconditionality of her attachment to her father. When he has mooted the possibility of their marrying, she asks her father for advice, reporting her own attitude as 'take it or leave it':

> And you mean to have him, do you?' said Silas.
> 'Yes, some time', said Eppie, 'I don't know when. Everybody's married some time, Aaron says. But I told him that wasn't true: for, I said, look at father – he's never been married.'
> 'No, child', said Silas, 'your father was a lone man till you was sent to him.' (144)

Eppie supplied the place that might have been a wife's. And in the event, Aaron himself has proposed that Silas must live with them and that, Eppie says, 'he'd be as good as a son to you – that was what he said' (145).

By placing a wedding at the end, Eliot gives a conventional kind of fantasy conclusion to the novel, and works hard to get it to blend in smoothly with the less conventional fantasy of domestic happiness and personal redemption that she has developed up to that point.[5] After the fulfilment of fatherhood has been so perfectly sent to him – or after fatherhood has been sent to him as his fulfilment – it cannot, in the terms of the novel, be once again sent away.

NOTES

1. George Eliot, *Silas Marner* (1861), ed. Terence Cave (Oxford: Oxford University Press, 1996), 138. Further references will be given within the main text.
2. Marianne Novy has pointed out how *Silas Marner* differs from classical adoption narratives in this respect, validating the adoptive parent over the birth parent, once found, by giving the (now adult) child the choice between them. See *Reading Adoption: Family and Difference in Fiction and Drama* (Ann Arbor: University of Michigan Press, 2005), ch. 5.
3. William Wordsworth, 'Ode: Intimations of Immortality from Recollections of Early Childhood' (1807), line 67, in *Poems, Volume I*, ed. John O. Hayden (Harmondsworth: Penguin 1977), 525.
4. Like others of Eliot's novels, *Silas Marner* is set in the past – a time that is vaguely dated, within the novel, to 'the early years of this century' (4) –that is, to the early 1800s'. Before the Adoption of Children Act of 1926, which established a legal framework for full adoption, adoptions in England most often took the form of *ad hoc* arrangements, usually but not always within families; the absence of records in such cases makes the history quite conjectural. A more formal system of 'placing' children for adoption through the mediation of agencies began to take shape in the 1920s; their work was one of the spurs to the passing of the 1926 Act, but informal adoptions continued to occur in the 1930s and during the war. See Jenny Keating, *A Child for Keeps: The History of Adoption in England, 1918–45* (London: Palgrave Macmillan, 2008), and Stephen Cretney, *Family Law in the Twentieth Century: A History* (Oxford: Oxford University Press, 2003), 596–627.
5. Margaret Homans's provocative reading radically undermines the fantasy, by suggesting that the marriage of Eppie and Aaron, who will live with Silas, is not so much a sign of continuing cottage simplicity in the pastoral mode

as an early stage of gentrification, since Silas has been enclosing some previously common land where he lives. Rather than opting authentically to remain with the lower-class level of her adoptive class, as it seems on the face of things, Eppie, along with her new husband, Aaron, will be as if aspirationally moving on up towards the property-owning classes. See Homans, *The Imprint of Another Life: Adoption Narratives and Human Possibility* (Ann Arbor: University of Michigan Press, 2013), 58–85, especially 78, 81–2.

4

How Not to be Parented

Speech Creatures in *Pamela* and *Pride and Prejudice**

In this chapter, Jane Austen's Mr Darcy shows up in a different guise from the endlessly enigmatic single man of romantic legend: instead, and alongside a very different character from another classic English novel, he appears as a spokesman on the subject of emotional education. The 'speech creatures' of my title come from Malcolm Bowie, whose delightful creation they were in his book *Psychoanalysis and the Future of Theory*. The phrase quietly injects some new and consciously psychoanalytic life into the usually more reason-oriented understandings of Aristotle's 'animals who have *logos*': have reason and language.[1] Speaking is the distinctive but ordinary thing that we human animals do that is different from what other animals do; we do it all the time and we often make stories with it. In the context of Bowie's broader argument, these speech creatures come to appear as beings in search of ways – psychoanalytic but also artistic – to articulate a future (rather than to return to or discover a past, which would be the more common psychoanalytic emphasis). The men whom this chapter will be considering, in the novels by Austen and Samuel Richardson, do that; but they are also speech creatures in a very simple sense, in that they both make significant summarising speeches at a culminating point in their narrative development. In these speeches, rather grand and self-congratulatory ones as it happens, *Pamela*'s Mr B. and *Pride and Prejudice*'s Mr Darcy each offer a story of personal development in which they declare themselves, in remarkably similar terms, to have been reformed or refashioned thanks to the influence of the woman with whom they are now about to share their life.

At the point of their acknowledgement of the salutary effects of the beloved, Darcy and Mr B. are, to put it mildly, not obviously comparable characters. Mr B.

---

* First published in *Paragraph* 32:2 (July 2009).

has been pursuing Pamela for hundreds of pages, in anything but respectable ways, including at different times abduction and house arrest; attempted rape through the impersonation of a woman; a bid to lure her into a 'sham marriage'; and, last and least heinous, perhaps, the offer of a very good package, including an income and a settlement for her parents, if she will be his mistress. His proposal to marry her for real comes at the end of all this: not just in concession to Pamela's unrelenting resistance but, as his speech makes clear, in professed apology for and repudiation of all his former manoeuvres. He will not just act differently; he *is* a different man.

Mr Darcy, at first sight, could not be more of a contrast. He has not exactly made his amorous feelings for Elizabeth Bennet plain to her or anyone else, whereas Mr B. has been running after Pamela quite openly, and involving his entire entourage in the numerous plots to win, or at least seduce her. For Elizabeth, if not quite for the reader, the first hint of Darcy's attachment is his blundered first proposal of marriage, real marriage. Darcy is a model of moral correctness, not only in his own person but in his taking upon himself the welfare of others. His parents are dead, and he has dealt successively with two potential or actual seductions by the dastardly Mr Wickham – the first, before the time of the novel, when Wickham nearly got away with Darcy's own sister, and the second when, halfway through it, he elopes with Elizabeth's flighty young sister, Lydia. Mr Darcy acts *in loco parentis* to sort out the rakes; Mr B. actually is one, or was one.

One thing the two men do have in common is a class difference from their intended – much greater in the case of Pamela and Mr B. Pamela is a servant, who waited on Mr B.'s mother, now dead; the Bennets are gentlefolk but by no means as wealthy or as high in the middle-class rankings as Mr Darcy's all but noble family (they don't possess an estate that remotely resembles the grand Pemberley). In both novels it is the girl from an inferior class who is able to teach the man what virtue should be – in Pamela's case, the virtue that a girl has to preserve against her 'ruin'; in Elizabeth's, consideration of another person's feelings, not just of their relative rank (Darcy says he assumed initially that Elizabeth would accept him without question). The 'love of a good woman' plotline, so beloved of chick lit throughout history, is typically spiced by a difference of class that both obscures and reinforces the power gap inherent in the difference of sex. The education the men will ultimately receive is thus an education not just from a woman, but from below; and in both cases it is cast in a form that accentuates the learner's initial resistance to it through a pride or stubbornness, which is itself subsequently seen as having been part of the problem that needed to be resolved.

After that preamble, it is time for the two men's speeches. Here then, first of all, is Mr Darcy, towards the end of *Pride and Prejudice*; he and Elizabeth

Bennet have been going over the history of their previous misunderstandings and Darcy has been reproaching himself for his lack of 'proper feeling',[2] before Elizabeth taught him differently:

> I have been a selfish being all my life, in practice though not in principle. As a child I was taught what was right, but I was not taught to correct my temper. I was given good principles, but left to follow them in pride and conceit. Unfortunately an only son, (for many years an only *child*) I was spoilt by my parents, who though good themselves, (my father particularly, all that was benevolent and amiable,) allowed, encouraged, almost taught me to be selfish and overbearing, to care for none beyond my own family circle, to think meanly of all the rest of the world, to *wish* at least to think meanly of their sense and worth compared with my own. Such I was, from eight to eight and twenty; and such I might still have been but for you, dearest, loveliest Elizabeth! What do I not owe you! You taught me a lesson, hard indeed at first, but most advantageous. By you, I was properly humbled. (377–8)

And here, compare and contrast, is Mr B., half a century and more before *Pride and Prejudice*, towards the end of *Pamela*:

> We People of Fortune, or such as are born to large Expectations, of both Sexes, are generally educated wrong. You have occasionally touch'd upon this, *Pamela*, several times in your Journal, so justly, that I need say the less to you. We are usually so headstrong, so violent in our Wills, that we very little bear Controul.
>
> Humour'd by our *Nurses*, thro' the Faults of our Parents, we practise first upon them; and shew the *Gratitude* of our Dispositions, in an Insolence that ought rather to be check'd and restrain'd, than encouraged.
>
> Next, we are to be indulged in every thing at School; and our *Masters and Mistresses* are rewarded with further grateful Instances of our boisterous Behaviour.
>
> But, in our wise Parents Eyes, all looks well, all is forgiven and excus'd; and for no other Reason, but because we are *Theirs*.
>
> Our next Progression is, we exercise our Spirits, when brought home, to the Torment and Regret of our *Parents themselves*, and torture their Hearts by our undutiful and perverse Behaviour to them; which, however ingrateful in us, is but the natural Consequence of their culpable Indulgence to us, from Infancy upwards.[3]

The two passages share a critique of the speaker's education, beginning at home. Both men believe they initially experienced a kind of anti-education, through which they failed to learn a necessary self-restraint. In a word – a word that is very popular in the period – 'I was *spoilt* by my parents', says Darcy; while Mr B. speaks of 'their culpable Indulgence to us, from Infancy upwards'. According to Darcy, his father 'allowed, encouraged, *almost taught me* to be selfish and overbearing'. In Mr B.'s case, 'an Insolence that ought rather to be check'd and restrain'd, than encouraged' is attributed to 'the Faults of our Parents'. Not only: It was them! They did it to me! – the modern accusing cry of the child turned dysfunctional adult. But also: They actually *taught* me this! – in a perversion of proper education.

This education is among other things irrational, in Mr B.'s judgement: 'for no other reason than that we are *Theirs*'. Why on earth should anyone prefer their own children? The parents are to blame not just for their indulgence per se, but because their behaviour is based entirely – 'for no other reason' – on personal preference and prejudice: '*Theirs*'. It is also significant that the parents are acting together, as one, in their *Theirs*: there is no distinction between the parts or the partiality of the mother and the father, the one or the other, who in this blinkered, counter-educational context have operated as a unit.

Enter, then, the re-educating saviour. This parental malformation has had to be unlearned with the help of the beloved woman. 'You taught me a lesson, hard indeed at first', says Darcy; while Mr B. has found inspiration in Pamela's journal. In both cases, there is a stepping down from an initial assumption of class privilege. 'We people of Fortune, or such as are born to large Expectations' are the ones who are open to the misdirected lessons. Darcy was 'almost taught . . . to think meanly of all the rest of the world' and was then, in a suitable reversal, 'properly humbled' by Elizabeth, where 'humbled' has connotations of rank as well as humiliation: he no longer understands his wealth as entailing superiority.

The emphasis on the power and importance of early education is characteristic of the period – the long eighteenth century that I am invoking to encompass both novels – though perhaps less characteristic of autobiographical pronouncements such as these. Mr B. and Mr Darcy both take up the idea that education is all, and then, as if at a distance, apply it to themselves. They see what their education, or mistaken education, made of them; they are then able to formulate a new man who has been differently made – who has been re-educated in another mould and can now, from his new vantage point, see the errors of his first formation.

Yet despite the broad similarities between them, Mr B. and Mr Darcy frame their declarations in very different ways. In one case, the point is presented as a social critique of the typical upbringing of 'We people of Fortune', who 'are generally educated wrong', while in the other there is no movement or extended application beyond the particular family set-up within which Mr Darcy was taught, or mistaught, a self-evident hierarchical certainty. That miseducation can now be seen as such, but no claim is made for its application to other grand families; instead, the revised lesson Darcy has learned has to do with correcting his hitherto demeaning judgements of 'the rest of the world'.

Mr B.'s critique goes on to take the form of a general theory of unhappy marriages as an ostensible vindication of his earlier pursuit of alternative ways of getting hold of Pamela: 'For nobody was more averse to this State [of matrimony] than myself, and now we're upon this subject, I'll tell you why I was so averse' (443). He is citing his own upbringing as a case to illustrate how mismatched couples get together who, because they have never learned to consider the needs of others, are bound to fall out. This is how the passage continues, right after the statement about the parents' 'culpable Indulgence to us, from Infancy upwards':

> And then, next, after we have, perhaps, half broken their Hearts, a *Wife* is look'd out for: Convenience, or Birth and Fortune, are the first Motives, Affection the last (if it is at all consulted): And two People thus educated, thus trained up in a Course of unnatural Ingratitude, and who have been headstrong Torments to every one who has had a Share in their education, as well as to those to whom they owe their Being, are brought together; and what can be expected, but that they should pursue, and carry on, the same comfortable Conduct, in Matrimony, and join most heartily to plague one another? (444)

Let us note in passing that broken-heartedness begins in a parental disappointment, not an erotic one. It is the parents, not the (potential) lovers or spouses, who have 'half broken' hearts, and this state in them leads to the making of a marriage for their children that is itself broken, or never united, from the start. The problem is not only the separate wilfulness of the two parties, but also their disappointed wishes:

> So great is the Difference, between what they both expect *from* one another, and what they both find *in* each other, that no wonder Misunderstandings happen; that these ripen to Quarrels; that Acts of Unkindness pass, which, even had the first Motive to their Union been *Affection*, as usually it is not, would have effaced all manner of tender Impressions on both sides. (444)

Mr B. pursues his miserable everyday tale of unhappy endings, with 'Appeals to parents or Guardians' – the couple are still in the position of children – and attempted, though usually unsuccessful 'Reconciliation', 'by Mediation of Friends'. But 'it hardly ever holds, for why?' (444):

> The Fault is in the Minds of *both*, and *neither* of them will think so; so that the Wound (not permitted to be probed) is but skinn'd over, and rankles still at the Bottom, and at last breaks out with more Pain and Anguish than before. Separate Beds are often the Consequence; perhaps Elopements; if not, an unconquerable Indifference, possibly Aversion. (444–5)

Finally, they are no fun to be with as a pair, 'but, separate, have freer Spirits, and can be tolerable Company' (445).

The first thing that is striking about Mr B.'s withering analysis is its gender neutrality: the same as with the parental couple, though in that case the couple is implicitly at one – at least in their parenting practices. We have here two people, both brought up in the same mistaken way; their incompatibility and mutual hatred arise not from a difference of expectations according to sex, but from the same unreasonable expectations because of the same wrong education: they have both been allowed to have their own way in everything.[4] The passage also pinpoints the determining interaction between (to put it in a different vocabulary) fantasy and reality, such that the clash of demands coming from 'the Minds of *both*' is then the cause of real 'acts' of unkindness.

The likely story of the bad marriage is, he claims, what has kept Mr B. at a distance from the institution up till now, and it is anatomised with regard to the failures of upper-class education as it applies to both boys and girls. Only a Pamela, from a humble background, has been able to show him another possibility, and at the point, a little earlier in the narrative, when he finally succumbs (to her own repeated refusal to succumb to his various forms of extra-marital pressure), his speech is a declaration of conversion:

> You cannot, my dear Life, be so happy in me, as I am in you. O how heartily I despise all my former Pursuits and headstrong Appetites! What Joys, what true Joys, flow from virtuous Love! Joys which the narrow Soul of the Libertine cannot take in, nor his Thought conceive! – And which I myself, whilst a Libertine, had not the least Notion of! (359)

This outpouring of rapturous righteousness should not blind us (or Pamela) to the more pragmatic modulation that takes place when Mr B. later argues about the social sources of bad marriages. But even here, already, the ostensibly principled stance – Virtue versus Appetites – is offered in terms of widening experience: what the 'narrow Soul of the Libertine cannot take in', not simply what he fails or refuses to see as 'true Joys'.

Mr B.'s exemplary story of the course of untrue love is based on solidly social generalisations, on what can easily be explained in view of the typical 'indulgence' accorded to the children of the wealthy, 'We People of Fortune'.

And as well as proposing a lack of differentiation between the way that boys and girls are raised in this regard, it also includes an appeal to the rightness of what would come to be known as the 'companionate' marriage. The problem for Mr B.'s young married couple is that they wind each other up to the point of mutual loathing: they can't be good mates. Behind that lies the premise that friends, at least friends of a kind, is what married people should be; and in his enumeration of the usual criteria, Mr B. could almost be making a historical as well as an ideological point: 'Convenience, or Birth and Fortune, are the first Motives, Affection the last (if it is at all consulted).' Out of this list, affection is certainly the last in the sense of the latest to be introduced as a premarital consideration for 'People of Fortune', and its importance, at least its assumed or ideological importance, would grow over the coming decades to the point that affection would come to seem the first and most obvious, not the last and least consulted of conditions.[5]

With a further unwittingly future bias, Mr B.'s list is also forward-looking in the very fact of its being a list, a set of heterogeneous factors all considered compatible and specifiable in relation to the objective of finding suitably matched marital partners. (A distant descendant of this mode of thinking is the present-day online tick-box culture whereby, in a comparable way, the potential mate or date is presented and evaluated according to a preliminary checklist of relevant criteria.) Mr B. is personally willing, however, to prioritise just one of these criteria, the last and the latest; his argument, in fact, is that parity of 'Birth and Fortune', far from ensuring compatibility of any kind, is more likely to lead to break-ups, given the present conditions of bad education. Over and above the historical shift that is downplaying the importance of class and money in favour of the importance of individual inclinations, this other premise is crucial too: emotional education makes the man, and the woman.

★

In summary, then: both *Pamela* and *Pride and Prejudice* feature remarkably similar conclusive utterances on the part of two specially speechy creatures. Austen's Darcy and Richardson's Mr B. are both men of a certain standing who know their elevated place in the world and have expected and been accustomed to get what they want, but who now take it upon themselves to repudiate that earlier sense of entitlement and omnipotence. The convergence of their discourses is the more striking, as we have seen, because on the face of things the two men are such different types. Yet both of them, both the rake and the paragon of moral rectitude, stick to the same object of desire; and both get her, in the end, on terms that alter the conditions of their former wishes and imagined powers. Both stories represent this adjustment as a cause for celebration, not for regret or resentment: they see themselves as having gained as persons as well as gaining the woman they wanted all along.

There are a number of ways in which we might connect and compare the self-discoveries of Mr Darcy and Mr B. to some psychoanalytic versions of how a man grows up. First of all, there is the humbling aspect of Darcy's plea. For Freud, the baby's dependence (and the parents' over-love) put it in the glorified position of 'His Majesty the Baby'. Becoming an adult is a matter, in part, of learning the true state of things: that you are one among others, not the centre of power and authority. Freud's 'Family Romances' paper describes an interesting transitional moment when the hypothetical Everychild is said to imagine that in reality they are the offspring of parents (or a parent) of higher birth than the ones they know as their own. Freud links this fantasy of adoption to the beginnings of a more objective view of the world, in that it starts with the child comparing his own parents to other people, and coming to see that they are not, after all, the great beings he originally took them for (the parental corollary of the royal family of 'His Majesty the Baby').[6] Darcy's problem, in these terms, is that he did not move on from the most infantile starting point of the assumption of personal and familial superiority; or rather, that when he did come to make a comparison, which he did, it only confirmed that superiority, and did so too through the encouragement if not the instigation of the parents themselves, who 'almost taught me . . . to think meanly of all the rest of the world'. The further refinement, 'to *wish* at least to think meanly of their sense and worth compared with my own' makes explicit both the fantasy – coming from the parents themselves – and the downwards comparative aspect, in reverse of the norm: here the boy finds no superiors beyond the parental world.

Darcy is thus, in this context, belatedly 'humbled'. Not only does he now declare that he has revised his opinion of relative worth; he also declares the realisation to be a matter of personal transformation brought about by seeing his own childhood formation in a different light. Mr B., too, ironises upon the miseducation of 'People of Fortune'. The change now, for both of them, is a matter of taking a distance from the models of identification and behaviour that were first presented to them. There is also an element of jubilation. Both are proud of their new reformed, reconstructed self; and both are grateful to the influence of the female mentor who has taught them, directly in Pamela's case, to see their errors. They sound 'therapied': they take pleasure in telling the story of how far they have come and how messed up they were before.

But here too some of the equally revealing distances from the psychoanalytic model show up. Normally, the lover and the analyst are not, in reality, supposed to be one and the same, even though the transference in the analytic situation is described as indistinguishable from falling in love. The whole effectiveness of the analytic process depends on its being set apart as a kind of experimental world in which the patient's former and current relationships can come to be experienced and understood in new ways; a real relationship – real in the sense of its taking place beyond the talking and beyond the consulting room – is expressly forbidden. There is, however, one place in Freud's writing where he discusses and celebrates a case in which the potential lover, sure enough, takes on the role of the mentor and reformer, and ends up getting together with him. This exception is the study of Wilhelm Jensen's novella *Gradiva*, in which the lively modern girl who succeeds in getting the unworldly archaeologist to notice and fall in love with her becomes, for Freud, an equivalent of the psychoanalyst: she brings about her patient's cure, and what he gets at the end, as in the cases of Mr B. and Mr D., is the girl herself as well.[7]

Another difference between psychoanalysis and the *Pamela* and *Pride and Prejudice* scenarios is that though the parents figure strongly in both Darcy's and Mr B.'s declarations, it is not as objects of love or hate or even identification, but rather as incompetent teachers. In Mr B.'s account, there is a seamless transition from home to school, with nurses, parents and teachers all occupying failed pedagogical roles. The child's response to them is behavioural, not affective. The 'parents', moreover, form a solidly dual subject in both Mr B.'s and Darcy's case (with Darcy's father standing only slightly separate as 'my father particularly', the one who was extra nice). There is no hint here of a proto-Oedipal division, in which the boy's differentiation between the parent he loves and the one he regards as a threat would be fundamental.

And if we turn things the other way round, to consider the Freudian set-up in the light of the spoiled child syndrome of Darcy and Mr B., we see that the two Freudian parents occupy opposite educational roles: the mother is the one who initially indulges the boy, and the father is the one who comes along and sets limits to what he can have. But the parents of the 'spoiling complex' have no particular separateness and, *a fortiori*, no particular sex *qua* parents. In the same way, strikingly, Mr B. and his sister have received what is represented as the same spoiled upbringing; and in Mr B.'s theory of the unhappy marriage the problem, once again, is that both the bride and the groom have been indulged in the same ways, so that neither has an inkling of how to make compromises in living with someone else. There is nothing sex-specific about any of it. The pair who are parents are united in the same mode of miseducation, and the pair who get married are disunited in the same inability and unwillingness to make room for one another's needs.

Another difference between spoiling complex and Oedipus complex is that in the former, the initial mal-formation is entirely due to the parents (and their surrogates). It is also the parents in *Pamela* who are broken-hearted as a result of the child's childhood: initially, the emotional wreckage is all on their side. In the Oedipus complex, on the other hand, everything starts from the child's feelings – except for occasional moments when Freud acknowledges that there is some input from the parents' own inclinations. And the child has no choice or agency in the matter: the Oedipus complex is what happens to him, it is the necessary and inevitable first sticking point of the human child, beyond which, with luck, he (and really only he – girls never get out) will come through as a better formed, better adapted social being. With the spoiling complex, things are much more contingent precisely because the first formation is dependent on variable parental proclivities. 'We People of Fortune' are brought up in a certain way; but there are other possible ways, and this is by no means a necessary one, as well as being an undesirable one from the point of view of future social and personal utility.

Both spoiling and Oedipus complexes rely on an assumption, so automatic today that it is difficult even to see it as such, that the child's first years are fundamental to the development of whatever kind of adult he or she will become – an assumption, that is to say, that the person's nature is not so much given or born, but shaped by their first emotional environment. There is also, for both complexes, the possibility of unlearning and re-forming, later in life. But the Oedipus complex offers the bleaker picture, in that the bad first education is inescapable and the best outcome that can really be hoped for, even after the analysis that might unravel what first went wrong, is what Freud called 'ordinary unhappiness'.[8] Darcy and Mr B., if not Jane Austen and Samuel Richardson, live in more optimistic stories.

NOTES

1. Malcolm Bowie, *Psychoanalysis and the Future of Theory* (Oxford: Basil Blackwell, 1993), 44.
2. Jane Austen, *Pride and Prejudice* (1813), ed. Tony Tanner (1972; London: Penguin, 1985), 376. Further references will be given within the main text.
3. Samuel Richardson, *Pamela* (1740), eds Thomas Keymer and Alice Wakely (Oxford: Oxford University Press, 2001), 443–4. Further page references will be given within the main text.
4. Mr B., as it happens, does have a wilful big sister called 'Captain Babs', who when they were children 'was always for domineering over me and I could not bear it' (412). She tries to prevent his union with Pamela and engages in a spirited argument about a different question in relation to sexual sameness, when she puts the case – which Mr B. rejects – that it ought to be the same for a lady to marry her 'Father's Groom' as it is for a gentleman to marry, as Mr B. has, his mother's waiting maid (see 421–2).

5. Ruth Perry has argued convincingly that the second half of the eighteenth century was the period in which this crucial shift took place, in practice as well as in principle, from marriages primarily 'arranged' by the future couple's families for reasons of inheritance and family concerns, to marriages for which the personal attachment between the two of them was the paramount consideration. See *Novel Relations: The Transformation of Kinship in English Literature and Culture 1748–1818* (Cambridge: Cambridge University Press, 2004).
6. See Freud, 'Family Romances' (1909), SE IX, 237–41.
7. See Freud, *Delusions and Dreams in Jensen's 'Gradiva'* (1907), SE IX, 1–95.
8. Freud used the phrase – *'gemeines Unglück'* ('common unhappiness') – at the end of the final part of *Studies on Hysteria* (1895), GW I, 312; SE II, 305.

PART II
CONSUMER CULTURE

5

Soft Sell

Marketing Rhetoric in Feminist Criticism*

> Many commodities are strictly women's propositions, and the advertiser, to secure the largest returns, should know the foibles of the sex and base his campaign upon that knowledge.[1]

Taken from an American advertising textbook of 1916, and appealing to and for a type of sexual differentiation reinforced and promoted by the expansion of marketing on both sides of the Atlantic during this period, this quotation still has a recognisable air. A vulnerable collective victim, 'the sex' with its special 'foibles', is targeted by a quasi-militaristic masculine offensive, 'his campaign'. In this case, the author in fact goes on to suggest that the sex's particular foibles are the result of occupational differences, rather than being natural; he does not, for instance, suggest that marketing is only directed to or against women, who are simply a particular case of an object that might be any group. But in any case, the mutability of a sex's foibles, and the fact that foibles are not confined to one sex, is no obstacle, rather providing unlimited possibilities for successful operations and conquests on the part of 'the advertiser', whose sole concern is the maximisation of profit, 'to secure the largest returns'. Marketing doesn't depend in principle on feminine foibles, as opposed to any others, but it has generally done pretty well out of the kind of fruitful engagement suggested by the offering of 'strictly women's propositions'.

This type of exploitation (in the most literal sense) has long been, in return, a ready target for feminist criticism. Sometimes consumerism has been seen as the principal source of women's oppression in the twentieth century, as a force which, by promoting a falsely feminine identity, distracts them from

---

* First published in *Women: A Cultural Review* 1:1 (April 1990).

what would otherwise be their true identities, as humans and/or as women. Such criticisms echo and are sometimes explicitly linked to Marxist and other accounts of a deterioration of the collective identity of working-class communities through the baleful encroachments of consumer culture. That this process has often been referred to in terms of 'feminisation' indicates the dominance of the quasi-sexual manipulation model of the opening quotation.

This is not the only line of reaction or resistance. Parallel to the operations of the rhetoric of marketing, there have in fact been two different constructions of the consumer to whom it appeals. In the first, of which the summary above is a version, the consumer is someone attacked by advertising as a powerless victim, her (or his) susceptibilities exploited in such a way that s/he is left with no effective choice. In the past this was usually a critical representation, whether from a liberal or a Marxist position, stressing the passive 'feminisation' of the consumer of whichever sex. The second construction of the consumer represents him (or her) not as a victim, but as the advertiser's double, engaged in conscious planning and decision-making. The sharpest British personification of this second figure emerged by the 1960s with the magazine *Which?*, designed for the thinking consumer of economical household goods. Instead of being seduced into unnecessary spending on worthless trinkets, this rational consumer is connoted as being a saver – of labour and time, as well as of money – and a sensibly functional person (he or she is more likely to buy tinned tomatoes or a refrigerator than nail varnish or whisky). And despite appearances, not one but both of these models are implied in the types of response to consumerism described just now: one as the place of the consumer, who is deluded, the other as the place of the critic, who is not.

For some time, then, the consumer has been a fairly hybrid being, half of it (more or less a feminine half) being that unhappy, or perhaps stupidly happy, victim of advertising's forces; and the other (more or less a masculine half) being a sober, rational sort of being who knows what he wants and makes the best possible decision based on the information available to get it. Meanwhile, although both these constructions remain in outline, they have undergone some extraordinary mutations of emphasis in the past few years.

The first, critical account has recently been given a more affirmative turn. Shopping is no longer seen as the despised symptom of patriarchal or capitalist alienation, but rather as part of a newly legitimate – politically acceptable – 'postmodern' interest in pleasure and fantasy. Those days are gone when consumerism could be comfortably identified as oppressive or regressive without more ado, and from some safely assumed position of exteriority. (This change is also criticised as being another weak acceptance of the status quo – a giving in on the part of the sex, and the other sex too, to a dominant order that has lately succeeded in pulling the wool, or the lurex, over a great many more critical eyes.)

In tandem with this (but probably seated on a different and more old-fashioned bike), the rational consumer has undergone a massive diversification of influence, with the great extension of the use of the term 'consumer' in everyday political language. The semantic territory of this figure has widened to the point where it has become synonymous with all sorts of other characters who might have been thought to have quite other concerns. In education, health, housing, water-drinking, egg eating, voting and many other fields, we are all addressed as 'consumers' now, and the term is assumed to imply individual rights and respect that are lacking for those who are merely regarded as parents, patients, voters, omelette eaters and so on. The consumer is fast becoming the model of citizenship itself.

A telling illustration of this is to be found in some recent remarks on behalf of the National Consumer Council, arguing for consumer education as part of the new National Curriculum in England:

> Too many young people leave school knowing how to do algebra and geometry but with little or no knowledge of how to compare interest rates on different types of loans. They may be able to write an essay on Jane Austen – but unable to write a sensible letter of complaint. Throughout pupils' education, they should be encouraged to think of themselves as consumers, the council said.[2]

This takes up a long-established opposition between literature and other subjects as the irrelevant versus the practical or the socially useful. Austen's name probably serves better than those of many other writers regarded as great to conjure up the required image of trite gratuitousness, mere feminine society banter removed from the nitty-gritty of real-life problems. But what is interesting is that the 'useful' or 'socially relevant' side of the comparison should now be taken up not, for instance, by contemporary history or ethical questions, but by consumer rights and financial skills. The consumer the pupil is to be encouraged to think they are is characterised simply by the capacity to demand a decent service or product, epitomised in that unforgettable specification of the 'sensible letter of complaint'.

There has thus been an increasing use of and focus on languages of consumerism. Yet it is clear that the various types of the consumer imply different models of the mental processes of the person persuaded to buy, choose or want this or that. The consumer represented as the mindless credit-card junkie or the helpless victim of 'subliminal' techniques is a rather different subject from the one construed as a savvy selector of the cheapest toothpaste or the best school for his child. These languages are not necessarily compatible, involving potential clashes between the 'consuming passions' of the postmodern shopper and the reasonable rights of the citizen-consumer (though one 'postmodern' representation would imply a third possibility, whereby the consumer is not passive *or* rational, pleasure-seeking *or* calculating, but either, alternately, according to mood or context).

Advertisers have been interested in subjectivity from a consciously pragmatic point of view (to find out what will work as a persuasive tactic). Theorists of subjectivity have not been particularly interested in the techniques of advertising or in the debates within marketing's special branch, already established at the beginning of this century, 'the psychology of advertising'; nor have they turned their attention to the models of subjectivity implied by critics or advocates of consumerism. But despite this apparent separation, models of marketing and the consumer do make an unacknowledged appearance in some writing about subjectivity in general, and not least in contemporary feminism.

Much feminist writing about subjectivity of the past few years has sought to open up possibilities outside what it identifies as the political limits of psychoanalysis. Where psychoanalysis was brought in at an earlier moment to rupture the Marxist centrality of class to the exclusion of other categories, it is itself often perceived as being both monolithic and potentially unhistorical in its insistence on the primacy of sexual differentiation, and in a form that necessarily makes femininity into an impossible derivative of what is always a masculine norm. (I leave aside the details of this question, which I have represented only from the point of view of critics of psychoanalysis.)

In place of this, models of identity are put forward now that seek to be more flexible in their understanding of the ways in which identities, including sexual identities, may be formed and may undergo changes. Class, gender and race, as well as a variable range of other categories, are all seen to share, though not necessarily equally, in the formation of identities. At the same time, the identity of the subject is seen less as a forcible imposition, whereby she is constrained either passively to take on or hopelessly to struggle against something fundamentally negative, but rather as potentially desirable: enabling as much as it is constricting. Foucault is often cited as the inspiration for such a conception of a multiplicity of identifications produced through the operation of numerous heterogeneous discourses that pull individuals in particular provisional directions. The political edge is maintained by stressing that the possibilities are restricted by the nature and number of discourses 'available' for identification; and the need for more or different ones is part of the argument. The aim is that no one discourse or its corresponding mode of identity should be granted priority: there can be many 'femininities', for instance, though some, according to political criteria that are given as a starting point, are deemed to be better than others.

There is, however, a particular discourse that often does emerge as dominant in such descriptions, and that is none other than the discourse of marketing and consumption. To take one example, from Chris Weedon's *Feminist Practice and Poststructuralist Theory*:

> Discourses, located as they are in social institutions and processes are continually competing with each other for the allegiance of individual agents . . .
>
> Some forms of subjectivity are more readily available to the individual than others and this will depend on the social status and power of the discourse in question.
>
> The nature of femininity and masculinity is one of the key sites of discursive struggle for the individual and we need only look at a few examples of forms of subjectivity widely on offer to realize the importance of this battle.[3]

Discourses behave here in a way that is identical to marketed products. As with companies' attempts to secure brand loyalty, they are 'competing' for 'the allegiance of individual agents'. One factor in deciding whether a discourse is picked up is its 'social status', just as a prominent marketing model of the consumer is based on her or his assumed need to be or appear to be higher up the scale, whether this is represented negatively, as a fear of falling ('keeping up with the Joneses'), or positively, as a desire to rise (upward mobility). There is a perpetual 'battle' (the military undertone of the advertising 'campaign'), where what is being fought over is the capitulation or resistance of the consumer as territory to be subdued on a 'site' of struggle. By implication, discourses are not modified by the purchaser, but come ready-made to be picked up and used as they are. Some 'are more readily available' than others, more 'widely on offer'.

Does it make any difference to the argument to point to its hidden persuasions? The trouble arises not from the presence of this particular discourse – there is no *a priori* reason to think that it is more insidious than any other – but from the fact that it is taken as not in need of the analysis being given to other discourses and their processes of what Weedon calls 'naturalisation'. Charged as it is, the discourse of marketing has been taken up as neutral, and used as the framework within which to understand the operation of all discourses and the relations of subjects to them. Since the languages of marketing and consumerism have been making their way into more fields of everyday life and talk than ever before, it becomes crucial to look out for them, not to take them as natural. But by the same token, marketing cannot just be regarded as a weed that could simply be rooted out of the discursive garden. For one thing, it comes in many shapes and forms, in varying degrees of intensity and distinguishability. For another, like any other discourse, it did not spring up independently, but developed out of a host of others – the military campaign and the planned seduction are two – with which it still enters into complicated relations, and from which it cannot wholly be separated.

So there is no straightforward getting away from marketing – we could not and need not stop using words like *offer* or *available*. But there should be no straightforward assumption of its normality, either. In the light of the new pervasiveness of languages of marketing and consumption, far beyond their first fields of application in advertising and shopping, it becomes all the more necessary to analyse the ways in which they work or sell. Feminists (who, by the way, are now a key target group for advertising, which can appeal to their particular foibles) should not simply take on trust, as read, the language of advertising, which has never made any secret of having a special interest in the exploitation of women, but which, and by the same token, has always been most attractive to them too.

This is not simply a proposal that we should look carefully at the labels before committing ourselves to something that may turn out to be not what it seems at first. Instead, it seems to me that the question of whether or not you 'buy' an argument is already part of the problem, suggesting that an argument is something comparable to a finished product, to be taken or rejected as is, yes or no, according to whether it seems to satisfy our existing demand. The purchase of an interesting text extends beyond the first rapid glance of appraisal.

All this too might indicate that there are more general questions to be asked about the rhetorics of feminist criticism: about the ways in which it does or doesn't 'sell' what it is presenting as its version of feminism; about how it sets that version apart from other versions of feminism or femininity to be rejected; about the mode of address to the readers, which varies from the academically authoritative to the cosily 'women together'. Sometimes, as with Betty Friedan, feminism has made its appeal precisely in the name of an alternative to a false femininity identified as imposed by consumerism. For the first issue of a feminist journal whose name is not so different from that of a mass-market magazine that used to be considered the epitome of housewifely feminine conformity, these questions seem irresistible.[4]

NOTES

1. Henry Foster Adams, *Advertising and its Mental Laws* (New York: Macmillan, 1916), 317.
2. Ngaio Crequer, 'Pupils "need lessons to be consumers"', *Independent*, 8 August 1989.
3. Chris Weedon, *Feminist Practice and Poststructuralist Theory* (Oxford: Basil Blackwell, 1987), 97, 98.
4. The mass-market journal referred to was *Woman*. The new journal was *Women: A Cultural Review*; its first issue, in which the present article appeared, was published in April 1990.

6

Make Up Your Mind

Scenes from the Psychology of Selling and Shopping*

SCENE 1: THE UNIVERSAL SHOWROOM

To set the scene, and to gain your attention (all commentators are agreed that this is the first difficulty faced by anyone with any kind of proposition to put over), let me begin by quoting a grand evolutionary statement that culminates in the fulfilment of the characteristic twentieth-century mode of being. On the first page of a how-to book for prospective door-to-door salesmen published in 1927, there occurs the following passage, which moves into realms far beyond the contingently practical:

> In a commercial sense, by 'selling' we mean disposing of or exchanging commodities for profit.
> Of late years, however, 'selling' has taken on another meaning. We are learning to recognize that nearly all human relations involve gaining attention, arousing interest, using persuasion. These are fundamental terms understood in the world of commercial salesmanship. The fact that they have been taken over into other phases of life besides those of commerce, indicates that the human mind is growing and broadening. We are beginning to realize that the act of living itself, in all its varied relationships, is, in reality, a vast business of selling and salesmanship.
> The woman who walks into a drawing-room takes care that her dress, words and manner shall please others she may meet there.
> The man who seeks admission to a club tries so to deport himself, and to impress his personality upon others, that he will be welcomed as a member of the organization.

---

* First published in *Shopping with Freud*, Routledge, 1993.

In either case, the woman or the man is 'selling' herself or himself. That is a meaning of the word that has crept into the language and is readily understood by everyone . . .

The young lover 'sells' his personality to his sweetheart; the wife, the idea to her husband of how beautiful she will look in a new fur coat.[1]

The passage both claims and exemplifies an expansion of terms associated with commerce beyond their original fields of reference, to take over new territories now seen to be their natural destination. A linguistic change covers and enacts a global change, as the wider meaning of 'selling' stealthily invades: it 'has crept into the language' to gain currency and purchase. All the world's a showroom, every man or woman is an advertisement for himself or herself, aiming to 'impress' and please his or her consumers. Two sexes are invoked with differentiated modes of behaviour – a man is wooer of women singly and men collectively, a woman a wearer of dresses financed by a husband, and so on – but these differences are subordinated to the overarching and organising category of the scene of the sale in which both adopt their respective roles.

By the same token, everyone is also, in relation to everyone else, a consumer, taking in as well as giving off impressions; 'paying' or withholding attention and interest. The primary aim of a book like *Salesmanship Simplified* – and there were numerous such books during this period – doubles up on its own argument: it is to sell selling – as a trade and as a way of life – to readers who are thereby addressed as consumers at the same time as they are being sold an identification of themselves as salesmen. This reciprocity also points to the way in which the generalisation of 'selling' – the passage above self-consciously puts it in quotation marks, under exposure – was also, by the same token, the generalisation of consuming. As another book of the period puts it from the other side of the transaction: 'The consumer is beyond economics, before economics, and beneath economics. For consuming is living.'[2] To the same degree that selling was becoming both a practical and a speculative theme, so was its natural opposite number. Viewed from the other side of the counter, consumption became the salesman's constant question: what will make this person buy? And it is for this reason that discussions of consumer behaviour, whether they emanate from within the business world or from those who situate themselves outside it, tend to move rapidly and overtly into general questions of psychology. To know the conditions and workings of the mind is to know how to act upon it, how to make an impression.

There is an intimate connection, institutionally and intellectually, between psychology and marketing during the first forty years of the twentieth century, and beyond. As psychology became separated off from philosophy on one side and neurology on the other as an independent discipline, the primary questions with which it was concerned were often identical to those that preoccupied advertisers, who wanted to know how people acted and thought in order to know what would get them to buy. Psychologists at this time were laying out areas of investigation that overlap to a striking extent with those that concerned advertisers from a pragmatic point of view; and the developing institutional fields known as 'consumer psychology' or 'the psychology of selling' form a bridge between the academic and the practical that makes science directly available to men and women engaged in selling, just as the interest of these professionals in psychological questions fed back, through actual funding and through other, less tangible channels, into the kinds of question that the 'pure' – not directly commercial – psychologists were asking.

Standard psychological topics at this time included the nature of choice and decisions, and how these might be affected by 'suggestion' as opposed to reasoned arguments; the distinctiveness of a collective or 'crowd' mind and how its operation differed from that of the individual mind in isolation; the differentiation between instincts given from birth and acquired habits, and the types of action to which each gave rise. All these are topics central to the consumer-oriented questions of marketing proper; and in this sense, the local questions about consumers become inseparable from more general questions about the determinants and the nature of human choices and actions.

The output of texts about psychology and marketing at this time was vast, and their range encompasses every gradation from the academic to the popular. There are numerous books reporting on experimental and other findings for the benefit of those on the policy-making side of selling, but there is also a large body of 'how-to' books for prospective door-to-door salesmen, or department-store assistants, which include material on psychology and how to use it in dealings with customers as a central part of their presentation. Considered from the perspective of the seller, it seems obvious that the issue of what makes a consumer choose to buy or not buy stands alone. But in fact, as in the opening quotation in this chapter, large claims are made, in popular as well as academic textbooks, about the inherent interest of psychology, as well as about the capacity of consumer psychology to stand for psychology in general.

A 1921 handbook for department-store assistants puts it like this:

> In a retail store, you have a wonderful chance to study human beings. Don't you think it is interesting to look at men and women and to wonder about them? Who are they? What are their chief characteristics? Why do they act and talk as they do? Where are they going? For what purposes do they buy various articles?

This does not mean that you must be 'nosey'. It simply means that as an alert individual you must study people.

It is the most absorbing game in the world, even more interesting than reading stories or novels. You are dealing with all types of individuals. Each one talks and acts differently. Why?[3]

In the quotation from the salesmanship book, all the world is a showroom; and it would then follow, as stated here, that the showroom is a microcosm of the whole world. This world of the most accurate psychological evidence is explicitly a place of fiction – of games and stories. Where previously you might have learned psychology from reading, now you will get it – and it will be 'even more interesting' – from the customers in a store.

Walter B. Pitkin's post-Crash discussion of consumer psychology draws on a similarly literary analogy, obliquely making a case not only for the pertinence of classifications in psychology based on categories from imaginative writing, but also for the priority of the consumerly to the literary as a psychological paradigm. The author makes a distinction between 'romantic' and 'classical' consumers:

> It sounds silly to speak of consumers as displaying 'classic' and 'romantic' taste. Yet they do this, and in a sense even more intensely than most literary critics have done. The ordinary person is, in this sense, a romantic through and through. His cravings . . . are many, relatively weak, not sharply organized around one or two dominants, and hence somewhat blurred both intellectually and emotionally. He may even find it hard to distinguish his ego from his cosmos.[4]

The difference between the two, and the tendency for the romantic to supersede the classical, is best exemplified for this book by the history of the automobile. Writers of this period, and particularly this one, tend to see the motor car not merely as an example of a desirable commodity, but as the epitome of the desirable commodity, their test case for how and why people might be moved to buy things. Pitkin continues:

> The original Ford car was built on classic lines . . . The vehicle had just one purpose and it fulfilled that better than anything else ever had; it aimed to transport its owner from point A to point B at a velocity never before attained with the same degree of safety and economy. It made not the slightest attempt to serve any other human wish; there was nothing of beauty in its line, still less in its color; it contained no cigar lighter, no mirror, no

powder puff, no clock, no compass, no barometer, and no radio. It was the expression of a single-track mind which had solved a single problem. And that is the very essence of the classical. Ford did one thing at a time and did that with austere completion.[5]

The classical mind, for producer and consumer alike, is thus based on principles of utility, security and above all economy (in time, money and mental effort: only one track). It directs itself from A to B by the shortest possible route, whereas the romantic mind is all over the place in its one place, treating the car as a luxurious interior stocked with gadgets to suggest and satisfy every momentary hedonistic whim.

From Pitkin's miniature history of the classical and romantic versions of the motor car can be extrapolated two standard models of the consumer, which have been subject to relatively minor modifications over the years in discussions of consumption from outside the economic field itself. One – like the romantic – is the consumer as dupe or victim or hedonist or any combination of these, infinitely manipulable and manipulated by the onslaughts of advertising; the other – like the classical – is the consumer as rational subject, calculating and efficient and aware of his aims and wants.

The first may be collectivised as the stupid population of a place called consumer society; such inhabitants are often seen as having undergone a process of what is called feminisation: they are 'like women' in their capriciousness and hedonism, though without this necessarily implying that such characteristics are natural to women. The second type is collectivised as either a noble opposition to the blandishments of consumer society, as with advocates of co-operative retailing or subscribers to magazines like *Which?* or *Consumer Reports*. Or, in a move that exactly parallels the extension of the selling model outside the technically economic sphere, they are citizen-consumers.

Here I am thinking of developments in 1980s Britain, where the word 'consumer' acquired a newly positive status in Thatcherite rhetoric. Before, people were students or patients or voters; now, they are *consumers* of education or health care or political representation, and the term connoted rights and initiative by implication not available to the various characters identified by the separate terms. The 'classical' model is also, implicitly, the identity that makes the consumer the double of the strategic salesman as planner; or, in another regular permutation, the 'classical' identification may exist unacknowledged in coolly rational critiques of the manipulative powers of advertising. In a world where every other mind is assumed to be infinitely vulnerable and impressionable, the critic of marketing techniques has somehow alone succeeded in preserving the balance.

The two types of consumer are complementary insofar as they turn upon a fixed opposition between control and its absence, between behaviour that is knowing and conscious of its aims and behaviour involving a mind incapable of, or uninterested in, resistance. A perfect accord, which is also a ready-made tension, exists between the passive and the active, the feminine and the masculine, the infantile and the adult, the impulsive and the restrained, the spender and the saver — and so on, through many familiar polarities.

Advertising psychology is concerned with what the mind is in the light of the question of what will bring it to the point of purchase: in other words, with how people make choices, come to decisions. Because the emphasis is always on how minds may be moved, on how people change their minds, there is never any question of a static, self-contained consciousness, immutable and self-centred — and this applies as much when the mind is considered as operating rationally and in full knowledge of its aims and wants. A different form of persuasion or motivation will be appropriate in this case, but the rational mind, or the mind in its rational mode, is considered to be no less subject to influence or solicitation: it simply has to be persuaded that its wants are not whimsical but sensible.

SCENE 2: MAKING UP THE MIND

'To most women', says Ruth Leigh, addressing prospective department-store assistants, 'making up their minds is a difficult and unpleasant task.'[6] The phrase beautifully summarises the ambiguities of the consumer situation, or — and it amounts to the same thing, as we shall see — of the enterprise of psychological description. In a moment, we shall be examining just how this making up of minds was supposed to occur — by what stages, and in what order of events. But even in its initial formulation, the standard phrase is as suggestive and multivalent as the process it supposedly puts a stop to is complex and indeterminate. To make up your mind is to come to a decision; but that 'making up', especially when openly assisted by another party, seems in all kinds of ways to detract from the exercise of independent reason that the phrase initially seems to indicate. Let us look in more detail at four of its possible meanings.

To make up is, first, to supply a lack, as in phrases like 'to make up the difference', 'to make up for lost time'. There is something missing from what would otherwise be complete; an implicit subtraction is rectified. But a second kind of making up is almost the opposite of this one. To make up a face is to add something to it, with a positive connotation of enhancement or adornment where the first kind of making up merely involved the avoidance of something negative. These two modes of making up correspond, roughly but readily, to the classical and the romantic consumer: to the mature, masculine saver determined to avoid a loss and the infantile, feminine spender, unregulated in her desires. In terms of the forms of advertising address, the first mode involves the suggestion of fears or needs. The buyer must identify himself as lacking, and so purchase the product in order to put things right or protect what is vulnerable. The second mode is in the form of an invitation to pleasure or excess: to have or be something more, something else, something new.

Classically, and romantically sometimes, forms of marketing address that are making an 'emotional' appeal (as opposed to an appeal to the consumer as a man of sense) can be divided between these two modes: the warning (look what you lack) and the promise (look what you can have or what you can be). In the first case there is a threat to an implicitly attainable or former integrity that you risk losing; this may take the form of physical appearance or social standing, or both. In the second, there is the hope of a lift of some kind, or a pleasure, in the context of a mobility that may be upward or merely unfixed, and is not predicated on a given identity or wholeness to be either restored or achieved.

In a third sense, making up implies putting together from pieces: an advertisement or salesman works to co-ordinate, bring into an ensemble, a mind that would have no being or direction without this integrative or unifying intervention. The decision to purchase, in this sense, parallels the effect which the product is supposed to procure, by marking a provisional moment of settlement and unity. We shall be returning to this moment of the sale – a moment which must always be anticipated, but which it is only possible to locate retrospectively.

There is also a fourth and crucial aspect of making up your mind, which is its buried connotation of fictionality. To make up is to invent. The seller makes up the mind of the buyer, casting her (it is generally her) in a role, and giving her an ideal script to go with it. By the same token, the seller also puts himself (it is generally him) in a role, plays a part and makes up a mind to the same extent as the buyer.

This process of making up and acting out is described and prescribed in great detail in the early texts of salesmanship practice and consumer psychology. These accounts of buyers' minds and selling processes shift the emphasis away from the contrast between two different psychological modes, since they involve an overt dramatisation through which the mode is not fixed for either protagonist, although fixity can be a frequent source of appeal. There is a give and take, a to and fro, an exchange in all senses, in which both consumer mentalities are simultaneously implicated, and always open to modification or reversal.

In order to take a closer look at these issues, I propose to concentrate on a particular preoccupation of these texts: the step-by-step process that is supposed to lead up to any decision to purchase. This provides a particularly sharp illustration of the ways in which representations of consumer psychology and selling psychology 'on the ground' – in the shop or the housewife's home – may illuminate and complicate what looks like the simple dichotomy between rational and non-rational consumers or, by implication, between rational and non-rational human beings.

I have two other selling points. First, as the idea of the classical and romantic consumer will already have suggested, there will be more to say about the relations between consumption and literature. And second, since this is also the period when another new kind of psychology was developing I will also, at the end, draw together some questions about the scenes and structures of Freud's version of the mind which these excursions into the world of selling may have suggested.

SCENE 3: THE PRIEST, THE JUDGE, THE SOLDIER AND THE LOVER

Let us now look at the step-by-step process of this remarkable performance, the sale. That it is a drama, in the full, theatrical sense, is made explicit by the constant use of this word in presentations of the method of selling; one book, for instance, has a whole chapter on 'Dramatization'.[7] Salespersons are to think of themselves as acting a part and as endeavouring to carry a performance through to a happy ending, with attention at every stage to the 'cues' from the prospective buyer. Here is one example, from Henry Dexter Kitson's *The Mind of the Buyer*, a 1921 theory book for practitioners in the field:

> Stage the sale so that there will be no disturbance while it is in progress; for any disturbance, no matter how trivial, may mean the introduction of a new idea into the mind of the buyer and a dislodgment of the balance of brain energy. In view of such danger, the salesman should carefully isolate the buyer and separate him from things and people. This is the great psychological advantage of using a show room.[8]

The ideal, then, is a situation sealed off so that nothing can make its way into the buyer's mind but what you, the salesperson, put into it or make up for it. Script and props alike should be kept under strict control.

The process of the sale is compared to several paradigmatic stories, according to a number of distinct stages. First, the stories, of which there are four: each is used as an example, a model for sellers to follow, but also, at the same time, subsumed as no more than an isolated and possibly anachronistic species or branch of selling, which is the general store of all verbal and non-verbal forms of persuasion. The story of the sale, and the practice of sales talk, are the latest modes, and also the mode to end all modes.

The first comparable story is the religious conversion. From Kitson again:

> For an excellent example of the tactics to pursue at this stage [the matter in hand is the sale of tyres] the seller may profitably study the methods used by a professional evangelist in 'selling' religion. He begins by showing the prospective convert (buyer) how great a lack there is in his life.

The same book draws also on the second of these paradigmatic scenes, which is that of a trial:

> The situation at this point may be likened to a court-room scene in which evidence is submitted and arguments are presented for and against. As each bit of evidence is submitted, the judge (buyer) must test it.[9]

Unlike every other identification, the courtroom scene casts the buyer-judge as a rational adjudicator; in the other three cases, though in very different ways, to buy is to be overcome – without reason.

The other two model narratives are the commonest and the dominant ones. One of them, the military paradigm, surfaced in the allusion of the quotation above to the 'tactics to pursue'. This one is all-pervasive in the idiom of salesmanship, written in, as it is, to the language of every advertising 'campaign'. The buyer, or the 'target' market is an enemy whose resistances must be overcome in a battle that ends in its capitulation.

Equally charged is the last of the four selling stories: the scene of seduction. The seller approaches the buyer with blandishments designed to lead her (or him) against or in spite of whatever will to resist she or he may have, to pay the price and bestow the final favours as ultimate consumer. This paradigm tends to be closely intertwined with the previous one in accounts of the likely progress of events between seller and buyer, to the point that it is practically impossible to separate one from the other. But military and erotic scenarios have a long history of overlapping, as object of desire and object of attack coalesce in the 'victim' of love's wound or a lover's onslaught.

SCENE 4: THE SCENE ITSELF

We turn now to the detailed unfolding of that quintessential twentieth-century psychological drama, the sale. For as with all narratives – so a brilliant purveyor of literary mythologies once led us to believe – while there may be numerous subgenres and thematic variations (in this case the battle, the seduction, the religious conversion and the trial), there is a certain structure to which they all, in their different ways, conform.[10] The sale is classically represented in four romantic stages; for what it's worth, they were invented by one E. St Elmo Lewis – 'in about 1898', as my source intriguingly puts it.[11] The four stages, given in terms of the mind of the buyer or 'prospect', are: Attraction, Interest, Desire and Sale – or, more logically, Action. From the point of view of the seller, the two outer stages are known as the Approach and the Close. There may be narrative expansions, overlaps and delays in the laying out of the sequence: Kitson, for example, slips in 'Confidence' after Desire, and tags on 'Satisfaction' at the end – but basically the outlines do not change. If you open an introductory marketing textbook today you will still find the four stages there, though they are likely to be rapidly abandoned amid a passion-killing barrage of econometric data.[12]

The first stage, attracting attention, is by common agreement equalled in difficulty only by the final 'close'. It is on these two, the beginning and the end, that I am going to concentrate, leaving out all the infinite delays and diversions that are possible in the interim, be they pleasurable or frustrating. Not that interest is boring, or desire unattractive; but for the moment we only have time to deal with the principal selling points. Occasionally, indeed, so the literature tells us, there really is little more to it than a happy conflation of the start and the finish:

> In some instances it may happen that both individuals simultaneously experience the impulse to exchange and in perfect unison pass through the various stages leading up to the final act of transfer of ownership, without either exerting any influence on the conduct of the other.[13]

But these wondrous coincidences are really no more than exceptions that prove the rule of normal difficulties.

We begin, then, with stage one: attracting attention. In a common representation, derived from the psychology of William James, the mind is represented as a constantly flowing stream of consciousness; the seller's first task is to succeed in throwing in his or her commodity, or rather the idea of it, so as literally to make waves, to make an impression. Discussion of how to play this first moment – what one book calls 'the method of arresting and penetrating the mental stream of the buyer'[14] – brings in fundamental questions about the mind's dispositions, and how they operate in relation to what comes their way from the outside. These dispositions are usually divided into the natural and the acquired, or instincts and habits. Kitson lists a number of stimuli that will naturally cause the mind to turn its attention to the proffered idea. These include repetition (say it often; the power of the trade name); extensity (big billboards are good, and for some reason 'Americans as a people are almost obsessed by the idea of immensity. They regard it as practically a virtue in itself'[15]); intensity (especially a loud noise that will shut out all the rest); colour; and movement (the cinema is the chief example here, but the car, as always, is often cited too).

If the approach is made by a man rather than by an ad – if, as one book puts it, you 'call in person' rather than 'call in print'[16] – different tactics apply, and these in turn depend on whether you are selling in a store or whether you are trying to cross the threshold of a private home in order to make your 'demonstration'. In particular, when the buyer is in a store, or leafing through a magazine, she or he can be supposed to be expecting and open to an approach, which is not the case when a salesman simply rings a doorbell and tries to barge into a housewife's hallway uninvited. There is a running or at least ongoing argument between advocates of personal selling and selling by other means; Henry Foster Adams, an advocate of the second, unequivocally relegates the man to the status of an unreliable advert, since the latter 'never gets sick' and can work 365 days in the year.[17]

Before moving on to the next stage, we may pause on the doorstep to look at a nice literary evocation of an approach, which half succeeds, but ultimately fails to take hold. Inevitably, it has to do with cars.

In Virginia Woolf's novel *Mrs Dalloway* (1925), Peter Walsh, on leave from a post in India and newly involved with a woman there, has just been to visit Clarissa Dalloway, with whom he was in love thirty years before – as she, perhaps, with him: 'Now I remember how impossible it was ever to make up my mind, thought Clarissa – and why did I make up my mind – not to marry him, she wondered, that awful summer?'[18] The 'prospect' is on foot, walking the streets of the city in that state of unfocused attention from which an 'approach' will have to recall him:

> And there he was, this fortunate man, himself, reflected in the plate-glass window of a motor-car manufacturer in Victoria Street. All India lay behind him; plains, mountains; epidemics of cholera; a district twice as big as Ireland; decisions he had come to alone – he, Peter Walsh; who was now really for the first time in his life in love. Clarissa had grown hard, he thought; and a trifle sentimental into the bargain, he suspected, looking at the great motor-cars capable of doing – how many miles on how many gallons? For he had a turn for mechanics; had invented a plough in his district, had ordered wheelbarrows from England, but the coolies wouldn't use them.[19]

The appeal made by the cars displayed to passers-by meets a response, to the extent that Peter's reflections turn towards scenes of grandeur, immensity and performance. The image of the car has elicited from its spectator an appropriate accompanying fragment of what advertisers at the time were calling 'reason-why' copy, as though he is spontaneously taking on the role of the consumer addressed as interested in fuel economy. But in the conflation of miles per gallon, colonial power and the size of the Indian subcontinent, it is not the propositional situation of the car shown in the window that comes to the front of the reflections in his own mind. Superimposed on the car, he sees the enlarged image of 'this fortunate man, himself', his own technical expertise and decision-making authority in the vastness of India among its inferior inhabitants; at the same time this puffing up of himself acts as an accompaniment or background to the insistence on being in love now and uniquely, and thus not with Clarissa, who is explicitly and repeatedly put down or put out of the way, but who in fact, and precisely through this contrary effort, floats so visibly in the syntactical stream of these thoughts. Psychological processes are prompted by those of the window display's mode of appeal, which claims his attention, but not enough to make its own features take over from those that derive from Peter's personal story.

SCENE 5: THE MOMENT

In the *Mrs Dalloway* case, the approach fails: a moderate attraction fails to develop into the positive interest of the second stage, let alone to the desire that is a prelude to purchase. But we will move on none the less, to see what happens subsequently if the buyer's attention is successfully secured. As though encountering no impediments, we may skip past interest and desire to reach the grand finale of the drama.

Everything in the final, crucial stage depends on gauging and acting on an elusive something called 'the moment'. The discussion of the moment looms large in both the practical and the theoretical discussions of selling; and just as selling can be generalised to encompass all facets of human psychology, so the moment of the close becomes nothing less than the key to explaining every change, every event, in human history, individual and cultural. Here is one account:

> The 'psychological moment' is not confined to the business of selling. It occurs in all kinds of human relationships, from such relatively inconsequential affairs as the feeding of a baby, to such momentous events as the precipitation of a World War. It occurs when the astute evangelist feels it proper to urge his hearers to hit the sawdust trail and when the seducer feels that he may, without fear of rebuff, press his victim to take the first drink.[20]

The writer goes on to quote Shakespeare, an early marketing theorist it turns out, who 'referred to it in the well-known lines: "There is a tide in the affairs of men,/Which taken at the flood, leads on to fortune"'.[21] It is in fact common for writers on consumer psychology to bring in literary examples as proof or illustration of their psychological arguments. Shakespeare is frequently cited, but so are a whole range of other authors, from Coleridge to Twain to the ubiquitous Benjamin Franklin.

Following their lead, we could turn to another literary comparisons, *The Picture of Dorian Gray* (1891). Here is the aristocratic dandy, Lord Henry Wotton, measuring his effect on Dorian, the innocently suggestible prospect, to whom he has been 'talking up' the beautiful portrait of him that has just been painted: 'With his subtle smile, Lord Henry watched him. He knew the precise psychological moment when to say nothing.' And later on, the 'psychological' reference is made precise and authoritative:

> There are moments, psychologists tell us, when the passion for sin, or for what the world calls sin, so dominates a nature, that every fibre of the body, as every cell of the brain, seems to be instinct with fearful impulses. Men and women at such moments lose the freedom of their will. They move to their terrible end as automatons move. Choice is taken from them.[22]

In a somewhat exaggerated form – the psychology of advertising tends to replace the vocabulary of sin with blander invocations of transgressive behaviour like 'wicked' perfume, or cakes that are 'naughty but nice' – this is an exact description of the result aimed at by the salesman. The moment of choice, of the exercise of the will, is in fact a relinquishing of the will; the whole task is to get the prospect to the point of capitulation, when there is no longer any question. Action is then spontaneous, irresistible; the mind has become purely biological or mechanical (the automaton).

In *The Mind of the Buyer*, with the same physiological emphasis as in Wilde's references to fibres, cell and brain, Kitson puts it like this:

> [In] employing the power of suggestion, we attempt to insert some object (whatever we have for sale) more or less abruptly into some person's mental stream . . .
>
> The next event – the production of muscular efforts – is more difficult to describe, and to achieve. It is here that the greatest amount of mystery centers; and here that the greatest amount of skill is demanded of the seller. How can a psychical thing like an idea change over into physical energy and assume the form of a motor act? And how can the seller facilitate such transformation?[23]

The 'mystery' of the sale is all focused on this final 'conversion' – successful persuasion as the changing of impression to expression, of the psychical idea into the physical act. One technique for obtaining it is to assume that you already have: for instance, by asking about the preferred means of delivery, or passing over the order book for signing. Tell-tale physical signs may be studied in the form of 'small involuntary movements'.[24] But the changeover can only be registered in its effects; the skill is to pre-empt it by taking it to have happened already. There is no plain sale.

SCENE 6: A CUSTOMER IS BEING BEATEN

All commentators agree that, as *Salesmanship Simplified* puts it, 'The close is the climax of the drama you have enacted with your prospect. Make it the big moment, as the climax of a drama deserves to be.'[25] It is regularly described as 'consummatory'. But it remains nebulous, unassimilable to the structure. Appearing only at the point of its having been passed, the moment signals this fine barrier between the two, after which there is no going back – but also, potentially, nothing to do, no movement at all. So once the moment has come – once back across the threshold or outside the showroom – what happens next? What is this thing called consumption?

It turns out that the close is by no means the end of the story: the drama is successfully concluded only if it leaves behind the anticipation of a repeat performance, and for this it is necessary that the prospect feel that she, not the salesman, has won:

> She will be a booster for you because she believes she hasn't been sold, but has forced you to give her the best of the deal . . . While a woman, easily sold, will forget about you within a half hour after you leave her home.[26]

Both buyer and seller, then, should imagine that the choice was theirs, and by the same token that they have triumphed over the other. Ruth Leigh counsels implicitly against neglectful post-close behaviour:

> Remember this point: to maintain a customer's patronage permanently you must remain as interested and attentive to her after the sale as before . . . The most valuable advertisement any store can have is a customer who departs in a pleasant frame of mind, thinking: 'Well, that saleswoman must have been interested; she tried hard to please me.'[27]

You have to ensure that the customer will be coming back; the only criterion of a sale's success is that it will generate another sale and another. This means that the question of consumption itself – whether the product fulfils its promise or answers the supposed need or wish, how it is used or used up – is altogether left out of count in a drama that subsists, or rather profits, entirely by its own momentum and its own imagined climactic moments. Satisfaction? Forget it – or rather, seek it, again and again.

SCENE 7: WINDOW DRESSING

So now there is nothing left but to rerun, or repeat, the whole routine in terms of another mind that has to be made up in a different way: that of the seller. In a section headed 'Finding a point of common interest', *Salesmanship Simplified* goes back to the beginning and makes it more complicated than it seems to outward appearances:

> Now, 'the approach' is not exactly the physical act of walking up to the door and greeting a prospect. It is really the approach of your mind to hers. And though you oppose each other when excuses or temporary objections are made, you must find some common point of interest upon which your minds can meet . . .
> Create the impression that you are considering her interests above yours.[28]

The subordination of the physical setting to the mental one, literally a case of mind over matter, fits with the artifice of the 'showroom' scene, where nothing extraneous must be allowed to intrude upon the mind of the prospective buyer. The 'meeting' is of minds set apart from the environment in which it happens to take place. As we have seen, the process leading up to the point of purchase is invariably represented in the form of a mental story with a supposedly physical end, or a fantasy that culminates in a hypothetical real event: it is a question of making a mark or an impression on a mind, such that something that looks like action, in the form of the decision to purchase, can be seen to have ensued.

Detailed instructions about how to orchestrate the performance occur in Ruth Leigh's book, *The Human Side of Retail Selling*, which is addressed primarily at women department-store assistants serving female customers (interestingly, in 1921 she uses the word 'salesperson' with the generic female pronoun throughout). It includes clear advice about how to present yourself, in every sense, to the customer: how to make an introduction and how to appear. On the question of 'Your expression', for example, Leigh says that this 'must be an indication of your attitude and personality', and goes on:

> No matter how tired you are, smile pleasantly at the approach of a customer. Do not smirk or give a bored smile of duty, but smile in a sincere,

engaging way that will make a customer feel that she is welcome in the store. Unfortunately, however, salespeople's smiles can be overdone; they can make or break sales.[29]

There is a finely drawn line here between not enough (too tired to smile at all) and too much (the 'overdone' performance). The right kind of smile is expressly put outside the category of 'duty'; it should be a sign or 'indication' of both your real nature and your present disposition ('your attitude and personality'). The expression of what you are and what you are feeling is thus also a double act. The duty smile is a first level of acting whereby actual tiredness is overlaid with simulated warmth; it is recognisable as a sign that points to something other than what it is, and incompatible with it. The correct smile, in contrast, is beyond that call of duty, responding to the even more stringent demand that the smile be in accord with what it suggests ('Your expression *must* be an indication . . .').

This is a version of the double-bind instruction familiar in much popular psychology of the period, notably Dale Carnegie's *How to Win Friends and Influence People* (1936). You have to work at looking as though you are sincere, but you will only succeed in this if you really are sincere in the first place. Thus the exhibition of sincerity, acted out, becomes the sign of its naturalness, making up as completion rather than artifice.

Leigh lists no fewer than six types of smile 'in which salespeople mistakenly indulge' (the pitying, the sarcastic, the knowing, the idiotic, the bored and the 'heaven-help-me'): every disposition that is not the appropriate one is subject to a classification that renders it typical and impersonal, not 'you'. This corresponds to a parallel classification of 'types' of customer, which the salesperson should learn to recognise and to deal with accordingly. There are no fewer than nineteen of them, ranging from 'The Bargain Hunter' to 'Mother and Daughter Customers' to 'The Customer "Just Looking Around"' to 'The "Nosey" Customer'; and concluding with a couple of paragraphs wearily headed 'Each Customer a Problem'.[30]

Here too, as with the salesperson herself, it is not just a matter of judging from appearances: part of the 'problem' is to assess whether your customer is merely acting the part of some particular character that may not be her true one after all: 'The aloofness of customers is often a pose to mask their attitude toward the merchandise.'[31] In this respect, the customer has become a salesperson too, and the pair are matched as equals, each of them acting in order to create a particular 'impression'. Any distinction between the appearing and the hypothetically real self fades away, since every characteristic, of buyer or seller, can be classified as one of a fixed set of types, and put on or off according to the situation. The strategy for maintaining the upper hand, for out-masquerading the fellow *poseuse*, is then a simple one: put yourself in her place: 'Consider the approach from the angle of the shopper, and you will appreciate it more fully'; 'Present goods from the customers' angle by picturing their needs. Talk in terms of "*you*", not in terms of your store or its merchandise.'[32]

A similar call for conscious identification occurs for the door-to-door tactics of *Salesmanship Simplified*:

> The best way to discover whether you are being turned down because you do not make a favorable first impression is to stand in front of a mirror when you're ready to start out and scrutinize yourself carefully.[33]

No more is said; the assumption is that you can see yourself as you will be seen, and whatever it is that is making the negative impression will do so also upon the you that is now looking at you. The business of identification to the point that you know exactly what your customer is looking for and looking at is then the logical next step, as the salesman evaluates himself from the position of the prospective buyer, the recipient of the impressions he makes or fails to make. He will thus become his own consumer, first – in the impulsive, malleable position – identifying himself with the one who takes the impression, and then, in a second moment, rationally evaluating the means by which it has been produced so as then to adjust it if necessary.

And as if in response to this demand, manuals for budding salespeople always include a section on what is usually called 'self-development' or 'personal qualifications', in addition to the section on the psychology of the consumer. The self-development section is literally about how to get your act together. In the same way as a purchaser, the seller is to take on and take in new goods, in the form of additional qualities. The objective is to fit yourself out with as many positive features as possible, which can then be put forward or promoted in the appropriate situation.

What this then implies is that the seller's mind itself becomes a shop, or shop window, stocked with ideas and dispositions to be brought out and displayed when required, to attract attention or make a favourable impression. One early textbook of 1911 puts it especially clearly, heading its introductory section 'Inventory of Qualities', and continuing: 'Business success requires inventories of the mental stock as well as inventories of the business stock. These mental inventories show what qualities a salesman possesses and in what qualities he is deficient.'[34] You should be constantly building up your stock, by means that range from reading to exercising to studying other subjects (Leigh's advice to store assistants is to learn psychology from looking at customers).

Consumer and salesperson have thus come full circle, interchangeable in their shared perpetual quest for the appropriate personal display in what has been identified as a world of generalised salesmanship: you buy the better to sell; and in selling you put yourself in the place of, identify with, the buyer.

SCENE 8: THE ULTIMATE SCENE

Now that the main business of the sale has been dealt with, I would like to suggest one or two further lines to follow. First, I have hinted throughout at points of correspondence between the psychological models used by early writers about the selling process and those of Freud, who is their contemporary. There is, in fact, something called the 'Freudian' model of the consumer that is still invoked in marketing textbooks. Its history goes back to this period, and it is extrapolated from a possible understanding of one aspect of Freud's thought – the unconscious and the role of instincts and defences. This Freudian model of the consumer vies with three others derived from other thinkers of the time: the Veblen model, in which an instinct for prestige is seen as primary; the Pavlov model, which stresses the automatic nature of responses to certain types of stimuli; and the Marshall model which, in identifying the consumer's mind with that of a rational entrepreneur, saving costs and making calculated choices among options on the basis of all the information available, is the precursor of Margaret Thatcher's citizen-consumer or the intended reader of *Which?* or *Consumer Reports*.

But my point has to do less with the particular representation of psychoanalysis in marketing theory than with the ways in which Freud's own writings, looked at through the lens of consumer psychology, might be seen to be offering another version of the modern marketing mind. It is a commonplace to talk about the 'economic' model in Freud, but this is rarely linked to either the economics of his time or the psychological preoccupations of that economics in the area of marketing. The starting point for looking at this would be the whole framework within which psyches are seen by Freud to function according to principles of value, cost and saving, of exchange, investments, compensation, promises of satisfaction, incentive bonuses and so on. Sometimes this involves trade-offs between rational buyer and rational seller, as when (in the text on Wilhelm Jensen's novella *Gradiva*), repressed wishes are said to 'purchase' (*erkaufen*) their half-entry into consciousness, by way of the distortions and disguises of dreams.[35] But everywhere in Freud, psychological modifications occur according to quantifiable criteria of gains and losses: you pay your way, and changes occur only 'at a cost', 'at a price'.

Alongside this recognisably rational operator – a *homo economicus* of the classical sort – is a polymorphously hedonistic, romantic part, untroubled by any sense of duty or obligation to defer its gratifications. Pleasure (or else, the restoration of equilibrium) is the aim, through the transformation of wish into actuality. There is a drama of attractions and interests, desires and choices, in which minds are forever seeking and forever failing to acquire what will satisfy their longings once and for all. The choices and wishes of love appear in the same linguistic guise as those of consumption: one of the words used is the verb *auszeichnen*, which is primarily used for selecting something in a shop.[36]

Or take that much-told Freudian story of the discovery of sexual difference – in particular, the one about the girl who sees something she instantly realises she hasn't got, and wants it; who reduces her rating of her mother when she realises that she too hasn't got it; and so on. The question is how this logic of comparison shopping and impulse buying can seem to make sense – both as an argument, and in psychological terms. This is related to the way that motivation in Freud tends to proceed, as does the logic of salesmanship discussed in relation to 'making up', according to instances of threat and promise: threat of the loss of an imagined wholeness, or promise of the restitution or acquisition of something presently absent. This distinction is often drawn by sex, so that the girl, repeatedly, is said to 'cling to the hope' of acquiring what she feels she has been deprived of, while the boy is forever threatened by the loss of what he believes he has.

Another strand of Freud is concerned with artificial settings and stagings. That 'other scene' of the unconscious is 'another showplace', *ein anderer Schauplatz*, sealed off from the details and interferences of reality. In the discussions of fantasy and identification, there is always a dramatic structure involving reversible poles of identity, and the 'scenes' of fantasy involve mutually dependent and oscillating positions: masculine and feminine, active and passive, voyeur and exhibitionist. As with the dramas between consumer and seller, there is no fixed identity. The adoption of one position is always premised on the suppression and possibility of the other.

The analytic situation itself is another artificial scene in which two participants play out a complicated set of roles in relation to one another. And in the same way as in the process of the sale, though over a much longer period, an analysis has to do with coming to a moment of decision or recognition which in itself is shrouded in mystery. In the course of his case histories and his discussions of analytic technique, Freud frequently remarks on the uselessness of the analyst's seeking to persuade the patient by rational means of his version of the story. The analyst may offer hints or suggestions, but in the end, the patient has to come to accept the interpretation for herself, to adopt it as her own: she must not experience it as something introduced from outside, imposed on her. She has to realise the truth for herself; but this moment of 'conviction', how or why it occurs when it does, retains, like the 'moment' of the decision to purchase, a quality of unpredictability, even though it is the crucial turning point on which the success of the analysis depends. At another level, just as salesmanship experts will say that judging the moment of the sale is a matter of practice and intuition that cannot be rationally learned or taught, so Freud, when dealing with standard objections to psychoanalysis, will regularly end with an appeal to the experience itself as the only criterion that will settle it: in both cases, you have to have been there, and there is thus a magical, indefinable quality to the decisive point.

In making these comparisons, I am not suggesting that psychoanalysis is to be equated with consumer psychology, or that the texts of consumer psychology have the complexity of Freud's. Marketing was never meant to cure anyone of anything, and if Freud had only wanted to maximise profits or patients, he went about it in a rather complicated way. But nor does the interest of consumer psychology lie simply in the provision of a bit of cultural background, the better to set off what is unique about psychoanalysis. To make a distinction between on the one hand a popular, commercial psychology with its limited interests and crude aims, and on the other an authentic, original and more generally applicable psychoanalysis is to assume that the consumer-oriented aspects of modern minds can be separated off as secondary, contingent formations. The point is instead about the general devaluation of consumption, as obvious – we all know what it is – and as secondary to more serious or complex concerns. For if the consuming-selling mind really is a dominant paradigm, then there is all the more reason to look at how it is situated or played out within what is arguably the richest modern account of mental processes.

The type of opposition in which consumption is both subordinated and taken as in need of no further explanation operates in other intellectual areas as well. In literature, the most disparate critical figures agree on dismissing a kind of reading they associate with 'mere' consumption, in favour of another kind which – for want of a less commercial phrase – is the genuine article. I am thinking here of obvious examples like F. R. Leavis, but also of less obvious ones like Roland Barthes. Barthes is not someone readily associated with hostility to mass culture – *Mythologies*, after all, while linking it to a delusive ideology, is all about its fascinations, about the importance of analysing the seductions of consumer culture. But at other moments, when he is not writing directly about it, Barthes too tends to use the notion of consumption as a given, and as a negative term in need of no further analysis.

In the much-read essay 'From work to text', for example, Barthes makes a distinction between the work as an 'object of consumption' and the text as something else. He goes on: 'The Text (if only by its frequent "unreadability") decants the work (the work permitting) from its consumption and gathers it up as play, work, production, practice.'³⁷ 'Consumption' here is almost literally the dregs; the use of the word 'decant' draws out one of the supplementary meanings of *consommation* in French as what you drink in a bar or café. The speedy, automatic and above all simple nature of consumption is being used as the contrast to everything valuable to be found in what may be left over when you have consumed.

What interests me is not so much the opposition of value in itself, though there would be much to say about this, as the way that consumption is able to function as the simple straw term against which the positive term can take its meaning and its value. And indeed it could be argued that the very deployment of consumption as the category of comparison makes the proof of its significance, for it implies not only that we all know what it is, but that it is something so common, so ubiquitous and so constant that it can serve as the general background against which to set what is valorised as out of the ordinary, in this case reading literature.

A different approach to the comparability of literature and consumption occurs in this passage from the poet Ezra Pound's *ABC of Reading* (1925). He is talking about 'criticism' and taking an etymological line, pointing out that the Greek word from which it is derived has to do with choice:

> KRINO, to pick for oneself, to choose. That's what the word means.
>
> No one would be foolish enough to ask me to pick out a horse or even an automobile for him . . .
>
> If you wanted to know something about an automobile, would you go to a man who had made one and driven it, or to a man who had merely heard about it? . . . Would you look at the actual car or only at the specifications?
>
> In the case of poetry there is, or seems to be, a good deal to be looked at. And there seem to be very few authentic specifications available.³⁸

Consumer choice is here being used as analogy to literary choice, not as a debased subspecies. It is assumed that the process of coming to a purchasing decision would be the one that the reader will have most knowledge of; that it is a complex and reasonable process; and that the example of this kind of expertise should function as a convincing argument for the kind of expertise to be acquired in the matter of another kind of picking out, in relation to poems. The passage may be understood as Pound's advertisement for poetry-reading, and it is made classically rather than romantically: the appeal is not to a consumer likely to be rapidly seduced by some chance fancy, but to one who gathers together all the information relevant to a purchase that is planned in advance.

Pound's pitch does not imply any detraction from literary value or complexity, but nor does it take consumption as read. When we wonder whether we 'buy' an argument, we acknowledge — and conscious irony does nothing to diminish this — that selling and consuming are inseparable from the modes in which modern minds think or speak themselves. As the elaborate psychologies of self-advertisement and the selling process indicate, there is nothing outside the shop — but this is something which, in all its everyday banality, we should perhaps not just take or leave as a given. We should 'pay' some attention to our surroundings and notice them for what they are — otherwise we will find ourselves entering the same shop every day.

NOTES

1. *Salesmanship Simplified: A Short Cut to Success*, ed. William T. Walsh, Managing Editor, Opportunity Magazine (Chicago: Opportunity Publishing, 1927), 9.
2. Walter B. Pitkin, *The Consumer: His Nature and His Changing Habits* (New York and London: McGraw-Hill, 1932), 35.
3. Ruth Leigh, *The Human Side of Retail Selling: A Textbook for Salespeople in Retail Stores and Students of Retail Salesmanship and Store Organisation* (New York: D. Appleton, 1921), 110.
4. Pitkin, 57.
5. Pitkin, 61–2.
6. Leigh, 169.
7. H. K. Nixon, *Principles of Selling* (1931; 2nd edn rpt, New York: McGraw-Hill, 1942), 179–93.
8. Henry Dexter Kitson, *The Mind of the Buyer: A Psychology of Selling* (New York: Macmillan, 1921) 180.
9. Kitson, 133, 134–5.
10. The allusions are to Roland Barthes, author of *Mythologies* (1957) and 'Introduction to the structural analysis of narrative' (1966).
11. Nixon, 63 – where the name is mis-spelt as Louis.
12. Kitson, 5.
13. Nixon, 44.
14. Kitson, 32.
15. Kitson, 33.
16. *Salesmanship Simplified*, 93.
17. Henry Foster Adams, *Advertising and its Mental Laws* (New York: Macmillan, 1916), 5.
18. Virginia Woolf, *Mrs Dalloway* (1925), ed. David Bradshaw (Oxford: Oxford University Press, 2000), 35.

19. Woolf, 41–2.
20. Kitson, 169–70.
21. Kitson, 170.
22. Oscar Wilde, *The Picture of Dorian Gray* (1891; Harmondsworth: Penguin, 1973), 27, 210
23. Kitson, 153, 154.
24. Kitson, 179.
25. *Salesmanship Simplified*, 159.
26. *Salesmanship Simplified*, 161, 162.
27. Leigh, 172.
28. *Salesmanship Simplified*, 177.
29. Leigh, 35.
30. Leigh,128.
31. Leigh,122–3.
32. Leigh, 131, 141.
33. *Salesmanship Simplified*, 184.
34. ICS [International Correspondence Schools] Reference Library, Self-Study and Development (Scranton: International Textbook Company, 1911), Part 2, *Essentials of a Good Salesman*, 1.
35. Freud, *Delusions and Dreams in Jensen's 'Gradiva'*, SE IX, 58; GW VII, 85.
36. See Freud, 'Mourning and Melancholia', SE XIV, 249, GW X, 436.
37. Roland Barthes, 'From work to text' (1971), in *Image Music Text*, trans. Stephen Heath (1977; New York: Noonday Press, 1989), 162.
38. Ezra Pound, *ABC of Reading* (1925; New York: New Directions, 1960), 30–1.

7

The Uses of Shopping

Richard Hoggart Goes to Woolworth's*

From the time of *The Uses of Literacy* (1957), and all through the numerous autobiographical works that he wrote in his later years, the cultural critic Richard Hoggart (1918–2014) was always writing about shopping. Quietly resituating the adverse stance of the literary world of his time, Hoggart was happy to ponder and wander the shops. This essay looks at the changing consumerly experiences that Hoggart describes and at the distinctiveness, for a man of his time and cultural places, of this lifelong interest.

Hoggart takes shops, like books, as objects of analysis. In various ways, and with varying questions, he observes the goods on offer, the customers, the staff – and occasionally, himself. It is as if shops are to be 'read' by means of equivalent skills to those required for thinking about a poem or a work of fiction: they may be quotidian and familiar, but they are multifaceted, and call for interpretation. And for both cases, literature and shops, this kind of close critique is seen as a job worth doing.

Take this passage from the book about English working-class culture that made and maintained Hoggart's name, *The Uses of Literacy*. It recounts a shopping expedition to a new kind of shop:

> The louder furniture stores are of unusual interest, especially because of an apparent paradox. At first glance these are surely the most hideously tasteless of modern shops. Every known value in decoration has been discarded: there is no evident design or pattern; the colours fight with one another; anything new is thrown in simply because it is new. There is strip-lighting together with imitation chandelier lighting; plastics, wood and glass are

---

* First published in *Textual Practice* 35:12 (January 2021).

all glued and stuck and blown together; notice after blazing notice winks, glows or blushes luminously. Hardly a homely setting.¹

Everything here hangs on the 'first glance'. We know from the outset that there is going to be at least one further appraisal but for the time being, Hoggart is letting his rhetoric run with every cliché known to the critique of mass culture in the 1950s. In this preliminary stage, he gives us a wholesale abolition of both taste and familiarity, with 'Every known value', no less, thrown out. It's now all fake, 'imitation' lighting flashing away, newness for newness's sake – the standard objection of a lack of substance in mass-produced consumer goods. 'Hardly a homely setting', comfortably rueful and a bit sarcastic, then comes back to soften the initial screech at 'surely the most hideously tasteless of modern shops'. Home, we understand – and it's a significant assumption – is what a furniture shop should feel like.

Yet this is only the preamble, for there are second and third glances to come. These turn on the salesmen who come across to begin with as a continuation of the general alien environment:

> Nor do the superficially elegant men who stand inside the doorway, and alternately tuck their hankies up their cuffs or adjust their ties, appear to belong to 'Us'. They are not meant to. With their neat ready-made clothing, shiny though cheap shoes, well-creamed hair and ready smiles they are meant (like the equally harassed but flashier motor-car salesmen) to represent an ethos.²

All show and surface, just like the goods they are selling. On the one hand, there is no substance beneath. And on the other, this is a performance. The salesmen are standing for something (they 'represent an ethos'): this is a show with a meaning. But also, quite simply, they are acting, putting it on, smiling to order.

But then, in a third glance (or rather with a longer listening), these men of unsubstance turn out after all to be decent underneath, to be just like you and me; the sound of them is familiar even if the look of them is not:

> The proprietors realise that working-class people will be dazzled by the exuberance and glitter of their display, will be attracted and yet a little awed. The manner of their salesmen is usually, therefore, understandingly colloquial . . . 'I know what it's like, madam', or, 'I had a young couple just like you in only last week'; all in the tone of an understanding son who has done well and become cultured. . . . [T]his type of shop – the huge, glossy affair aiming specifically at working-class customers – specialises in this approach.³

Hoggart's portrayal both is and is not an indictment of 'this type of shop'. For all the apparent turn or return to the sense of a relateably local boy who can after all be comfortably found inside the smart suit, the subsequent sentences are clear about the decisive agency of 'Those who direct them' and the way that the appeal of 'the personal' is a deliberate and deceptive ploy; it is described as 'a pretty Trojan horse'.[4] But most striking in the passage are the many levels of the description. There are the superficial presentations, of the décor and the stuff for sale and the salesmen's outfits. There are the likely phrases to be used. And behind those there is the analysis of customer expectations, of how the 'understandably awed' are at the same time 'attracted'.

On the part of the understated observer, the man of the first and the subsequent glances, who listens to the patter with a placing ear, there is an identification with each one of these always at least double parts. He puts himself in the place of the customer reacting to the new kind of shop; in the place of the entrepreneur considering the customers' likely reactions; and implicitly, also, in the place of the youngish salesman, who is in one way part of the new furniture and in another a representative of home. This observer-narrator, Hoggart in person, does not draw attention to his own presence, either in the argument being laid out now, or in the original scene in the store. But I think we can fairly infer that in the 1950s Richard Hoggart was someone who spent a good deal of time in shops, and thinking about shops. And this was only the beginning – or the nearly middle, perhaps – of a life-long enthusiasm for this particular mode of social study. It changed its form along with the man himself as he aged, and also along with newer new types of establishments that came into being; but it was a constant in all his writing about contemporary culture.

In his extended analysis, Hoggart describes the complex social dynamics of the furniture store of the 1950s with an attentiveness and elaboration not found in the quick-fire arguments against 'consumer society' that were commonplace in the 1960s. Much later, after retiring in 1983, he had lost none of his fascination for the specific encounters fostered by new types of shopping environment. In particular, he seems to have spent a great deal of time at the supermarket checkout – and not unhappily; reading his book of the mid-1990s on Farnham, the Surrey town where he lived by then, you sometimes wonder if he was ever anywhere else. Time and again, some insight or inference is attributed to what has been seen or heard from that useful vantage point, acknowledged and recommended as such. This is no ordinary view. Throughout the course of supermarkets' existence – a shorter time than Richard Hoggart's shopping life, but a good many decades by now – the checkout has been regarded as a perpetual problem, and the prevention of long queues as a problem of seemingly boundless scope for generations of marketing professionals. But for Hoggart, it is as though the default understanding of this point of obligatory pause had been entirely forgotten. The checkout is not an unwelcome hold-up so much as the best available place from which to watch and listen to how people talk and behave as they wait.

There are numerous examples in Hoggart's writings of the *ad hoc* checkout case study; here is one, from the Farnham book. The topic, quite specifically, is middle-class, middle-aged women, presented as a recognisable social type in which Hoggart takes a particular interest: 'I come back again and again to women of that age and class.'[5] He goes on:

> Another tiny but illustrative incident. I was in a supermarket one Friday morning, waiting behind such a middle-aged woman who was next to be served. The man who was checking out his groceries emptied the trolley and moved perhaps a yard away from it so as to have more space to sort out his shopping bags. He did not at that moment pull the trolley with him.

At this point, despite the framing as a 'tiny' event, the intricacy of detail might lead, generically, to the expectation of some kind of sudden assault. But the passage instead continues:

> The hard-hatted lady next in line called to him without hesitation, in a voice which would have carried twenty yards, not the one yard needed to reach the man: 'Do you intend to leave that trolley *thare*?' It was premature, rude, stupid. What made her think she could call out in that tone of voice to anyone?[6]

There are more sentences in this vein, countering the hypothetical objection that this might be simply one specific woman, or an off-day for this particular woman; the paragraph concludes instead with the summary conviction that the incident 'speaks of, reveals something of the common style of, a whole class of women, especially those of a certain age'.[7] The move from the individual to the representative is typical for Hoggart; and it is to the supermarket, in particular to the checkout, that he goes for the telling piece of evidence or corroboration about contemporary social types – or stereotypes.

Hoggart almost never draws attention to the peculiarity of his predilection for shopping, whether as a subject of thought or a practice in daily life; for the most part he just gets on with both, or with the constant conjunction between the two. The predilection is rare in the first case, as a subject of study and thought: shopping has regularly been left out of social history, even when social history is dedicated to giving a serious place to the time-taking, everyday occupations that fall outside the established historical categories. But in the second case, as a practice in his own daily life, Hoggart's habit was unusual for the simple reason that he was not a woman.

He was quite aware of this gender eccentricity himself. In the early 1990s, he writes: 'Most professional men of my generation hate shopping for food, furniture or clothes; I enjoy it.'[8] This sentence (from the middle volume of his three-part autobiography) could have served as a text – in the old-fashioned pulpit sense – for the present essay. Almost everything I seek to understand about shopping and Richard Hoggart unfurls from its few simple words. First of all, there is the way of categorising himself by as many as three amalgamated markers: social class, gender and generation. The category of generation is potentially double; it may refer either to people of roughly his age, at any time (he is in his early seventies when he writes this), or else to his specific cohort, those with the shared formation of being born at a particular period and therefore living through the same times at the same stages of their lives. Second, class variations in consumption practices are a constant preoccupation for Hoggart, to the point that he occasionally sounds barely distinguishable from a market researcher, with lengthy listings of likely car models and supermarket choices for different socioeconomic groups. A glimpse of this tendency can be seen in the present example, with the semi-automatic listing of 'food, furniture, or clothes'. More often, though, there is a more textured mode of differentiation and that, we shall see, is what follows straight after the declarative sentence.

The third category, gender, is the most surprising aspect of this distinctive shopper's self-description, or self-labelling. That is because at least until recently, and most certainly for people of all social groups from the same generation as himself, shopping of all kinds, whether hated or enjoyed, was almost exclusively the task or the privilege of women. In the twentieth century, the man shopper for anything, in any class, is the rarest of birds. It was women who 'did' the shopping, in the sense of the regular job or chore; and it was also women who 'went shopping', for pleasure, for an outing – in the other sense of shopping, not as a task but as an open-ended leisure activity. In neither mode, doing the shopping or going shopping, are men much to be found, whether in image or in reality.

Most pointedly, Hoggart's coming-out or going-out shopping sentence works across the hinge of its summary semicolon, both slick and silent: most hate it, whereas (semicolon) I enjoy it. In that concisely marked contrast, Hoggart declares his own distinction, his difference from the majority of men of his time and place. And proud of it!

The paragraph continues, though, in a different direction, with an acknowledgement of the other world from which this late twentieth-century individual emerged:

> Most professional men of my generation hate shopping for food, furniture or clothes; I enjoy it. The related interest [he means his own] in things which claim to be 'bargains' now seems increasingly comical to me, as it has done for years to the rest of the family. This is the bran-tub spirit (there may be gold there), the Woolworth's syndrome, and as congenitally working-class as the addiction itself to those stores. Until I began to write this story – and found Woolworth's appearing again and again in different contexts – I did not fully realise their importance in the theatre of working-class life during the first half of this century.[9]

The rhetorical and logical steps of this passage are both characteristic and fascinating. It is narrated as a process of self-discovery, by means of autobiographical writing that then transfers immediately into general social truth, applicable not just to Hoggart himself, to the particular author, but to the entire working class. I read my own story, the story I have just written; I see what it is; and what it is, as I thereby see, is the story of 'working-class life', equally unnoticed until now.

In Hoggart's marketing identification mode there then follows an account of why Woolworth's appeals or appealed to working-class people – by the fixed low prices along with the 'open displays . . . piled high'.[10] But then – when you thought he had said this was in the now 'comical' past – he reverts to the bargains:

> Against all current reason, the love of bargains has stayed with me and with others I know from similar backgrounds: the love of advertisements which don't try to be psychologically cunning but say straight out, 'Look, this is a bargain; come and get it'; ads for food, cars, clothing, furniture; small ads in shop windows and classified ads in local newspapers. The big department store sales are attractive because they do have genuine bargains and you can now afford any you reasonably want. But so are bring-and-buys, jumble sales, displays of gear for making your own beer and wine, church and chapel bazaars, auctions (especially shabby auctions in small country towns), discount and second-hand shops and particularly those where they accept goods, agree on a price and put it in the window, taking a percentage if it's sold; and now car-boot sales.[11]

This is a joyous accumulation, a piling up and buying it cheap over and over again – as not just more and more stuff, but more and more words to say it and ways and places and times to grab it are poured onto the page, like the classified listings in freebie local papers.

Two more sentences show the place of mail order as the direct precursor of online browsing:

> Today's bargains are centred above all on the postal service and must appeal, do appeal, more widely than to émigrés from the working-class world; but they hook us particularly thoroughly. I make the routine objections to junk mail, but can scarcely bear to throw it away unopened.[12]

'Scarcely bear': he does it but hates to have to. The small tensions of tiny daily things are palpable in this sentence, which records a permanent self-division – the one who makes 'routine objections' as opposed to the one who really takes pleasure in these things – from a third perspective, that of the rueful and indulgent self-observation of this trivially complex being.

This is by no means the end of this excursion among the varied shopping scenes of Hoggart's memoirs. The following page has a paragraph listing just about every item he can remember having succumbed to as a mail order bargain, with parenthetical ratings as to its usefulness or otherwise, and an irrepressible sense of fun, as one silly item after another is mentioned and then discarded:

> I have not yet sent for a small electric shaver for the hairs within the nose and do not expect to; nor for an ioniser (*Which?* says it's not at all sure about them). I would hate to find I have won a Personal Organiser. I have bought a car-boot tidy (not very useful), Able-Labels (handy), little quartz travel alarm-clocks, an anti-wrinkle steamer (not worth the trouble) . . .[13]

The list goes on. But all these many things, the useful and the not useful, the fantastical and the really practical, are then set aside as basically irrelevant in light of their underlying function: 'one should allow something for the pleasure of sending off, and of opening the packet; it might be a real bargain.' And then, setting off in another analytical direction: 'What causes all the little spurts of pleasure as bargains are sniffed out?'[14]

But here, it is time to leave behind the dubious arrivals through the letterbox and go back to the real shops evoked at the start of the autobiographical shopping pages, where Hoggart referred to what he called 'the Woolworth's syndrome' and his surprise at finding that store appearing so frequently in the present memoir – as though it took writing and representing to see what was really going on with the raw name that seemed to surface so often. Woolworth's, of course, is not just any old shop; in this passage, it is glossed as being central to what is engagingly called 'the theatre of working-class life in the first half of the twentieth century'. Woolworth's puts in an appearance of one kind or another in practically all Hoggart's books, including the one on Farnham, where it figures in its later declining mode. It is a passage that combines Hoggart's characteristically dual rhetorical mode for descriptions of shops. On the one hand he offers a light form of nonetheless serious interpretation: 'The allure, and that word is not excessive, of the old-style Woolies lay in both its sense of being an Arabian bazaar and in its psychological accessibility. It didn't frighten you; it belonged to your class.'[15] On the other hand, further on, he seems to abandon what now seems more like a scholarly façade – while also knowingly winking in the act of doing so. Thus we now get a new sort of list, consisting of what you can no longer buy in the place. It is punctuated not by cool writerly semicolons, but by a self-mockingly dramatic exclamation mark: 'I have by now lost count of the useful things Woolworth's no longer stocks. . . . Woolworth's not stocking household polishes and shaving cream! It's against nature.' You may think this is mainly bluff and self-parody, and probably it is; but the paragraph changes tack once again to end with this solemn concessive overview: 'Still, in many branches, their gardening and DIY sections remain valuable and competitive.'[16]

Hoggart did not ignore more recent incarnations of the cheap city centre variety chain store selling anything and everything. *Townscape with Figures*, in 1994, opens with a scene in front of the Farnham branch of Argos, where old men hang about in the same way, Hoggart says, that in past times they might have found an outdoor home round a town square. The store itself, though, is presented as representing a sad decline from the lovably showy frivolity of Woollies. 'Among British town shops Woolworth's used to be, was for decades, the chief working-class point of reference; now it has lost its magic.'[17] Argos's stock of what he calls 'consumer durables and nondurables and unendurables'[18] is mostly hidden from view:

> no display but that huge coloured book representing all the stuff stacked on shelves at the back, called up by computer once you have made your choice. Late twentieth-century marketing which has creamed off much High Street trade and will itself, they say, be succeeded in ten or twenty years by home-computer-shopping.[19]

How accurate he was about the distinctive Argos set-up as a precursor of internet shopping. And also, how he would have loved Poundland and the rest of the internet-bucking fixed-price bricks-and-mortar stores that emerged in the 2010s, against all entrepreneurially expert predictions.

But the starring role of Woolworth's throughout Hoggart's *œuvre* – and his life – has another meaning and purpose, which may be summarised with the help of another kind of familiar name. The critic Q. D. Leavis was the wife of the famous critic F. R. Leavis; her book *Fiction and the Reading Public* was published in 1932. It is a social history of working-class reading in England, and true to my thesis its index has no entry for anything in the orbit of shopping or retailing, let alone individual stores. There is Smollett but not Smith's – and there is 'Woolf, V.', but not Woolworth's. Yet the book begins with a prolonged and detailed account of the many different types of shop that presently stock reading matter for borrowing, hiring or sale. Among these named outlets is none other than Woolworth's, which enters the picture with these mostly uncontentious words: 'Where multiple stores have a branch there is usually to be found a bazaar of the American firm, Messrs. Woolworth; here for 3d. or 6d. nearly everything necessary to existence may be bought, including literature.'[20] So far, apart from the moderate sneer of the 'Messrs', this could be neutral or even extolling. But the account of the literature on offer soon deteriorates into palpable condescension as Leavis describes various cheap series of popular classics and not yet classics. 'There appears to be money in "literature associated with the film"'; the inverted commas around that phrase do special work.[21]

Later on in Leavis's book, a typical Woolworth's store is brought into focus, in language that could not be more different from Hoggart's:

> Here, while passing from counter to counter to buy cheap crockery, strings of beads, lamp-shades, and toffee, toys, soap, and flower-bulbs, and under the stimulus of 6d. gramophone records filling the air with 'Headin' for Hollywood' and 'Love Never Dies', the customer is beguiled into patronising literature. If it is a country town, the bazaar is packed on market-day with the country folk who come in once a week to do their shopping, so that Woolworth literature supplies the county with reading; if it is a city, the housewives of the district make their regular tour on Saturdays, though a constant stream passes along the counters handling the goods throughout the week.[22]

The comparison of rural and urban shopping habits is suggestive, not least for the unelaborated contrast of the 'country folk' with the city's 'housewives'. Momentarily, Leavis does seem to be interested in the determinations of shopping differences, with geography and gender both getting a glance at this point. But the main concern of the summary is to insist on the deviously persuasive ambiance – 'under the stimulus . . . the customer is beguiled'. Linguistically, it is a quaintly hybrid description, in which the exotic suggestion of beguiling, straight out of the caption to an orientalising advertising image, fails to bond with the semi-behaviouristic perspective of the word 'stimulus'. And is this also the first ever scholarly reference to in-store muzak? If something called literature appears along with the rest of the assorted merchandise on Woolworth's tables, that is only because – as Leavis has already concluded from a librarian's report of borrowing practices in relation to mass-market literature – 'the reading habit is now often a form of the drug habit'.[23]

Quite simply, Q. D. Leavis's critique is here the mirror image of Hoggart's. Contrast her description with his, in the first volume of his autobiography, where he says: 'To go round a Woolworth's in any town or city you land in, no matter how far away it may be from home, is like having a quick fix from a drug you became addicted to very early.'[24] Apart from the obvious reversal between the good and the bad shopping trip, there is also the simple difference of placement. For Hoggart, every Woolie's is a home from home; whereas Leavis remains on the outside, observing the strange powers of an orchestrated environment that touches her personally not at all. Shopping has nothing to do with, nothing to offer, the critic objecting to substandard literature; there is just no connection. With Hoggart, on the other hand, those two personae, the present writer and the one-time youth, are not divided, even if they are not one and the same.

Hoggart himself points out the link, or rather the disjunction, between his own perspective and Leavis's, in a late interview with Nicolas Tredell. Referring to what he is calling his 'documentary' writing method, he speaks of one prompt for *The Uses of Literacy* having been his 'dissatisfaction with Mrs Leavis's contrasts, in *Fiction and the Reading Public*, between popular novels and a much earlier generation of working people; it did not seem a true match. Mrs Leavis', he goes on to say, 'did not realise that I was, there, . . . implicitly and politely making a criticism of her approach.'[25]

Q. D. Leavis's reference to housewives takes us back to what is surely, as noted earlier, the most striking and exceptional feature of Hoggart's shopping habit. In the middle decades of the twentieth century, as Leavis implies, household shopping – indeed shopping of almost every kind – was almost always done by women: both in fact and in public images of the practice, whether promotional or critical. Hoggart stands out, and knows he stands out, as going against that norm. But it is frustrating, given how much he does say, that in none of his memoirs does he tell us to what extent he actually did the Hoggarts' household shopping – that is, went and bought what was routinely needed from local shops, or later from supermarkets, as opposed to going shopping: wandering about Woolworth's of a weekend, or earnestly checking the pages of *Which?* for the best-value washing machine. Also annoying, if not exasperating, for my purposes and curiosities, is that two periods of living abroad – for a year in upstate New York and for five years, no less, in Paris, no less – pass with almost no mention of the shops in either of these places: shops so different in type from England's, and from one another. Especially given Hoggart's usual preoccupations, it is a remarkable lacuna.

The Hoggarts spent an academic year in Rochester, NY in the second half of the 1950s. At this time sizeable supermarkets were firm fixtures everywhere in the US; since their beginnings in the 1930s they had become the default mode of household food shopping. But they had yet to appear in significant numbers in Britain, and those that did exist were far smaller in selling area (and numbers of checkouts) than their American counterparts.[26] Even the most shopping-uninterested cultural commentators from Europe, and indeed from within the US itself, habitually seized on the American supermarket of this period as emblematic of new extremes of a consumer society only just beginning to cross the Atlantic; and for literary men the rhetorical contrasts are well established, even ready-made. The supermarket represents the antithesis of literary culture, and the visible, garish sign of its manifest decline. This is the decade of Allen Ginsberg's poem 'A Supermarket in California' and of the poet Randall Jarrell's essay, 'A Sad Heart at the Supermarket'. Jarrell's piece was first included in a 1959 collection of essays on mass culture by various writers; it was a title that he liked well enough to make it the name of a whole book of his own, as well.[27] What did Hoggart make of this extraordinary new shopping phenomenon, as yet unseen in England? There is barely a word – only a couple of oddly formulaic sentences. In the chapter describing this American year in the second volume of the three-part autobiography there is a general reference to 'wasteful and meaningless accumulation in the vast supermarkets', as if it is all too much, somehow beyond depiction. This vaguely economic and existential complaint is followed, a little later, by what sounds like a downmarket version of *The Stepford Wives*, when Hoggart refers to 'the sheer stylelessness of the almost ubiquitous bulging trousers, loose nylon blouses and TV-lipstick of thirty-five-year-old women trundling round supermarkets'.[28] And that is all he has to say about the so different American stores of the mid-1950s.

Just as striking is the absence of the shops and markets of Paris. For a few years in the early 1970s the Hoggarts were living on the boulevard Haussmann, with two of the city's iconic department stores, Printemps and Galeries Lafayette, just along the street from their splendid apartment. Yet of these or any other grand stores, or small stores, there is not a word.

Perhaps the shops that interest Hoggart have to have some connection to home. For if supermarkets are all but omitted from his account of the time when he encountered the vast American version, then this is more than made up for in the later works of his English retirement. In *Townscape with Figures*, as already suggested, it is as if Hoggart is almost never not in a large self-service store of some kind. He begins the book with that cluster of old men who regularly congregate outside Farnham's Argos; but he himself, from the evidence of the pages that follow, is surely the town's principal loiterer in and around retail spaces – as he is the first to admit. He refers to 'the conversation I heard today, at the check-out of course', and on the next page he responds to hypothetically sceptical readers by saying: 'I only ask them to keep their eyes and ears open at key points where the different social groups inevitably meet, for example at those "junctions" I have constantly returned to – railway booking offices and supermarket check-outs'.[29]

The final works also return to long left scenes. One of Hoggart's later collections of essays is called *First and Last Things*. A plain formulation that also has many possible resonances, the title is characteristic of his distinctive style; or, to use a favourite word of his, it is 'telling'. Simply, the book is about his early life and his later life. That is a description of most autobiographies; but here, for someone who had already written a long one, it is as if the first and last things are meant to suggest a changed choice of emphasis, a kind of paring down or filtering out. This new memoir contains not quite the last of the many life-writings, and for the most part what is presented in it only says once again, and in similar ways, what he had written before: in that sense the final version is simply a repetition, now growing a little weary, of the first. But as he goes through the old stories one more time it turns out that there is still, after all, some possibility of surprise – for the seasoned Hoggart-reader, but also, most movingly, for the writer himself. It is only now, he says, speaking once again of his childhood, that I have remembered I had a dog. It was kind of them to let me have her. In that moment of the present telling, so much is contained – is potentially there, and is revealed as having been held back, unknowingly, for all these years and decades. How is it possible to forget that you had a dog, even a dog of your very own? But he did, he finds that he did; and only now, at the very end, she has returned to his consciousness during the process of writing – but far from it being the first time – about that ancient period of life.

The long lost dog – unnamed, undescribed, but a she – returns to memory late in life, a creature of the past who suddenly appears in the midst of the ageing present. It is rare for Hoggart's recollections to be so laden with possible individual meanings. Most often, it is as though his own story, while it is deeply felt – to use that formulation so dear to mid-twentieth-century literary criticism – must remain, if not impersonal, then representative, its value for recording to be found in its indication of a certain kind of working-class experience. The little lost dog, though, both her discovery now and her having been there at the beginning, for once disturbs the settled ways of that style. It is something that is Richard Hoggart's story alone, an object of early love that had disappeared from his own picture.

The stories of shops and shopping that Hoggart tells were mostly of that generally comfortable and affectionate type that is the hallmark of his relationship to the places of his past when he brings them out as illustrations of the styles of life he has known – *The Way We Live Now*, in the Trollopian title of yet one more of the final books. But there are two consumely moments in his memoirs whose power to speak of what they do not actually say has more in common with the episode of the dog than with the many scenes of chain-store cheerfulness or cheeky checkout curiosity. One is from young boyhood, and the other from the time of old age. The word 'moments' here is meant as an echo of Hoggart's own quasi-Wordsworthian term for a small number of recollected childhood experiences of fulfilment, of having had a sudden sense of perfect being in the here and now. Such moments are recounted at long intervals in the three-volume autobiography.

The first of these moments has many of the pleasurable associations of the childhood moments to which he gives that name himself. It concerns a neighbour from the first place where Richard lived, with both the siblings from whom he was to be separated in later childhood, following the death of their mother. This neighbour was a small-scale baker who sold cakes from home on Saturdays: 'The smell in the yard was then all warm, yeasty, currany and sugary.' When there were some cakes left over, they might be given to the Hoggarts. 'Even now, the smell and taste, the cushiony butteryness of a toasted teacake, not only seem marvellous but instantly bring back, with warmth, life in Potternewton Lane, even if I am having tea in a posh hotel.'[30] The story is about consumption in the primary sense of eating – and eating for pleasure rather than need: this special delicacy that, Hoggart says now, has forever imbued the toasted teacake, however grand the setting of its serving, with an aura that comes from that first fine Saturday perfection.

This primal and Proustian moment of consumerly pleasure is homely in every way. The shop is more or less next door, it is 'on the premises' of someone's house, and in any case it is not like a regular shop with regular hours. The moment is a treat, yet a regular treat. But the delicious vignette of repeated teacake heaven is striking for a further reason. In the chronology of Richard Hoggart's life as told, it is the very first instance of anything to do with a shop, the first hint of buying and selling as a part of life. Yet while it comes from a sort of shop and was baked to be sold, the teacake has not been bought; it has been given. Given to a family known to be 'hard-up' (Hoggart's word) but also, you infer, given out of kindness and neighbourly hospitality, and consciously against the grain of monetary concerns.

The second moment comes from the other end of Hoggart's life, and it appears in the very last of the memoirs, a short book called *Promises to Keep*. This moment is given as having occurred in the late 1980s – quite early in the retirement years. The Hoggarts, Mary and Richard, are on a trip to Australia, and the later narrating Hoggart begins by setting the scene of an ordinary coach excursion – while also highlighting his own special knowledge and role in relation to the historic site they are about to visit:

> We joined a group to see the remarkable cave paintings, so remarkable that they have special international status with UNESCO. They came within my portfolio during my time in Paris.
>
> Apart from the two of us, almost all the passengers were middle-aged American couples. After about an hour the coach stopped and the driver waved at a single small cave with a few faint drawings on its walls. I was astonished, since the important cave to which the coach company promised a visit was about two hours from Darwin and had a substantial series of well-preserved paintings on several walls.
>
> I went to the driver, indicated that I knew what had happened and asked him to drive on. He mulishly and silently ignored me. The other passengers were now back in their seats after looking at the feeble drawings. I told them we were not at all at our chosen destination and that I was sure of this because of my UNESCO connection. I asked them to join me in asking the driver to go further.[31]

The next sentence is set out like a display quote, a miniature paragraph in the centre of the page, and in italics:

> *They sat stolidly in their seats, most with their heads down, and all silent.*[32]

Hoggart comments beneath it:

> Collective cowardice, reinforced by their shared national habits; 'do nothing so as to avoid a fuss.' How 'English' the Americans can be. I tried again, with the same result. I was both surprised and shocked. The driver engaged the gears and we went back to Darwin. No moral courage there.[33]

He is not done yet. The next paragraph begins: 'Perhaps I should have made an even greater fuss on the spot', and goes on to analyse his own by then passive behaviour, 'enough of the English disinclination to cause a fuss' along with an 'anger at "being done"'.[34]

In the end, none of the characters in this episode does anything different: neither the fellow tourists, nor the coach driver, nor Hoggart himself, who gives up the effort at protest. The passage is partly about the failure to modify an evident wrong, or to interest others in the fact that they are being conned. It is about the helplessness and frustration of a futile consumer complaint: no one is listening, everyone just wants a quiet life ('most with their heads down and all silent'). But most of all, the sadness of the passage lies in Hoggart's own loss of authority. The man who not long ago was head of a major wing of a famous international organisation, UNESCO, is now unable to get a few passengers on a bus trip to pay him attention; worse than that, they seem to cower away, to try to pretend he is not making a fool of himself. The travellers are nowhere in particular, in an outback where one cave is much like another; they are notionally Americans but they may as well be English, Hoggart suggests, to judge from their comfortable coach potato capitulation. Like the contented visitors to 'the most photographed barn in America', promoted as such, in Don DeLillo's novel of 1985, *White Noise*, these people, Hoggart apart, or possibly Hoggart and Mrs Hoggart apart (we don't know), are happy to think they have seen what they want to have seen; they don't want to know that they haven't.[35]

It is as if there are no active witnesses to what amounts to a collective outrage. The driver takes no notice, the passengers take no notice of either the initial exchange or the speech that is made for their educational and consciousness-raising benefit. It is as if the recounting in the present book is meant as one more attempt to expose the holiday scam. A last resort. But the telling of the story now only reinforces the picture of powerlessness, of a Richard Hoggart reduced to appearing as an eccentric old man haranguing an unlistening and ignorant coachload of tourists in the back of beyond. Geographically and culturally he is transported away from his consumerly comfort zones, as he dwindles into the far distance.

One other scene, less extreme, seems like an echo of this one. Again, it is part of an otherwise unrecounted vacation in the retirement years; again, it takes place not just far from home, but far from present-day human settlement – in the only motel for miles and miles somewhere in the remotest reaches of America: 'We were driving across the dire agoraphobic wastes of Death Valley, California, at the turn into the 1990s.'[36] It is at this ghastly and god-forsaken intersection that Richard and Mary find themselves; the place is unwelcoming and filthy and the only available food is something that goes by the name of a Desert Stew. Rather than that, he says, 'We retreated to an unkempt, chill cabin outside'.[37] Hoggart was not of the TripAdvisor generation – but even so, this is clearly a one-star experience. There is no choice; there is no warmth; there is no more to say. It is as if he had come to the end of all the vitality and variety, of all that Richard Hoggart had been as a writer and as an enjoyer of the consumer experiences of his time.

But it would be wrong to finish with these sad images of an exiled, ancient, and (to put it less tragically) straightforwardly dissatisfied consumer: with Richard and Mary ending up in far-off places imbued with the disappointments or downright deceptions of some forms of international tourism. The Australian coach trip has a distant affinity, and therefore a visible contrast, with the lovingly detailed description of a wholly different kind of tourist experience at the other end of Hoggart's life, which is the charabanc day trip to Scarborough described in *The Uses of Literacy*. There, in a couple of pages, Hoggart packs in all the pleasure of the outfits, the fish and chips, the ice creams, the banter, all the hour-by-hour rituals of the once-in-a-summertime seaside enjoyments of his Leeds childhood. Even the inevitable queue for the ladies' is a chance for fun – and a moment that gets its moment in his account. Embarking on his account of the journey back at the end of the day, he then goes on:

> If the men are there, and certainly if it is a men's outing, there will probably be several stops and a crate or two of beer in the back for drinking on the move. Somewhere in the middle of the moors the men's parties all tumble out, with much horseplay and noisy jokes about bladder-capacity.[38]

'Somewhere in the middle of the moors' – as with the Australian site, it is out of range, but here are no ageing, well-off passengers, couples keeping their careful, frosty distance. Instead, back there in the early middle of the twentieth century, we are given a community of sometimes women, sometimes men, and sometimes all together, the children along for the ride as well, all spending their pennies together, idealised in the memory and the gentle analysis of the sometime small boy. All in it together: one coach, one day, one still vivid narrator of stopping and shopping pleasures.

NOTES

1. Richard Hoggart, *The Uses of Literacy: Aspects of Working-Class Life, with Special Reference to Publications and Entertainments* (London: Chatto & Windus 1957), 90.
2. Hoggart, *The Uses of Literacy*, 90.
3. Hoggart, *The Uses of Literacy*, 90.

4. Hoggart, *The Uses of Literacy*, 90–1.
5. Hoggart, *Townscape with Figures: Farnham: Portrait of an English Town* (London: Chatto & Windus, 1994), 51.
6. Hoggart, *Townscape*, 51–2.
7. Hoggart, *Townscape*, 52.
8. Hoggart, *A Sort of Clowning: Life and Times, Volume II: 1940–59* (1990; Oxford: Oxford University Press 1991), 188.
9. Hoggart, *A Sort of Clowning*, 188.
10. Hoggart, *A Sort of Clowning*, 89.
11. Hoggart, *A Sort of Clowning*, 189.
12. Hoggart, *A Sort of Clowning*, 189.
13. Hoggart, *A Sort of Clowning*, 190.
14. Hoggart, *A Sort of Clowning*, 190.
15. Hoggart, *Townscape*, 110.
16. Hoggart, *Townscape*, 111.
17. Hoggart, *Townscape*, 24.
18. Hoggart, *Townscape*, 4.
19. Hoggart, *Townscape*, 5.
20. Q. D. Leavis, *Fiction and the Reading Public* (1932; London: Chatto & Windus,1968), 14.
21. Leavis, *Fiction and the Reading Public*, 16.
22. Leavis, *Fiction and the Reading Public*, 17–18.
23. Leavis, *Fiction and the Reading Public*, 7.
24. Hoggart, *A Local Habitation: Life and Times: 1918–1940* (1988; Oxford: Oxford University Press, 1989), 121.
25. Hoggart, *Between Two Worlds: Essays* (London: Aurum Press, 2001), 306.
26. On the contrasting developments of American and (later) British supermarkets, see Rachel Bowlby, *Carried Away: The Invention of Modern Shopping* (London: Faber, 2000). On the (relatively) small scale of newly opened British supermarkets in the late 1950s, see also Bowlby, *Back to the Shops: The High Street in History and the Future* (Oxford: Oxford University Press, 2022), ch. 7.
27. See Allen Ginsberg, 'A Supermarket in California', in *Howl* (1956: San Francisco: City Lights, 1986); Norman Jacob (ed.), *Culture for the Millions? Mass Media in Modern Society* (1959; Boston: Beacon Press, 1965); Randall Jarrell, *A Sad Heart at the Supermarket* (London: Eyre & Spottiswoode, 1965).
28. Hoggart, *A Sort of Clowning*, 164.
29. Hoggart, *Townscape*, 177, 178.
30. Hoggart, *Between Two Worlds*, 213.

31. Hoggart, *Promises to Keep: Thoughts in Old Age* (London: Continuum, 2005), 93–4.
32. Hoggart, *Promises*, 94.
33. Hoggart, *Promises*, 94.
34. Hoggart, *Promises*, 94.
35. Don DeLillo, *White Noise* (1985; New York: Penguin, 1986), 12.
36. Hoggart, *First and Last Things* (London: Aurum Press, 1999), 192.
37. Hoggart, *First and Last Things*, 153.
38. Hoggart, *The Uses of Literacy*, 122.

8

Scenes of Shopping*

Near the end of William Cowper's *The Task* (1785), embarking on a quiet passage in praise of countryside contemplation, the poem suddenly shifts away from this kind of timeless retreat. We are in the city, and in a shop – or rather, in a series of similar fashion shops. What these represent, for Cowper, is the place not to be; they are where a man would find himself if he made the mistake of passing his time not in philosophical thoughtfulness but in the company of the sort of young lady who always has to be drifting about from one such place to another. These are the lines that describe that fool

> who gives his noon
> To Miss, the Mercer's plague, from shop to shop
> Wand'ring, and litt'ring with unfolded silks
> The polished counter, and approving none,
> Or promising with smiles to call again.¹

This person is a pain not only for her gentleman companion, tired out by having to accompany her shop-hopping, but also for the man on the other side of the counter. She is 'the Mercer's plague', no less: a special female contagion tormenting the innocent shopkeeper who cannot resist her uncharming charm: 'with smiles', she says she'll be back. She has taken up his time, asking for one roll of fabric after another to be taken down and shown to her. But she hasn't bought a thing. Both men, it is implied, would agree on the serial annoyances of this young woman, with her multiple shops and multiple silks. Time and again she presents herself as being on the point of purchase, inside a shop and with merchandise ready to buy – but she never settles for any particular item.

---

* First published in *Back to the Shops: The High Street in History and the Future*, Oxford University Press, 2022.

We can unroll and replay this scene from many perspectives. First of all, it is a set-piece drama of gender relations. Not just one but two men are made to succumb to the whims of a flighty female who does what she wants with both of them, wasting the time of the man of leisure and the man of business alike. She benefits neither: the shopkeeper makes no money, while the gentleman seemingly has no pleasure in sharing *her* pleasure, her 'wand'ring' movement from one shop to the next and her indirect 'litt'ring' of the counter with everything she has wanted to handle and have a close look at. So the two of them are in the same position, in relation to both her, and their lost time – in one case probably valuable time.

But there is no mutual acknowledgement of this. Because at the same time the two men are also in quite different positions in relation to both the shop and the woman who has entered it. They are on either side of the counter, in two clearly separate classes, with one giving her the service of a specialist trade and the other the chivalrous, socially equal attentions of the *beau*. And just as the roles of each player are allocated according to gender and occupation (or lack of it), so they are specific to the situation inside a shop. The customer, the customer's friend and the salesman can all, so the poem implies, be given their likely characteristics and parts, with this particular type of difficult woman determining the playing out of partial, repeated events.

For the young lady is confidently represented as a stock type: 'Miss, the Mercer's plague', whose defining feature it is to act in this maddening fashion, trying everything and buying nothing. As such she is a literary forerunner of a much later and longer cast of typical shopping characters, who feature for instance in textbooks for shop assistants of the twentieth century. These contain colourful synopses of the likely behaviour of this or that sort of woman (it is always a woman) who will present you with her own particular obstacles to the smooth making of a sale. On the one hand the store assistant is elevated to the role of an expert who knows her or his psychological types, just as she knows about the goods she is selling. And on the other hand, this specialist knowledge of customer profiles is also a way of mitigating the annoyance of having to deal with such people. Converted into representative characters, embodiments of a single type, they are put at a distance and are halfway to being controlled and kept at a distance. You know what you are dealing with (and what you are dealing with has no surprises, no individual differences). More broadly, the same is true of the shopping scenario itself. In its basic elements – customer, shopkeeper, something to sell or to buy – it is scripted in advance with a number of key roles, a *dramatis personae* with both a set and a likely plot in view (the shop itself, and the purchase, made or thwarted).[2]

Cowper's vignette with its repeat non-buyer and its purposeless but apparently deliberate feminine drift (the girl's 'Wand'ring' habit) may look like a possible hint at the unmarried Miss who refuses to make up her mind, enjoying her power to receive an offer before smiling sweetly and moving on to the next one – swiping left, in eighteenth-century style. But it is placed, in the poem, as one of a series of negative illustrations for men of how not to spend time that would be better devoted to contemplation. The other bad occupations are playing billiards or board games, and going to auctions but never making a bid – the point in common with all of them being the waste of time and the last example closely resembling the practice of the unpurchasing girl shopper.

The problem of the non-buying customer had been raised before. In a number of *The Spectator* published in 1712, a shopkeeper's complaint is voiced in a fictional letter:

> I am, dear Sir, one of the top China-Women about Town; and though I say it, keep as good Things, and receive as fine Company as any o' this End of the Town, let the other be who she will: In short, I am in a fair way to be easy, were it not for a Club of Female Rakes, who, under pretence of taking their innocent Rambles, forsooth, and diverting the Spleen, seldom fail to plague me twice or thrice a Day, to cheapen Tea, or buy a Screen; *what else should they mean?* as they often repeat it. These Rakes are your idle Ladies of Fashion, who having nothing to do, employ themselves in tumbling over my Ware. One of these No-Customers (for by the way they seldom or never buy any thing) calls for a set of Tea-Dishes, another for a Bason, a third for my best Green-Tea; and even to the Punch-Bowl there's scarce a Piece in my Shop but must be displaced, and the whole agreeable Architecture disordered.[3]

The letter is signed by 'Rebecca the Distress'd'. In this all-female shopping world, all the sexual privileges of being a man are suspended: here are Women about Town (one of the 'top' ones, even), who keep their own shops, and here are other women strolling about in a group, on their 'innocent Rambles' which 'plague' the writer. She is bitingly sarcastic – *'what else should they mean?'* – in her criticism of these 'No-Customers' who bargain over the price of tea (then don't buy it) and mess up the shop's interior display of china, 'the whole agreeable Architecture disordered'. They behave in this way, she says, because they are 'idle', with 'nothing to do'; they only make more work (and no profit) for the shopkeeper.

For Cowper, the error in the shopping example is that of a male companion sharing in a purposeless female outing. There is no shadow here of a closely related scene, often described in nineteenth-century advice to would-be (male) strollers in the city, to avoid at all costs the company of a woman, who is bound to make you stop and shop (and spend your money at her request).[4] In contrast,

Cowper's young lady ought to figure as a delightfully cheap date; but perhaps at this early stage in the evolution of city shopping the absence of a loss of money fails to be noticeable in the face of the palpable loss of time, which is presented as a useful and finite resource even for those who are under no obligation to work.

Cowper's female 'plague' on the mercer also has her modern counterpart. In the passage about the time-taking, non-buying shopper, we might as well be in the early twenty-first century, denouncing the sort of customer who taps the expertise of a specialised high street retailer before making a more or less awkward exit and buying online instead. In *The Task*, though, there is no suggestion that the Miss is out to save money or seek information; it is not clear that she has any plan of purchasing at all. Instead, her behaviour seems to be tailor-made for the sort of enjoyable looking and not yet quite buying that would be enabled if not invited in the city shops of the decades that followed. Already, in Cowper's own time, there were showroom-style shops for the display of attractive china or glassware.[5] Such commodities were tasteful accessories that aspiring customers came to see for themselves, in a space whose own design and location became part of the products' prestige. Such developments can now be seen to mark the beginning of a culture of commodity display that would be more and more visible and accessible in the nineteenth century. The shops of a city centre became places to go and see, to spend time and not necessarily money just looking at what was there: admiring, perhaps desiring. *Shopping* became established as part of a lady's life: the word as well as the habit, in the sense of an open-ended activity, without a precise purchasing purpose.

Cowper's Miss is given short shrift, as a time-consumer for men who might have been otherwise occupied. She is clearly a nuisance, but the few lines given to her do not explore why she might have been acting the way she does. That balance is amply redressed by a work from a few years before *The Task*. Fanny Burney's novel *Evelina* presents a young lady whose initiation by other women into the social habits of modern London includes introducing her to a practice so new that it has to be garlanded with a special description as well as its own special word. Writing to her guardian back home, Evelina says: 'We have been *a shopping*, as Mrs Mirvan calls it, all this morning, to buy silks, caps, gauzes, and so forth.'[6] She expands on what is meant by this; it involves, it would seem, a male performance:

> The shops are really very entertaining, especially the mercers; there seem to be six or seven men belonging to each shop, and every one took care, by bowing and smirking, to be noticed; we were conducted from one to another, and carried from room to room, with so much ceremony, that at first I was almost afraid to follow. (27)

In Evelina's account, as in Cowper's, there is not just one article brought out in answer to the customer's request. But in this case, rather than being the result of a girl's not deciding or not wanting to make a choice at all, the showing of many possible things is all part of the flashy service:

> I thought I should never have chosen a silk, for they produced so many, I knew not which to fix upon; and they recommended them all so strongly, that I fancy they thought I only wanted persuasion to buy every thing they shewed me. And indeed, they took so much trouble, that I was almost ashamed I could not. (27)

'I fancy they thought': not only is Evelina reporting on a new experience for herself, as a woman *a shopping*; she is also putting herself in the place of the men in the shops and thus adding to their persuasive performance her own imagining of what they think she, the soon to be buyer, is thinking. Her 'almost ashamed' and not settling for the entire stock is Burney's cue for us to see Evelina's reading of these men as naively echoing their own design as salesmen: we know (so Burney allows us to think) that they are only too pleased for this first-time shopper to feel there might be something wrong in not buying enough, let alone in not buying at all. And there is also a personal element. Even though this is clearly recognised, by Evelina herself, as an elaborately orchestrated scene, complete with its stage moves as she is guided from one part of the shop to another, she also perceives the assistants as likely to suffer from real disappointment if she doesn't do what she thinks they think she would do with just that little extra push of completing 'persuasion': that is why she is 'almost ashamed', with a warmth of feeling that echoes what she takes to be theirs.

For a first shopping expedition, so early in Evelina's urban experience as well as in the history of modern shopping, Evelina is already up to her ears and eyes in all the interpretative intricacies of shopping psychology, as the passage goes to and fro between different understandings of what is going on, both in the shop and in the minds of the buying and selling characters. And it is not over yet!

> At the milliners, the ladies we met were so much dressed, that I should rather have imagined they were making visits than purchases. But what most diverted me was, that we were more frequently served by men than by women; and such men! So finical, so affected! They seemed to understand every part of a woman's dress better than we do ourselves; and they recommended caps and ribbands with an air of so much importance, that I wished to ask them how long they had left off wearing them! (27)

Being served by men is not different from what happened before, in the mercer's, where there were six or seven of them; for some reason it seems that the phenomenon is more to be noted as such in relation to the milliner's – selling not just finished hats, but all the accessories and variations implied by the 'caps and ribbands', which the men are said to be so familiar with. All the way to the 1970s BBC sitcom *Are You Being Served?*, about a provincial department store, this may well be the first in a long tradition, in more than one medium, of representations of the camp male shop assistant: obsequious, emphatic – 'so much importance'! – and fond of female fashion. And it is via that parade on the men's part of such an intimate familiarity with femininity that Evelina is led to situate herself as part of a community of actual women, 'we . . . ourselves'.

With the 'so much dressed' ladies at the beginning, the paragraph also indicates something about the subtle shift that is taking place in the invention of this new thing called shopping. The practice is seen as both excessive – 'so much' – and ritually social, like making a formal visit. This is the sort of occasion for which dressing up is clearly required; as opposed to buying things, even pretty, feminine things, which is not – or has not been till now – regarded in the same way, Evelina implies. But despite all the fussing and frippery, there is also a point to be made – in a firm, single-sentence paragraph of its own – about a quite different feature of this kind of shop: 'The dispatch with which they work in these great shops is amazing, for they have promised me a compleat suit of linen against the evening' (27). This is the first time there has been a direct mention of the size of the establishments, previously suggested only in the proliferation of their front-of-house personnel. But directly mentioned here it implies not excess, but a new kind of large-scale efficiency: they can make her a whole customised outfit by the end of the day, in time for tonight's event. In its own way it is the first fast fashion.

Evelina ends the account of her remarkable morning by describing a further new experience: 'I have just had my hair dressed. You can't think how oddly my head feels . . .'. Though this work is also, as with *shopping*, an occasion for noting a new word – '*frizled* they call it' (28) – there is no mention of the man, or woman, who does it, or where the transformation happens. Whereas the buying of fashionable clothing would come to lose the prestige of a personal service bestowed or inflicted on the well-to-do young lady, *hairdressing* – compacted into one word – would expand to become every woman's regular special occasion, a standard amenity on side streets as well as in city centres – and many women's adaptable lifelong job. In the late 1950s, the town planner Wilfred Burns referred to the tendency of housewives who had been hairdressers before marriage to open up a part-time business in a bedroom, with service 'provided outside normal working hours when it is most appreciated by a large number of working women'.[7] In Britain, the hairdressing salon was up there in numbers with the equally ubiquitous newsagent's and sweet shop in the mid-twentieth-century heyday of local shops and shopping. In terms of daft punning names, an English speciality, the hairdresser is almost the equal of the fish and chip shop, the original takeaway fast food outlet: A Cut Above meets The Codfather. Hairdressing salons and barbers are also among the few types of business whose presence on shopping streets has not declined in the twenty-first century. You can't get a haircut online.

By the time of Jane Austen's novels, a few decades after Burney's, ladies' shopping for new fashions is part of the fabric of middle-class life. Along with their mother, the Bennet sisters in *Pride and Prejudice* (1813) enjoy their London aunt's descriptions of the new season's latest styles, and when one of them visits her, the round of metropolitan entertainments includes not only an evening at the theatre, but also some daytime 'bustle and shopping': the word has by now become a regular noun.[8] But this is only a more glamorous version of what happens at home all the time, with the fun-seeking youngest girls, Lydia and Kitty, transfixed by the latest accessories in the windows of the milliner's in the small town near where they live. For them, these are natural objects of feminine desire, just like the young men in uniform who saunter up and down the same street – and they can walk into town to gaze at them whenever they want.

In Austen's *Emma* (1816) a comparable establishment is shown as a focal point for another such provincial place. It is talked up by the visiting Frank Churchill, who wants to impress Emma Woodhouse with his local knowledge. He describes the shop, with mock exaggeration (and also as a quick change of subject from Emma's grilling), as an essential part of local life – every day and for everyone:

> At this moment they were approaching Ford's, and he hastily exclaimed, 'Ha! this must be the very shop that every body attends every day of their lives, as my father informs me. He comes to Highbury himself, he says, six days out of the seven, and has always business at Ford's.'[9]

Not only does Frank's father supposedly have something to buy at Ford's all the time, but the claim has been made by a man to a man (even if it is now being reported, with possible ulterior intent, to please a lady). And now Frank himself proposes to follow in his father's regular footsteps:

> If it be not inconvenient to you, pray let us go in, that I may prove myself to belong to the place, to be a true citizen of Highbury. I must buy something at Ford's. It will be taking out my freedom. – I dare say they sell gloves. (179)

Local initiation, at least in jest, is making a purchase, at Ford's – and the particular choice of a specific 'something' to get is subordinate to this larger intention. At any rate, Emma warmly responds to both sides of Frank's declarations: 'Oh! Yes, gloves and everything. I do admire your patriotism' (179):

> They went in; and while the sleek, well-tied parcels of 'Men's Beaver' and 'York Tan' were bringing down and displaying on the counter, he said – 'But I beg your pardon, Miss Woodhouse, you were speaking to me, you were saying something at the very moment of this burst of my *amor patriae.*' (179)

There is no direct mention of the person performing the actions of bringing down and displaying, even though the naming of two of the sample styles of men's gloves could not be more precise. The narrator is specific about commodity specifications, and is also attentive to good-looking, effective packaging ('sleek, well-tied parcels') as part of the service. Frank and Emma, though, continue to talk for the length of a page before the storyline momentarily returns to the setting, and then only in an introductory clause, 'When the gloves were brought and they had quitted the shop again' (180). The transaction is passed over without details of what kind of gloves, or the moment of choosing, as if now it is merely a background to the main stream of a conversation about something else.

In keeping with Frank's father's alleged pronouncement of the shop's importance, this is not the first time that Ford's features in *Emma*. On its initial appearance, in fact, it is given a plug that sounds like a formal equivalent of what Mr Churchill said to his son: 'Ford's was the principal woollen-draper, linen-draper, and haberdasher's shop united; the shop first in size and fashion in the place' (159). This concise tour-guide aside comes in the middle of a long paragraph in which Harriet Smith is ramblingly recounting how she got caught in the rain, and entered the shop for shelter. The narrator puts in the sudden promotion without any diminishing distance: it comes over like paid-for content surrounded by fairly banal local news. Inside the shop, though, an emotional drama ensues, as Harriet finds herself sharing space with her just rejected suitor and his nice sister, and there is the problem for all concerned of how they should act and react. As with Frank Churchill's glove-buying moment, the shop scene's narrative interest is not about any actual or potential purchase (although the Martins appear to have made one); here Ford's becomes, in effect, just like any enclosed space, public or private, in which people negotiate an embarrassing meeting by chance. Anxious words and movements are painstakingly charted – 'I found he was coming towards me too – slowly you know, and as if he did not quite know what to do' (160) – until, the rain having stopped, Harriet finally gets herself out of the door. There is no suggestion, whether from the (again, unmentioned) proprietor or assistant, or from the narrator, or even from the guilty Harriet herself, that popping in to get out of the wet, and not buying a thing, is something that should not be done. The shop has its non-commercial uses.

Yet another scene at Ford's does involve, this time, a definite plan of purchase – 'Harriet had business at Ford's' (209) – but one that then turns out to be painfully protracted, as she fails to make up her mind. Harriet's delay is open-ended, but Austen is specific about its twofold cause, from both a multiplicity of desirable possibilities and the persuasive force of any remark: 'Harriet, tempted by everything and swayed by half a word, was always very long at a purchase; and while she was still hanging over muslins and changing her mind, Emma went to the door for amusement . . .' (209). After a while, along comes Frank Churchill in the company of his stepmother, Mrs Weston, this time presenting himself not as a natural patron of Ford's, but as a likely encumbrance: 'My aunt always sends me off when she is shopping' (210).

After her exchange with him, Emma has reason to hurry Harriet along, and goes over to 'the interesting counter – trying, with all the force of her own mind, to convince her that if she wanted plain muslin, it was of no use to look at figured; and that a blue ribbon, be it ever so beautiful, would still never match her yellow pattern'. The deal is finally clinched – 'At last it was all settled' – by the persuasive 'force' of the friend rather than by 'Mrs. Ford', who does this time appear by name in the subsequent discussion, recorded in all its dithering detail, about whether or not the purchase should be put into two parcels for two destinations. This is an issue to do with where it will be needed by Harriet, who moves between two places, and also, as pointed out by Emma, to do with the limits of customer service: 'It is not worth while, Harriet, to give Mrs. Ford the trouble of two parcels.' To which, after Harriet's agreement, deferential to both, the response from 'the obliging Mrs. Ford' is: 'No trouble in the world, ma'am' (211).

Emma's stationing herself at the door of the shop makes her more like an unoccupied shopkeeper than what she presently is, a regular customer waiting for someone else to make a purchase. A full picture, minute by minute, is given of the just about urban scene she can see:

> Much could not be hoped from the traffic of even the busiest part of Highbury; – Mr. Perry walking hastily by, Mr. William Cox letting himself in at the office door, Mrs. Cole's carriage horses returning from exercise, or a stray letter-boy on an obstinate mule, were the liveliest objects she could presume to expect; and when her eyes fell only on the butcher with his tray,

a tidy old woman travelling homewards from shop with her full basket, two curs quarreling over a dirty bone, and a string of dawdling children round the baker's little bow-window eyeing the gingerbread, she knew she had no reason to complain, and was amused enough; quite enough still to stand at the door. (209–10)

The 'traffic' includes a number of people, a generational cross-section of a small community, from the children to the old lady. They are mostly engaged in commercial or consumerly errands of one sort or another – beginning with the dogs and the bone. 'Mr. William Cox' has an office he lets himself in to, Mr Perry is just in a walking hurry of unspecified aim, but everyone else's movement or attitude has something to do with food buying. The old lady and the butcher are both carrying out the final stage of completed purchases that need to be conveyed from shop to home, while the children, not going anywhere, are collectively captivated by the sweet things to be seen in the baker's window. For Emma, even though 'Much could not be hoped' from it, this everyday spectacle is *enough* (twice said) to keep her where she is: it amuses her. It is enough, because it is various, each separate actor or group singled out with their particular activity as a seller of goods or services, or a buyer, actual or potential: the children 'eyeing' the cakes that are there but not theirs, tantalisingly visible but not accessible.

With Emma, there is nothing significant – nothing that changes the story – in what she witnesses of local shop life. She just looks, and takes pleasure in the looking. Like her own creator, Emma enjoys observing the ordinary ways in which life goes on in a little place; and at this particular moment in her novel what she takes in is the simple street scene of the shops and a typical morning's activities that they elicit. Butcher, baker and buyers, present and future: all the small-town shopping world passes before Emma's eyes as she waits in the draper's for Harriet to sort out her ribbons.

But Emma's perspective, viewed with a sense of the longer implications of what she sees, can also be critical. In its small way, Ford's of Highbury is a local beacon offering services more and less commercial of many kinds. It is where the customer, even a fairly insignificant customer like Harriet Smith, is able to stop off in a shower, to have what she's bought packaged up and delivered to her particular requirements – and to hesitate about whether or what to buy, for minutes on end. Among possible classifications of customer stalling, she stands in a different place from Cowper's young lady who leaves (again and again) with a charming smile, buying nothing. Harriet hates her own hesitation and is also chastised for it by her superior female companion.

In *Emma*, the shop itself is half personified as a focus of local affections and identifications. Ford's is a semi-public space in which the customer is given all kinds of personal attention and practical assistance, in addition to the basic buying of this or that article. It is solidly anchored on the main street, it stands for much more than the 'bricks and mortar' that have become the dismissive phrase for shops that exist in a place that is not the internet. In later times, the corporate tracking of 'customer loyalty' would take away the lightness of Frank Churchill's little joke. And so would the patronising – not patriotic – attitude to the 'small man' (or woman) of the standard high street shop, half indicated, perhaps, in the virtual absence of Mrs Ford or any other shop personnel from the scenes in *Emma*. He – or she – plays a vital social role.

NOTES

1. William Cowper, *The Task* (1785), in *Cowper: Verse and Letters*, ed. Brian Spiller (London: Rupert Hart-Davis, 1968), 522.
2. See for instance Rose Buckner, *Design for Selling for Bakers and Confectioners* (London: National Association of Master Bakers, Confectioners and Caterers, 1959), 68–81; Ruth Leigh, *The Human Side of Retail Selling* (New York: D. Appleton, 1923), 110–28; S. A. Williams, *Teach Yourself Salesmanship* (London: English Universities Press, 1944), 38–47.
3. *The Spectator*, ed. Gregory Smith (London: J. M. Dent, 1906), vol. III, No. 336 (Wednesday 26 March 1712), 62. The author of the piece is Richard Steele.
4. On this warning against female company for the nineteenth-century (male) *flâneur*, see Rachel Bowlby, 'Walking, Women and Writing', in *Still Crazy After All These Years: Women, Writing and Psychoanalysis* (1992; London: Routledge, 2010), 6.
5. The marketing of Wedgwood china, including a well-appointed London showroom, is the classic eighteenth-century example of this phenomenon. See Neil McKendrick, John Brewer and J. H. Plumb, *The Birth of a Consumer Society: The Commercialization of Eighteenth-Century England* (Bloomington: Indiana University Press, 1982).
6. Fanny Burney, *Evelina* (1778), ed. Edward A. Bloom (Oxford: Oxford University Press, World's Classics, 1982), 27. Further references will be given within the main text.
7. Wilfred Burns, *British Shopping Centres: New Trends in Layout and Distribution* (London: Leonard Hill, 1959), 43.
8. Jane Austen, *Pride and Prejudice* (1813), ed. James Kinsley (Oxford: Oxford University Press, 2004), 117.
9. Austen, *Emma* (1816), ed. James Kinsley (Oxford: Oxford University Press, 1995), 179. Further references will be given within the main text.

9

Buying the Baby, Growing Your Own*

In October, 1826, the campaigning writer William Cobbett was travelling up from Southampton back to London. On the way he found matter for argument at Netley Abbey, where he fulminated about the disappearance of the 'ancient *fish-ponds*' of the place – '"reclaimed," as they call it'. What had gone was a valuable and simple source of food:

> What a *loss*, what a national loss, there has been in this way, and in the article of *water fowl*! I am quite satisfied, that, in these two articles and in that of *rabbits*, the nation has lost, has had annihilated (within the last 250 years) food sufficient for *two days in the week*, on an average, taking the year throughout. These are things, too, which cost so little labour![1]

The perspective is one of planning on a national scale, with the deployment of averages, time periods and cost effectiveness to elaborate the case. Starting from one particular place, the view pans out to encompass innumerably more: all the ponds that Cobbett has seen on his travels, a justification for the generalisation that he has already made: 'You can see the marks of old fish-ponds in thousands and thousands of places. I have noticed, I dare say, *five hundred*, since I left home.'[2]

What is to be done? The solution would be straightforward, just like the yield that could then be obtained again from these sources – but it is a solution which, Cobbett declares, is thwarted from the start, and that is because of a new social practice that has effectively made the ponds redundant:

> A trifling expense would, in most cases, restore them; but now-a-days, all is looked for at *shops*: all is to be had by *trafficking*: scarcely any one thinks of providing for his own wants *out of his own land* and . . . his own domestic means.[3]

---

* First published as 'Sources', in *Back to the Shops: The High Street in History and the Future*, Oxford University Press, 2022.

Cobbett casually identifies a momentous change: from the default position of growing your own and using the local resources, to seeking what is needed elsewhere – and above all with *shops*, the word speared with those savage italics. Cobbett identifies the difficulty primarily as a matter of mind-set: today 'scarcely any one thinks of' being self-sufficient.

Then Cobbett says more on shops and what is wrong with them: 'To buy the thing, *ready made*, is the taste of the day: thousands, who are *housekeepers*, buy their dinners ready cooked.'[4] Apart from some now unlikely characters and turns of phrase – the housekeepers, 'the taste of the day' – this could be the beginning of a well-meaning post about 'cooking from scratch', as currently used to mean preparing food at home, as opposed to buying a ready meal from the shop (or having it delivered). As it stands, Cobbett's harangue could well be the earliest example of this argument. To be sure, this is not yet the world of Deliveroo, or even the not so long ago world of Vesta curries, those packets from half a century ago that are sometimes spoken of now with a sort of nostalgic horror. In their twentieth-century time, such things – loved and loathed – seemed like a new idea. In his monumental history of the past century of British retailing, published in the mid-1950s, James Jefferys ventured the thought that future developments in food sales might include 'even the sale of ready-cooked meat and meals'.[5]

So it is striking that two hundred years ago, Cobbett articulates his environmental and lifestyle concerns about the food we eat in terms that are not very different from those of today. He deplores the way that new modes of consumption have taken people away from local making – growing, rearing, and food preparation – and taken them out to the *shops* to get what they need (he is not, in this passage, condemning the desire for new commodities as such: that comes elsewhere). That *ready* meal epitomises a different relationship to what is eaten because it does away with the sense of a long and slow process in which nature and then people take the time that it takes to make the food. Ready is instant, is now; it has no distinct connection with the place of consumption or preparation. But for some reason, it is what people seem to want, and Cobbett's aim is to change their minds.

On another journey, the previous year, this time going through Surrey, Cobbett set off on a related train of polemic, this time prompted by a farmhouse rather than a fishpond. Again, an exemplary sighting: 'Here I had a view of what has long been going on all over the country.' What he spots this time is a sale taking place because the long-standing leasehold farmer is moving out. Cobbett's interest and upset is directed at the change in custom, which has led to a fine old table no longer being used or cared for, or even now kept at all. This table being put out for sale is the symbol of a whole way of life that has been abandoned:

> Every thing about this farm-house was formerly the scene of *plain manners* and *plentiful living*. Oak clothes-chests, oak bedsteads, oak chests of drawers, and oak tables to eat on, long, strong, and well supplied with joint stools. Some of the things are many hundreds of years old. But all appeared to be in a state of decay and nearly of *disuse*. There appeared to have been hardly any *family* in that house, where formerly there were, in all probability, from ten to fifteen men, boys, and maids: and, which was the worst of all, there was a *parlour*! Aye, and a *carpet* and *bell-pull* too![6]

Cobbett even imagines the future upcycled fate of the long table as part of an ornamental bridge for the residence of a stockbroker ('stock-jobber') – and decides to rescue it by buying it himself. He also goes into details about the end of the communal household that he supposes to have been there – the 'family' including the live-in workers and servants. All of them would have been eating together, with not much privileged difference in the master's entitlement, Cobbett thinks. But now the extra people have been cast out to live in separate small households, much more expensive to run, and not earning enough to do so; meanwhile, in the big house, the remaining immediate family of the farmer is playing out an imitation of an already degraded contemporary mode of life, epitomised by that ghastly new kind of room, the *parlour*. Like the *shops* it is shown up in italics and also, this time, for good measure, with scare quotes as well. Inside it is an array of the things that go with the different way of living:

> One end of the front of this once plain and substantial house had been moulded into a '*parlour*,' and there was the mahogany table, and the fine chairs, and the fine glass, and all as bare-faced upstart as any stock-jobber in the kingdom can boast of. And, there were the decanters, the glasses, the 'dinner-set' of crockery ware, and all just in the true stock-jobber style. And I dare say it has been '*Squire* Charington and the *Miss* Charingtons; and not plain Master Charington, and his son Hodge, and his daughter Betty Charington, all of whom this accursed system has, in all likelihood, transmuted into a species of mock gentlefolks.[7]

This transformation involves everything from the building work to create the *parlour* to the buying in of the upmarket china and glass that were beginning to be grandly promoted as aspirational commodities.[8] All of a piece, you can't put the old things in with the new, and 'That long table could not share in the work of the decanters'.

The italics added to the *parlour* and the inverted commas to the 'dinner-set' convey the condemnation in another way, now as a matter of a special language; the things are like self-citations, or brand names of themselves. So the fancy font twists the straight letter, and 'plain' Master Charington and his children have to be addressed with fussy titles. The 'plain' house and 'plain' name have been falsely changed into fake versions of a superior class, 'mock' gentlefolks; but this needless, almost absurd performance does harm as well, by its detrimental effects on the farm workers.

Cobbett goes on – and on – about the Charington farmhouse (owned, as it happens – and as he tells his readers – by the public school Christ's Hospital). To ears and eyes familiar, as ours may be, with property advertising and lifestyle features across many media, Cobbett seems to be instituting a sort of angry reversal of the genre before it has even begun. He moves away from the specifics of the place he visited to make a general critique of current new-build farmhouses. Once again, this involves a detailed imagining of exactly what the interior will be like:

> Those that are now erected are mere painted shells, with a Mistress within, who is stuck up in a place she calls a *parlour*, with, if she have children, the 'young ladies and gentlemen' about her: some showy chairs and a sofa (a *sofa* by all means): half a dozen prints in gilt frames hanging up: some swinging book-shelves with novels and tracts upon them: a dinner brought in by a girl that is perhaps better 'educated' than she: two or three nick-nacks to eat instead of a piece of bacon and a pudding: the house too neat for a dirty-shoed carter to be allowed to come into; and every thing proclaiming to every sensible beholder that there is a constant anxiety to make a *show* not warranted by the reality.[9]

All the features, decorative and rhetorical, of the earlier section are resumed in this one: the superficiality of the houses that are just 'painted shells', the calling ordinary things and people by fancy names; the mockery of 'showy' furniture – including, here, a sofa (no, a *sofa*), one of the must-haves of these softly sitting times. And there is more, with the tacky display of cultural objects: gilt frames and prints, not real paintings; novels and tracts, the latest ephemera of the too light or too serious – rather than decent old books. Instead of proper food, a solid two courses of meat then pudding, the people are just grazing on snacks – on 'two or three nick-nacks'. Not even 'ready' meals, which are bad enough. Then there are the artificial separations of space and employment, allied to mistaken ideas of rank. These people cut themselves off from the ordinary dirt of the outside; and they want nothing to do with actual work. Instead of farming, the sons are meant to get jobs in an office – jobs that are as inauthentic as the food their parents consume. 'Good God! What, "young gentlemen" go to plough! They become *clerks*, or some skimmy-dish thing or other.'[10]

Lamenting the fate of the fishpond and the farmhouse, Cobbett's two reports both work in the same way. They home in on one particular place where a change has occurred, by human intervention, from age-old consuming practices to new ones. The evidence of the change he has seen with his own eyes, and now describes. The new practice lacks all the virtue and good sense of the old. It involves purchases, whether of fixtures and furnishings or food – where previously no money was involved, because the table had been there forever and the meal was sourced and prepared at home. It involves, in the farmhouse case, the loss of a harmonious mixed community and the substitution of an unequal division in which the master class cuts itself off from real work and requires a fabricated language to go with its fabricated roles and possessions.

Cobbett's characteristic style moves from here (in this very place) to all over, as he starts with a show and tell – look what I saw! – and then makes it a microcosm of broad and regrettable ongoing changes. From the sight of this one particular place – and all the more because this one particular place is self-evidently real, is here and now – we are assured that the story that surrounds it is true. And that sense of righteous rightness is presented as all the stronger because Cobbett is already talking, directly, about contrasts between the true and the false, the real and the fake, which are inseparable, he suggests, from the language in which they are lived and spoken. The *Miss* Charingtons, as opposed to plain Betty Charington, belong with the *sofa* on which, inevitably, they are seated.

The changes that Cobbett describes are all interrelated. If 'now-a-days, all is looked for at *shops*', it is also the case that more and more elements of everyday life – more and more goods and services, new and old – are now being bought with money rather than made or maintained or performed by those who use them. An old table becomes something to be sold off and replaced, rather than something whose age, as it always has done, confirms its continuing value and usefulness. The home, having previously been a place of communal habitation for an extended working group, is now isolated as the residence of a nuclear family whose adults seek to mark their social superiority; new, paid-for projects of improvement and newly purchased objects of interior décor are to extend and demonstrate that status. The home is 'showy' rather than for living in.

The generalisation of the cases means that Cobbett goes out of his way to point out that these new consumers, consumers of the new, are not individually at fault. The choice is not their own:

> the blame belongs to the infernal stock-jobbing system. There was no reason to expect, that farmers would not endeavour to keep pace, in point of show and luxury, with fund-holders, and with all the tribes that *war* and *taxes* created. Farmers were not the authors of the mischief; and *now* they

are compelled to shut the labourers out of their houses, and to pinch them in their wages, in order to be able to pay their own taxes.

This twofold explanation – social emulation on the one hand and a tax burden on the other – departs from the emphasis elsewhere, which gives no explanation for what the farmers have been doing. The two reasons now brought forward are different in kind, as well – and also in forcefulness. The first, fairly plausible, is economic. The farm workers are thrown out of the house because saving on their wages is the only way for employers to pay their taxes. The second, much less tangible and much more complex, is vaguely psychological and social. It is hedged about with the uncertain double negatives of there being 'no reason' to expect that farmers 'would not' do what they are doing. And what they are doing is copying. In a phrase that is almost exactly equivalent to 'keeping up with the Joneses' (which enters the language much later), Cobbett says that this happens because the farmers want to 'keep pace, in point of show and luxury, with fund-holders' and all the rest of them. The old table is swapped for a new one because that's how the new moneyed classes behave – and implicitly, therefore, it is the stockjobbers and their ilk that the farmers want to be seen to keep up with. But why?

Keeping pace is equally curious as it introduces all of a sudden, and again without further explanation, the idea of speed and contest. Why would rural farmers be measuring themselves at all in relation to such a different class, that of the moneyed *nouveaux riches* of the city – let alone comparing a rate of advance? Moving away from a formerly stable situation would seem to be part of the image of false progress that Cobbett condemns the farmers for buying into. He doesn't approve of the attitude, but he presents it as if it were somehow bound to be: 'no reason to expect, that farmers would not'. But why would anyone ever have abandoned the food-rich fishpond and sent out to the shops instead? It's not even that they have taken to selling the pond's easy produce for profit. It seems that the pond and its contents lack the appeal of the shops, have just been let go: 'scarcely any one thinks of providing for his own wants *out of his own land* and other domestic means.'

This slightly slippery moment in Cobbett's arguments suggests that there must be more to say: hidden depths, perhaps. It may indicate that there is something in the social situations he is trying to give an account of that does not fit easily into the categories he wants to maintain. The farmers endeavouring to keep pace are a particularly strong illustration of this hesitation, since the idea of social emulation as a reason for going out to buy new stuff – especially stuff for the home – is today one of the dominant ways of explaining why and how people might do such a thing. It is the phenomenon brilliantly labelled *conspicuous consumption* in Thorstein Veblen's work of semi-satirical anthropology, *The Theory of the Leisure Class*. From the tasteful parlour to its appropriately accompanying lady and the display of cultured accessories, many of the elements that Veblen singled out to describe affluent Americans in 1900 are present in Cobbett's description of buying for show. Veblen's phrase is now used without any sense of the where and when of its origins; and the emulation and aspiration it describes are taken so patently to be how people really are motivated that they are not seen as needing any further explanation.[11]

In Cobbett's time, that general expectation is not yet the case, which is why the affirmation – he says it, but says no more – is so interesting. The logical jump occurs just when he is articulating the sense of a break that is taking place between the enduring and the emerging; between the permanent source (the old oak table, the ever-plentiful fish) and the quick new thing (the bought-in décor and dinners). But as an argument, this contrast is also what gives his writing its power. Something has happened – is happening – right in front of us, if only we have eyes to see it. Think about it! Do something!

Two centuries after Cobbett's time, what he says shouts out once again with the urgency of anger and activism about the environmental damage that humans have done and are doing to their immediate and larger worlds. Why did we turn our backs on local sources of sustenance? How can we step back now from the false appeals of the fast? Fast fashion, fast food – and yes, fast furniture. Once again, there is a wish to consider the long-term effects of short-term satisfactions – and to challenge the dominance of buying and selling, and throwing away, in almost every aspect of ordinary living. The scope of the challenge extends to the whole global economy, from the destruction of natural balances and resources to the perpetuation of glaring human inequalities: in Cobbett's picture, from the fishpond to the downgraded farm workers.

In the passages from Cobbett quoted above, history is an indefinite period of unbroken usage, and the present a sudden and stupid shock of the needless new. At other times, on other occasions, he offers instead layered and detailed accounts of the idiosyncrasies of one region or another as they have interacted with human history over time. There is both a use and a risk in the defining polemical illustration. A use because it shows what it shows so clearly, as if beyond the need for further evidence. A risk, by the same token, because it stands alone, without more ado: as if history, up to the present time of observing and writing, had been gently passing or flowing by, without disturbance; whereas now, dramatically, all is changed. But equally, there is both risk and use in staying only with the gentler gradations of change: as if nothing was ever contested, and everything happened along slow and settled pathways towards the destination of the present.

Cobbett's rage at the commodification of just about everything, and at the happy accommodation to that, continues to reverberate today, but in a different way precisely because the purchasability of almost anything has extended so much further since his time. Take the passage about the neglected fish, which doesn't end with the purchase of pre-cooked food:

> To buy the thing, *ready made*, is the taste of the day: thousands, who are *housekeepers*, buy their dinners ready cooked: nothing is so common as to *rent breasts* for children to suck: a man *actually advertised*, in the London papers, about two months ago, to *supply childless husbands with heirs*! In this case the articles were of course, to be *ready made*; for, to make them '*to order*' would be the devil of a business; though, in desperate cases, even this is, I believe, sometimes resorted to.[12]

Then, as now, the buying of babies can be presented as the ultimate scandal: if even a baby can be pre-ordered and paid for, then surely nothing is out of the reach of marketisation. Cobbett also highlights the promotion of the practice: they don't just do this, they *actually advertise* that they do it. Thus the fact that baby-buying might not be scandalous is itself a scandal. But at the same time as this final example is continuous with present-day sensibilities, the specific practices are not the same. In the nineteenth century, wet-nursing, the rented breast, is commonplace; although Cobbett clearly doesn't like it, he takes it for granted and treats it as the everyday habit that offsets the truly appalling – but unspecified – practices that may happen in 'desperate cases'. What is being referred to? The advertisement, here, is left to speak uninterpreted, in its euphemistically riddling way (the childless wife who must belong with the childless husband is not even mentioned). The ready-made baby probably means a clandestine adoption, while a baby made to order may involve some form of surrogacy or supposition (a newborn passed off as the offspring of another woman who is not in reality its birth mother). Just possibly the reference might be to artificial insemination. The difficulty now is not only to identify what Cobbett intended to suggest – if indeed it was any particular practice – but also to know whether he expected his readers to get it at the time.

Cobbett's pre-ordered baby does two things in his argument. On the one hand it is there to show the arrival at an extreme limit of commodification: even babies can be bought. On the other hand, it is meant to seem almost silly – the very idea of an advertisement to *supply childless husbands with heirs*! – and so to discredit or mock the more ordinary examples of buying just anything too. Seen in this company, the idea of the food to go could begin to look as ridiculous as the idea of the baby to go. Of course we should make them ourselves!

But the logic is also one of retreat to the small-scale rural unit. Which is all very well if you have a fishpond (or a fertile spouse) of your own, but sometimes it may be necessary to trade or at least to exchange with others to get what you modestly want or need. Not everything is already given for everyone by bountiful nature. But if it is, look no further.

NOTES

1. William Cobbett, *Rural Rides* (1830), ed. George Woodcock (Harmondsworth: Penguin, 475.
2. Cobbett, *Rural Rides*, 475.
3. Cobbett, *Rural Rides*, 475.
4. Cobbett, *Rural Rides*, 475.
5. James B. Jefferys, *Retail Trading in Britain 1850–1950* (Cambridge: Cambridge University Press, 1954), 207.
6. Cobbett, *Rural Rides*, 226–7.
7. Cobbett, *Rural Rides*, 227.
8. On the innovative marketing practices of Josiah Wedgwood's company in the second half of the eighteenth century see Neil McKendrick, 'Josiah Wedgwood and the Commercialization of the Potteries', in McKendrick, John Brewer and J. H. Plumb, *The Birth of a Consumer Society: The Commercialization of Eighteenth-Century England* (Bloomington: Indiana UP, 1982), 100–45.
9. Cobbett, *Rural Rides*, 229.
10. Cobbett, *Rural Rides*, 229.
11. See Thorstein Veblen, *The Theory of the Leisure Class* (1899), ed. Martha Banta (Oxford: Oxford University Press, 2007).
12. Cobbett, *Rural Rides*, 475.

PART III
FEMINIST DIRECTIONS

10

Fifty Fifty

Female Subjectivity and the Danaids*

Who the hell are the Danaids? Unless you have specialised knowledge, it is unlikely that you would have much idea beyond, perhaps, a vague sense of them as mythological and female. If you were really well informed, you might have them down as residents of Hades, and if you had got that far you would probably be able to name some of the others they work out with in that infernal gym: Ixion and Tantalus and Sisyphus, for instance You might even know that, unlike others doing time down there, the Danaids are not one but fifty: the fifty daughters of Danaus. (Or rather, as will become clear, the fifty daughters of Danaus, minus one.) They massively outnumber all the other celebrities from hell, and yet they fade into the background by comparison. Perhaps this is because they are not individuals. Or perhaps it is because they are women. Whatever the explanation, it would seem that the Danaids have not, at least of late, had a significant role as poetic figures or as subjects of common allusion; they have remained in or returned to obscurity – unrepresented, with barely the ghost of a mention in summaries of classical mythology.

But if this may be more or less true of the recent English-speaking tradition (there are counter-examples, as we will shortly see), it is probably not so for some European countries.[1] My tale of the Danaids is prompted, in fact, by a striking instance of this hypothetical Anglo-Continental division, when the Danaids, in the process of being moved from German to English, were simply lost in translation. Towards the end of *Studies on Hysteria* there is a passage in which, thinking about the problems of the newly discovered talking treatment for hysterical illness, Freud turns to consider a practical problem that has

---

* First published in *Freudian Mythologies: Greek Tragedy and Modern Identities*, Oxford University Press, 2007.

emerged: the sheer time it takes. In James Strachey's 1955 translation for the Standard Edition, Freud says: 'The physician will not be spared the depressing feeling of being faced by a Sisyphean task.'[2]

The Sisyphean task evokes a more familiar image from Greek mythology. Sisyphus, most people do remember, was the one who had to keep on rolling the boulder up the hill until, just when it was getting to the top, down it rolled again. It seems an evocative image for the effort and the frustrations of the therapist, always about to reach the end of the job but always thwarted at the last minute by the patient's force of resistance to moving on and her readiness to fall back into her previous situation. In terms of the history of psychoanalytic theory and practice, it is a prescient declaration, depressingly prescient: more than forty years after *Studies on Hysteria*, Freud would write the long essay called 'Analysis Terminable and Interminable', in which the same problem of the endless analysis is addressed, itself apparently a problem that had never been resolved. More than a century on, that ball is still rolling as analysts seek to respond to patients' needs or demands for less frequent sessions and a shorter overall period of therapy than that of the 'classic' Freudian analysis, five times a week for an indefinite length of time.

But actually, it turns out that Freud makes no mention of Sisyphus. Instead, where the English has 'Sisyphean task', the German has *Danaidenarbeit*, 'Danaids' task' – and, in addition, '*Mohrenwäsche*', or whitewashing.[3] The '*Mohrenwäsche*' or 'Moors' wash' (the inverted commas are Freud's) conveys the mildly racialised suggestion of an attempted cover-up, light on dark, its impossibility indicated by its having to be done over and over again, and never successfully. But in English you would never know, for it has disappeared without trace; no blank space or substitute appears to mark its absence or alteration. The 'Danaids' task', on the other hand, is supplanted in Strachey's translation by the Sisyphean task. Presumably Strachey did not imagine his educated English readers would know the meaning of the allusion, and so put in its place something comparable that they might be expected to understand.[4]

Like Sisyphus, the Danaids were condemned in hell to a perpetual punishment of performing a single repetitive task that could never be completed; and therein lies the similarity that justifies Strachey's substitution. The Danaids' job is doubly dispiriting. Over and over again they fill containers with water, and the containers have holes in them. It looks in one way like an image of the futility and the endlessness of domestic labour, constantly interrupted, never done, always to be begun again.[5] The equipment is damaged, and further effort only leads to further waste.

But apart from his never completed task, Sisyphus does not have much in common with the Danaids. In some accounts he is something like an ex-conman, who arranged for his funeral rites to be incorrectly performed so that after his death he could get back out of the underworld again on a technicality. Then Sisyphus can also readily be linked to the common image of the shrink as charlatan, in a way that the Danaids can't: in other words, he generates new associations. Yet despite the difference, the English mistranslation acquired a certain *ex post facto* authenticity. Sisyphus did not remain as part of a passing phrase in the text, but actually found his way into the index of the Standard Edition in his own right, through no virtue or crime of his own – that is, despite the fact that he is not actually mentioned by Freud! Yet still, the solitary figure of the man struggling with the resistant stone has a touch of the noble hero about him, and in the wake of Albert Camus's absurdist version of the Sisyphus myth, this was the dominant image at the time of Strachey's translation in the mid-1950s; the English translation of *The Myth of Sisyphus* came out in the very same year.[6] Compared with this, the crowd of women sloshing away is hardly a picture of existential endeavour or muscular machismo.

On the other hand, much is lost by dropping the Danaids. By only a small shift of focus, it is possible to see in those leaky vessels and involuntary flows a picture of femininity as a dismal subjection to both dysfunctional biology and uselessly repetitive, unskilled work. A French feminist of the early 1960s, Evelyne Sullerot, made the contrast between women's and men's daily lives in terms of the Danaids and Sisyphus – another sign of the Danaids' greater familiarity in continental Europe, especially since Sullerot was writing for a popular readership:

> Every day they [women] fill the Danaids' container. Sisyphus pushes his rock upwards, it rolls back down, and everything has to be started over again each day. He is seized by a feeling of absurdity, but he puts all the force of his arms into the effort and sees clearly that the important thing is not the rock but the struggle to which he is condemned. But we Danaids fill containers with holes in them: the substance escapes from us through our fingers.[7]

Sullerot was not the first feminist to throw in the Danaids *contra* Sisyphus. In an English poem of the early eighteenth century called *The Thresher's Labour*, the Wiltshire farm labourer and poet Stephen Duck had taken Sisyphus as an emblem of the endlessness of men's agricultural work: 'Like *Sysiphys*, our Work is never done; / Continually rolls back the restless Stone.' To which, in *The Woman's Labour*, her witty response to Duck of 1739, Mary Collier, a Hampshire washerwoman, directly riposted:

> While you to *Sysiphys* yourselves compare,
> With *Danaus*' daughters we may claim a share;
> For while *he* labours hard against the Hill,
> Bottomless Tubs of Water *they* must fill.[8]

It now begins to seem that in suppressing the Danaids in favour of Sisyphus, Strachey, consciously or not, might have been doing more than covering over an obscure mythological reference that he assumed would be lost on his readers; he was also removing associations that would have been other than desirable. For the analogy, after all, is with the analyst: it is the analyst's labour that is Danaidan. At a time when there were as yet no women analysts in reality, and when almost all the patients – every one of those in *Studies on Hysteria* – were women, Freud makes the suggestion that the doctor is like the Danaids, doing a menial feminine job without satisfaction or prospects. No wonder he calls this a 'depressing' thought; though the German *verstimmende*, with no conveniently available adjectival equivalent in English, has more the sense of being put into a bad mood – pissed off. An irritating idea, these Danaids, and perhaps Strachey did well to delete them from psychoanalytic history. Or perhaps not. What *is* the task of the translator?[9] This is one question raised by the Danaids' disappearance. Strachey's choice also raises more general questions about the nature of work. What is a task or a job, whether chosen or assigned (a difference that cannot always be maintained)? What is a man's job? What is women's work? Feminism has typically manifested itself as refusing the assignment of women to 'reproductive' tasks, bearing and raising children and maintaining the household. In this context the Danaids appear as a spectacular illustration of female labour reduced to utter uselessness: they have neither husbands nor children to tend, and their one, unvarying task is not just eternally repeated, but never accomplished at all.

But if, like the rest of Hades' prison population, the Danaids have no future, they certainly have a history, and this shows them up in a stronger shade of darkness. Behind their eternal drudgery lies another kind of act altogether. What they are being punished for is murder: all but one (in some versions two) of the fifty of them killed their husbands, the fifty sons of Aegyptus, on their joint wedding night. For the movie, there is obviously a choice of several titles: 'Fifty Ways to Leave your Lover'; 'Fifty Brides for Fifty Brothers'; or – the clear winner – 'Fifty Weddings and Forty-Nine Funerals'. The Danaids move from murderous protest to deadly resignation. With its implausible combination of murders, marriage break-ups and faulty household appliances, their story in its entirety resembles the bizarre generic *mélange* of the TV soap. It is a strangely naturalised combination of the dramatic and the domestic, of the utterly aberrant with the numbingly normal; of the one-off horrific catastrophe with the serial continuity of an unchanging existence that simply continues as it is.[10]

Literary and philosophical representations of the Danaids have picked out different aspects of their multifaceted story. They appear in various surviving Greek and Latin works, sometimes fleetingly (as well-known mythological characters) and sometimes in leading roles. To begin with, and most substantially, they are the subjects of Aeschylus' play, the *Suppliants*, which is concerned with the first part of their story. This play was the first in a full trilogy about the Danaids; the other two plays are lost. In the *Suppliants*, the fifty daughters of Danaus arrive from Egypt in Greek Argos with their father to demand asylum. Danaus's daughters are running away from their fifty cousins, their uncle's sons the Aegyptoi, whom they refuse to marry. As is usual in tragedy, they make their request for asylum as a supplication, in the name of the gods – but their arguments are various, including the claim to be Argive themselves in origin, the claim that women are vulnerable to some men and so need protection from other men, and the claim that women have the right to refuse suitors not to their taste. Eventually they are granted protection by the Argive polity, just before the ship bearing their hot pursuers docks in the harbour. After various negotiations, however, matters are settled for the time being and the Aegyptoi back off.

It is thought that the two subsequent tragedies in the trilogy, one of which was called *The Danaids*, must have dealt with the next stage of the story in which the Danaids do marry their cousins, after a fashion. The ending of the *Suppliants* suggests some counter-arguments to the Danaids' resistance to marriage, which perhaps open the way to a genuine capitulation that might have happened before the wedding and its tragic aftermath. The Athenian audience for the *Suppliants* would have been familiar with the myth of the Danaids and so would have known that the end of this play was 'to be continued', and roughly what was to happen; they would then have watched the two further plays the same day, as well as a fourth, more lightweight and bawdy satyr play, in this case probably about Amymone, another one of the fifty daughters. The absence of the follow-up plays makes it impossible to know how Aeschylus imagined the ethics and the erotics of the Danaids' murders – issues that Horace and Ovid, several centuries later, would sharply moralise by singling out the non-murdering Danaid as a romantic heroine and damning her sisters as wicked. But the *Suppliants* is nonetheless a rich and peculiar source, not least because of its unusual mode of characterisation.

The play is distinctive because its chorus, the Danaids themselves, is not, as is most common in tragedy, a background source of moral commentary and lyrical interludes, perhaps with occasional interventions in the action. Instead, it is a collective protagonist. This used to lead critics to suppose that the play must be Aeschylus' earliest; because of its active chorus and group heroine it was regarded as 'primitive' or 'archaic'. But the discovery in the early 1950s of a papyrus proving that the *Suppliants* was in fact produced much later than had been supposed, probably in 463 BCE, began to change this argument.[11] More recently, critics and translators have seen other qualities in the play and have challenged as anachronistic the criteria that demoted it because of its relative lack of complex characterisation in a recognisable modern sense.[12] But insofar as our interest in the Danaids has to do with the kinds of subjecthood that they exemplify, this collective agency may be the most interesting feature of the play. Here is a body of women – fifty women – demanding asylum in a state that they take to be hospitable to their concerns, and fleeing from what they identify as a threat of subjugation to masculine power against their will.[13] In this sense, the Danaids are a band of proto-feminists, using the state to help them *as women*, with their womanhood represented as a vulnerability in the face of unwarranted male demands; the Greek word used most in this connection is *hubris* and here seems to mean principally a violent lust.[14] Pointing up the issue of sexual symmetry, the same word *stolos* – a band or group, with connotations of a military expedition – is used of both collectives.

It could be objected that the Danaids are only following their father, refusing the men on his behalf as it were. But this does not detract from their adherence to a kind of daughterly feminism in which, although they shuttle from one form of paternal protection to another, from Danaus to the Argive king, they still know and claim a right to resist the violence of a different version of masculinity that they refuse. Like so many individual tragic heroines, from Antigone to Electra to Medea, these women are by no means shy of asserting themselves; they both declare and justify their refusals. In making their claims on both civic and sexual grounds, they deliver rhetorical arguments as good as they get. And even though they are obeying their father, the refusal and revulsion are clearly as much their own. They seem to see themselves as having equal rights – an equal right to men, but also the right to make claims *as women* in relation to the impositions of male sexuality and marriage.

Against this assertive and anti-sexual femininity,[15] masculinity has more than one manifestation in the play. The Aegyptoi are repeatedly spoken of in images of brute force, as opposed to the considerate humanity of Pelasgos, the king of Argos. Above and beyond both him and the Aegyptoi is Zeus, curiously combining the masculinity of both. He is at once the predatory male who went after Io (the Danaids' Greek ancestor), and also the arbiter and conciliator. He is represented (twice) as holding the scales of justice, *balancing* powers and rights in an image of the equitable political negotiation between conflicting claims. Here is Janet Lembke's translation of one of these passages; the chorus of Danaids is pleading with Pelasgos to do what they ask:

> We share
> one blood and
> spring from one vigilant God Whose hands

weighing human differences fairly dispense
vengeance to the profane
blessings to the reverent.[16]

In a literal translation, the lines might read:

> On both sides [*amphoterois*] Zeus our common ancestor inspects these matters, making now one side and now the other preponderate [this whole clause translates a single word: *heterorrepês*], appropriately distributing penalties to the bad on the one hand, holy things to the lawful on the other. (*Suppliants*, 402–6)

The to-and-fro oscillation of paired opposites is apparent: two sides to the scales, two sides to the sentence, this way and that way in an alternation marked by the characteristic prefixes *amph-* (both) and *hetero-* (the other of two).

But it is not clear that the scales are balancing like with like, or that the grounds for the arbitration are shared between the different parties; arguably, if they were, there would be no dispute. There are too many different claimants and hypothetical terms of engagement. These include: the Danaids (fleeing the Aegyptoi) versus the Aegyptoi (pursuing the Danaids); the Danaids seeking asylum versus the Argives defending themselves from possible attack; the claims of kinship versus the claims of what we might call international justice; marriages of convenience versus forced marriages; incestuous marriage versus exogamous marriage; religious versus civic duty. The Danaids ask for protection on a number of disparate counts: in the name of the gods; as foreigners with a right to asylum; as originally natives of Argos; as vulnerable women in need of male protection against male assaults; as women who resist marriage as subjugation: 'May I never become the slave of men's power' (392). Pelasgos is put in the double bind characteristic of the supplication scenario. If he and his people agree to the Danaids' request, then they will be liable to invasion by the pursuing army. But if they refuse, they will be liable to the wrath of the gods: as is customary, the Danaids are making their plea on holy ground. To drive home the point, they even threaten to hang themselves if they are refused, an action that would magnify the pollution or *miasma* incurred by the Argives. The Danaids' collective suicide threat would perhaps have been recognised by the audience as ironically linked to the mass murders they do ultimately commit. Whether it is a challenge or a cry of despair, or both, this move, in which the women graphically point to the damage they plan to do with their brooches, is something other than a reasoned argument about the justice of their case. Yet it comes just before Pelasgos departs on his mission to consult with the Argive people, who take a vote on the matter in a proto-democratic way, 'dêmou kratousa xeir hopê plêthunetai' (604), 'the people's hands ruling according to the majority'. This line is historically the first surviving occurrence of the combination of *dêmos* and *kratein*, the elements of 'democracy': which thus originates as a response to a collective female demand.

As an upholder of the law of the land, Pelasgos also believes in the local variability of justice, at least in some matters. It seems to be a moot point whether the Danaids' marriage to their cousins is illegal or, on the contrary, positively prescribed by law (to keep property in the family). That both possibilities seem to be conceivable, with nothing between them, is a perfect illustration of the arbitrariness of kinship rules, as described by Lévi-Strauss, with the only cultural universal being that there *are* such rules, not that their content is fixed in any way.[17] With a sense of cultural relativity, Pelasgos asks them about the practice where they come from, with the implication that that should be the paramount criterion. His questioning of the Danaids about legal matters is itself expressed in the form of a hypothetical court case: 'If the sons of Aegyptos are your rulers by the laws of your country [*nomô poleôs*], claiming to be your nearest relations, who would want to speak in opposition to them?' (387-9). The notion of personal preference in the matter of marriage partners might seem to be very far off the agenda, especially when there are fifty women and fifty men involved. Yet Pelasgos does specifically put the question of the women's feelings: 'poterov kat' echthran ê to mê themis legeis'; (336): 'Do you mean you can't stand them or that it's not the custom?'

One strand of the Danaids' case is their claim that Argos is their rightful homeland. They make much of their direct descent from the Argive Io, the daughter of the river Inachus. Her misfortune had been to attract the attention of Zeus, seen in this connection not as absolute judge but rather as habitual seducer. In the version that the Danaids recapitulate here, Zeus' eye fell on the lovely Io; Hera, Zeus' wife, turned Io into a cow; Zeus consequently turned himself into a bull, so Hera put Io under twenty-four-hour, hundred-eye surveillance from the watchman Argos. Zeus' response to this was to have Argos killed by his messenger Hermes. Then Hera set a gadfly, an *oistros*, onto Io, which stung her into perpetual flight. The original mad cow, Io then ran about in a frenzy all over the world, touring the whole of Asia before finally fetching up in Egypt. There she was caressed by Zeus, as a result of which she gave birth to a son called Epaphos ('touch'). Epaphos was the great-grandfather of Danaus and Aegyptos. In coming to Argos, the land of their great-great-great-grandmother, the Danaids then claim to be returning home.

Yet the presence of their ancestor Io in the Danaids' thoughts – they recount her story at length – shows up a rather curious elision in their immediate history. They think back through their foremother, apparently; but who, exactly, is their mother? Or rather, who are their mothers? For that matter, who are the mothers of Aegyptus' boys? A father can have any number of offspring, be it fifty or five hundred, but naturalistic limits are placed on women's reproductive capacity. The excessive numbers of Danaids (and Aegyptoi) and the absence of any mothers seems like a caricature of a fundamental biological dissymmetry of the sexes. No woman could single-wombedly bear a whole army of children in her lifetime, but a man could conceivably engender fifty offspring in a week or two. Or even, today, in a few seconds, since new reproductive technologies have made it possible to separate out sperms so as to fertilise any required number of eggs. Indeed, the fifty daughters on one side, fifty sons on the other, might now suggest a fantasy of high-tech multiple births, pre-selected for their sex.

The Danaids seem, from this perspective, almost inhuman in the very singleness of their multi-mindedness. If they have no mother or mothers, they never mention the fact, instead sustaining themselves on their dream of Io. They do not miss their mothers, and nor do they seek to find someone else to love one-on-one. Instead, they are driven, all together, by their one aim of avoiding the fifty ties, or the fifty-fold tie, to their cousins. It is this, and this alone, that unites them. The play gives no evidence of sisterly affection or particular relationships between the sisters. They think *as one*, with the conventional first-person singular speeches of a chorus; there are no factions or internal differences and no primary motivator. Unlike the relationship between Antigone and Ismene (in Sophocles' *Oedipus at Colonus* and *Antigone*), or between Electra and Chrysothemis (in Sophocles' *Electra*), there is no intersisterly politics here. The myth as commonly reported makes their father the instigator of their predicament, since he is in dispute with his brother, refusing his daughters in marriage either as the main issue or as a corollary to a general quarrel about their division of authority and land. But Aeschylus' play makes no mention of this background. The Danaids' own collective refusal of and revulsion against the Aegyptoi is the starting point; there is only this motive and it seems to originate with them, just as the lustful aggression they attribute to their cousins is another kind of datum, according to the Danaids the sole defining motivation on the men's side.

Richard Seaford discusses the Danaids as part of his compelling demonstration of a pervasive ambivalence in Greek tragedy about the moment of marriage, often subverted by elements of protest and lamentation.[18] Other commentators go so far as to suggest that the *Suppliants* is not only a play about these particular characters, or about ancient Greek culture or myth; it is about adolescent femininity in general. The Danaids are simply going through a phase, acting out a moment in female development when male sexuality is both feared and rejected as daughters remain, for the time being, daddy's girls.[19] The girl or *parthenos* is also, from this perspective, seen as untamed, like a wild filly that will later be brought willingly or unwillingly under control; critics point to other places in Greek literature where young women are represented as similarly frisky figures. The word that hovers here is *domestication*, a term that can encompass both the anthropological and the animal. Just as cows or foals are brought under the yoke, so nomad races settle down in one place, and so lively young girls will eventually settle down as women: civilised, homely, subject to routine. The consensus is that the Danaids have no *particular* cause for complaint; though their complaint, if the critic is a feminist, may be justified in general.[20] Their objection to arranged marriages, their flight from Egypt and seeking of asylum, amount to a dramatisation of the girlish condition, seen as complex and fraught with ambivalence.

If for the moment we follow the hypothesis of a normal female tendency to domestication preceded by youthful refusal, it is interesting to ask what it is that the Danaids want. What they don't want seems easier to answer. It is what they are running away from and what is pursuing them: the Aegyptoi. But they also seem to be attached to an idea of home, praising both places they claim as their countries, Argos and Egypt, in lyrical descriptions. There is a moment when Pelasgos, after the Egyptian herald has retreated, offers a guide to the local housing options:

> There are many kinds of home in the city. My own accommodation is by no means on a small scale. You can choose to live in large dwellings with lots of other people. But if you would rather, it's also possible to live in single-style units. (959–63)

They are to have rooms of their own, privately or publicly, singly or together. *Monorruthmos*, the word I have tendentiously translated as 'single-style', is a one-off word, this being its only occurrence in extant Greek literature; it is a compound of *mono-*, single, and *ruthmos*, rhythm or shape. The passage does seem to suggest a kind of lifestyle choice; the decision about where to live is a decision about how to live, and it is significant that the women are given a choice at all.

The Danaids' status points more generally to a double entitlement. Their claim for consideration is *xenikôn astikôn th' hama* (618): they are both 'towns-people' and foreigners or guests, to be cared for according to the laws of hospitality. The oddity of this is that these are normally mutually exclusive possibilities: either you claim rights as a citizen, or you claim the different rights of a non-citizen. The Aegyptoi, it might also be said, could make the same double claim: they are after all the Danaids' cousins, and they too are descendants of Io. But it is never suggested that they might do this. Instead, their name seems itself to determine that the Aegyptoi belong where they came from, in Egypt.[21]

The Danaids, as we have seen, identify themselves as Egyptian–Argive, or Argive–Egyptian, while the Aegyptoi remain unequivocally Egyptian. Mothers' lines of descent (Io, a great-great-great-grandmother, is on the paternal side for both Danaids and Aegyptoi) are never mentioned either; if the however many mothers come from different countries, as other sources suggest, we are not told so.[22] All these relational sleights of hand are overlaid by the play's use of a rhetoric of civilised versus barbarian.[23] The Aegyptoi verge on the bestial; they are uncontrollable. The Danaids are returning to the justice and calmness of Argos, and fleeing the violence of the *barbaroi*. But ethnic differences also feature in the exchanges between the chorus and the king. Pelasgos' first reaction to the Danaids is that they can't possibly be Greek because of the way they look. When Danaus is about to go round the town touting up support for his daughters' case, he takes an escort to avoid harassment. Yet despite this visual prejudice – clearly, they cannot 'pass' – the Argive identity awarded to or recognised in the Danaids is apparently not related to the colour of their skin.[24]

The *Suppliants* leaves the Danaids' story in suspense. The Aegyptoi have been driven back from Argos, and the women are installed as residents of their new home city, in a kind of sheltered accommodation where they will be safe from the invading horde of Aegyptoi. It is not the classic end to a tragedy: no one has been murdered or committed suicide; instead there have been pleas, threats and negotiations, and a provisional settlement, in both senses of the word. The Danaids' extraordinary acts of violence are unrepresented. If the other two plays in the trilogy survived, the murders would not of course have been shown on stage, but reported by a messenger. That the plays themselves have disappeared, and are thus only a matter of conjecture, reinforces the sense of the Danaids' doom. The murders are unwitnessed, a missing but reconstructed link in the dramatic history that seems to take the Danaids straight from Argos to Hades.[25]

Pindar's version of the myth, however, seems to forget Hades along with the need for punishment. The Danaids make a brief appearance in the ninth Pythian ode, not in relation to the murder or the punishment but to an interim moment of their father finding second husbands for them all. Or all but two: Pindar actually specifies the number forty-eight, *tessarakonta kai oktô* (113) without mentioning the original fifty. Elsewhere we learn about Hypermestra, the one who stayed married the first time around by refraining from murder, while a second sister, Amymone, seems to have been turned into a fountain after a brief encounter with the god Poseidon. The Danaid story is told in Pindar as a hint to a royal father about how to get your daughters married off quickly: Danaus was known to have organised a foot-race for suitors to come and compete, with the individual girls as prizes in some sort of pre-arranged pecking order. The speedy marriage, *okutaton gamon* (112), matches the race itself. Significantly, the women are called *parthenoi* (113), implying a status as both daughters and virgins; no mention is made in the poem of either their first weddings or their crime.[26]

In his 1902 study of the myth, Campbell Bonner pointed to the anomalies in this strand of the legend, 'the more flattering form', inconsistent with the trajectory that takes the women from crime to punishment.[27] He argued that the foot-race and second marriages must be a later addition, in fact a 'white-washing' to cover the story of the 'blood-guilty brides'.[28] A number of theories were being brought to bear at this time to explain the myth and to attempt to date-sort its diverse elements and explain their inclusion or rejection for different ideological ends. J. J. Bachofen's *Mutterrecht* (1861), the work that made the case for an ancient world of 'mother right' having preceded the patriarchal culture that superseded it, had taken the Danaid myth as one illustration of the transitional phase between the two. The women's refusal is consistent with the female choice of the first period; their punishment reflects the new regime of female subjection to men.[29] Jane Harrison considered the development of the myth in terms of a gradual 'moralisation' linked to this hypothetical sexual-cultural revolution: 'Of old the Danaides carried water because they were well-nymphs; the new order has made them criminals, and it makes of their fruitful water-carrying a fruitless punishment – an atonement for murder'; moreover their crime, from the punishing patriarchal perspective, 'is clearly not only that of murder, but of rejection of marriage'.[30] In both Bonner's and Harrison's studies, the water-carrying aspect of the punishment becomes a focal point of the argument. Did the Danaids begin mythical life as water nymphs, or were they retrospectively given that early identity as an explanation for their particular water-related punishment? For Harrison, the marriages-and-murders story is yoked onto the innocence of the primitive, mother-era version, in which the Danaids are 'well-nymphs'. For Bonner, the 'blood-guilty brides' is the *sine qua non* of the Danaid myth, both the oldest and the distinctive part.

From Campbell Bonner's perspective, three elements of the myth – the second marriages, the sister who did not kill (Hypermestra), and the water-nymph beginnings, linked to Amymone – are all to be seen as second in time and secondary in importance to the core marriage-murders. In Latin poetry, the versions of Horace and Ovid both concentrate on the exceptional Danaid in the murder story: Hypermestra. In Horace's *Odes* III xi, Hypermestra is 'splendide mendax' (35), 'nobly cheating' on her father, and she is offered to the poem's addressee as an exemplum of proper femininity.[31] Lyde, in the poem's present, is refusing to yield to the appeals of her lover (she is like a gambolling filly who fears touching); one alone among the Danaid sisters had the maturity to accept marriage. But the poem moves from Lyde to Hypermestra (who is not named) via a wayward sequence of connections. The argument goes like this: Lyde, you are not succumbing to my lyre. But even the criminals performing their punishments in Hades stopped work to listen when they heard the music: Ixion, Tityus and the Danaids. Hey, let me tell you about the Danaids! They all murdered their men, a wicked sisterhood, 'scelestas . . . sorores' (39–40), except for that one in a million, 'una de multis' (33), who superbly defied her father and saved her husband. She is an exemplary girl for all time, 'in omne virgo / nobilis aevum' (35–6). Hypermestra herself then appears, telling her new husband Lynceus to rise up and run away while there is time; she says she doesn't care if her father puts her in prison and banishes her to live among the savages for her act of clemency, and finally, as she urges him to hurry, she asks him to have an elegy in her memory engraved on her tombstone. She swaps her life for his, but also requests to be allowed to survive in story, as she is now doing in another way through this poem.

Hypermestra is presented as standing out from the crowd, and as a model of behaviour for all time. After her death, she will live on, her good memory preserved on the tombstone; her afterlife is counterposed to that of her sisters, who are not just averagely unexceptional women, but wicked ones. The framing of the poem does hint at a romantic involvement on Hypermestra's part: Lyde is being asked to succumb to the poetic music of her lover. Here, though, the speaker's logic becomes very shaky. By the end, the identification offered to Lyde is with the nobility of Hypermestra and her consciously chosen act in sparing Lynceus. But the bridge that takes the poem to Hypermestra is the suggestion that the lyre, and by extension the lover, are irresistible, not a matter of choice or virtue at all. This is an inevitable capitulation, not a virtuous commitment. And to make the point even more peculiar, the proof of this seductive power is that even the inhabitants of Hades, among them the Danaids, stopped what they were doing when Amphion came down to charm them with his music.

Ovid's poem about Hypermestra (*Heroides*, XIV) follows on from Horace's. It takes the form of a dramatic monologue, a letter written from prison by Hypermestra to Lynceus, explaining with a messenger speech's sense of dramatic tension and sensational titillation just what went on during the wedding night turned bloodbath. The sisters wait as 'armed brides', 'armatas nurus' (24), until the brothers-cousins-bridegrooms turn up 'merry' ('laeti', 31) with drinking and overeating; they can only lie down and sleep. Hypermestra all but does the deed, having heard the sounds of her sisters' acts in the middle of the night. There follows a lengthy passage in which Hypermestra reports her own lucid but contradictory nocturnal meditation on the ethics of the question. It is the fear of her father, described as 'violentus' ('violent', 43) and 'saevus' ('savage', 53) that moves her, 'three times', in the epic mode of ghostly hesitation, to raise the sword to kill him. But in her ultimate refusal to do the deed there is also an element of rebellion against this cruel father, with whom she and her sisters have to roam the world because of his dispute with their uncle: 'cum sene nos inopi turba vagamur inops' (62): 'with a helpless old man we wander about as a helpless crowd'. At this point Hypermestra could make a move to identify herself and her sisters with their cousins, equally subject to the demands of the old men's quarrel. But in fact she does the opposite. The brothers are treated as extensions of their father; they 'deserved this death': 'hanc meruere necem' (61).

What holds Hypermestra back is not love for Lynceus or even, primarily, duty either to him as her husband, or him as a human being. 'Timor et pietas' (49), 'fear and piety', are the abstracted considerations that determine her non-doing. Hypermestra does not see why she should have to accept the guilt of murder: 'quo mihi commisso non licet esse piae?' (64): what have I done that I'm not allowed to be 'pious'? – in other words, to be within the ethical law, free from the taint of a wrongdoing.

Up to this point Hypermestra is arguing in terms of human morality in general. But she also makes a contrast between men's and women's spheres of action:

> quid mihi cum ferro? quo bellica tela puellae?
> aptior est digitis lana colusque meis. (65–6)

> What do I have to do with swords? What is the point of warlike weapons for a girl? Wool and the distaff are better suited to my hands.

Men are killers and women are weavers; murder is not my job. This might seem, obliquely, to add force to the implied claim that the bridegrooms do deserve to die, being identified with their father's alleged crime, in a way that the daughters are not identified with their own father's actions. It also has the effect of further depersonalising Hypermestra's act, or her failure to act. Piety and respectful fear, those neutral civic virtues, are no longer the issue; *as a woman* she cannot do it, it's not an appropriate act.

Hypermestra in effect breaks up the sisterhood; her defiance of their kind of defiance makes the murders now appear as individually chosen acts, since there is one who has gone her own way. With the opposite emphasis, this same assertion of personal choice occurs in Euripides' *Phoenician Women*, in which Antigone threatens Creon with Danaidesque behaviour. She will murder her fiancé, his son, if he refuses to relent and allow her to bury her beloved brother: 'That night [of the marriage] will see me one of the Danaids' (line

1675). Antigone singles herself out (she uses the word 'one', *mian*) as a potential bad Danaid, not as the good one. Her situation resembles the Danaids' in that she is engaged to her cousin, but her indirect indication of her murderous thoughts is a remarkable instance of a mythical shift of emphasis. 'I'll do a Danaid on you', Antigone says in effect, using the story to get what she wants in the present time of her own story.

The Roman focus on Hypermestra suggests a poetic interest in the psychology of romantic love. But in fact, as we have seen, it is not really so. Ovid's poem is a prisoner's defence and request for assistance from the one she has rescued; there is only one allusion to amorous attraction, which is the telling of Io's story. Horace's ode, on the other hand, *is* a love poem, but the bizarre sequence of steps in the argument that leads to Hypermestra does not present her as a lover, only as the one virtuous Danaid.

Ovid's Hypermestra tells the story of Io, just as the Danaids collectively do in Aeschylus' *Suppliants*. In Ovid, the importance of the connection and the excuse for the narrative is not Io's Greekness but her troubled life of wandering far from home; indeed, Hypermestra seems to reverse the Aeschylean attributions by making her Greece a distant place of exile and Egypt, implicitly, home: 'regnoque domoque / pellimur; eiectos ultimus orbis habet' (111–12): 'We are driven from our kingdom and our home; we are cast away to the farthest ends of the world.' Ovid narrates Io's story at much greater length in the *Metamorphoses* (it also appears in Aeschylus' *Prometheus Bound*); and Hypermestra's abbreviated version leaves out features related in detail in the other text: Io's surveillance by Argos, set to watch her by Hera/Juno, and Argos's murder by Mercury/Hermes, Zeus/Jupiter's appointed hit-man. The shorter version also omits the specific source of Io's frenzied rushing about the world: Hera's maddening gadfly, which pursues her relentlessly until finally she collapses by the Nile. One element, however, that does appear in both Ovid's Io stories brings back the question of Freudian substitutions and Freudian versions of femininity. It is what we might call Io's anti-Narcissus moment.

After she has been changed into a heifer, Io looks in the water and what she sees is a cow. She cannot believe, but has to believe, that it's her; and in the *Heroides* version it is the shock of this sighting, not the goading gadfly, that sends her wild and wandering. She can't stand to look at what she recognises as now herself:

> per mare, per terras cognataque flumina curris;
>   dat mare, dant amnes, dat tibi terra viam.
> Quae tibi causa fugae? Qui tu freta longa pererras?
>   Non poteris vultus effugere ipsa tuos. (101–4)

> Over the sea, over lands and related rivers you run; the sea, the rivers and the land all give you passage. What's your reason for running away? Why do you wander over the broad seas? You won't be able to run away from your own face.

Narcissus' story, like Io's, is told in the *Metamorphoses*. Narcissus falls in love with the image he doesn't initially realise is his own; Io runs away from the image she can't bear to see, but does see, as her own. Narcissus dies after being captivated by his own beauty, and Io's life is ruined by her seeing and recognising the unbeautiful cow that she is. 'Ioistic' behaviour might make a counterpart or alternative to Freud's 'narcissistic' model of subjectivity, particularly in light of the resonances of sexual difference here. Io is no self-admiring Dorian Gray, his outward appearance, immaculate even as his image secretly grows old and repulsive.[32] Instead, she sees very well the change in her, the loss of her youthful beauty, and she cannot live with it; her life henceforth is a flight from the unattractive image of herself.

Io's feminine reaction also resembles Freud's account of the way that women encounter sexual difference: with an immediate acknowledgement but also a protest, in the face of an irrefutable visual perception.[33] Freud's own discussions of femininity as such occurred after his general theory of human development, based on the story of Oedipus, was well established. He had drawn on Greek tragedy for his paradigm of the common story for men, and when he turned to consider the distinctiveness of women's development, the Oedipus model remained the pattern; women's failure to fit it became the explanation for all their difficulties of adjustment in adult life. Women's problem was that they started off thinking they were like boys, but then had to face the fact that they weren't: this was the shocking realisation of 'castration'. After that, their lives could only be a matter of more or less manageable negotiation with a fundamentally thwarted existence, in which any solution, even the normal one of settling down as a wife and mother, was still to be regarded as following on from this determining disappointment.

In the 1970s and 1980s, Freud's model of female development provoked heated argument among feminists.[34] His theory gives women no identity of their own; whether they protest or succumb, whether they are feminists or paid workers or mothers, or any combination of these, everything they do, once they have realised that they are women, meaning not-men, is related to what now must be seen as their lost masculinity. They never get over it: to be a woman is to be a disappointed boy. This perspective seems to leave no possibility for escape from what is pessimistically presented as an inevitable doom. Modern women can do better, so the argument ran; they need not be caught in this pre-modern dungeon. But for those on the other side of the argument, the sense of entrapment did not appear as a negative quality, since it provided an account of why women, even when apparently emancipated, set free from their prison, still found themselves afflicted by personal unhappiness and sisterly strife in ways that seemed to defy rational explanation.

In thinking back through the Danaids it is not my intention to propose their story as a new paradigm of female development, but instead to suggest that its very contradictions and complexities could have added something to Freud's consideration of the difficulties of female subjectivity. The Danaids are formidably effective campaigners, attuned to the pragmatic need for 'spin' or *peitho*; they are also, like Oedipus (and like numerous tragic heroes and heroines) murderers; and, in a third incarnation, they are downtrodden domestics. Their story is not a single one, generically or morally; the perspective is always moving around, as if it were impossible to gain a distinct view of their position or condition. At different points they exemplify both the resentment and the resignation that Freud attributed to women as typical reactions to the discovery of their difference from men. Yet the Danaids never see themselves as having been deprived of masculinity: it is *as women* that they articulate a resistance to the *hubris* of men, a refusal of female subordination to male power.

Beyond this, the teasing fifty-fifty symmetry of the Danaids and their cousins, the girls and the boys, points to other issues in modern political and feminist argument.[35] How should we differentiate a group identity from an individual one, or a two-person one, and what is the validity or force of a group identity *according to sex* (as opposed to class, or ethnicity, or nationality, or any number of other categories)? Is sexual difference still, as Freud assumed, the primordial distinction in the acquisition of human identities? To speak of two sexes, of 'the' two sexes, with their 'equal' rights, fifty fifty, necessarily rules out the differences that may render their respective claims or qualities radically incompatible and not susceptible to such balancing of like with like according to a common criterion. The Danaids versus the Aegyptoi represent two groups identically matched, apparently equal (because equal in number), and yet two groups so different that they are ever and eternally two – ever and eternally either in love or at war.

In keeping with this suggestive multiplicity of the Danaids myth, three nineteenth-century versions bring out very different aspects of it. Schopenhauer used the endlessness of the Danaids' labours as an image for the insatiability of desire, as in this passage from *The World as Will and Representation*:

> For we untiringly strive from desire to desire, and although every attained satisfaction, however much it promised, does not really satisfy us, but often stands before us as a mortifying error, we still do not see that we are drawing water with the vessel of the Danaides, and we hasten to ever fresh desires.[36]

Here the Danaids are neutral both morally and sexually. That their continued labours are a punishment is not said, and they are not marked out as women; they are given as a general figure for the ceaseless renewal of wishing.[37] This is a pre-Freudian idea. In *The Interpretation of Dreams*, wishing is what gets the mental apparatus going and keeps it going, as well as setting up the elementary structures of an imagined sequential time; there is also, in the passage quoted, the suggestion of a subjective blindness like the Freudian unconscious. But Freud gives no mythical identity to his universal desiring and dreaming subject: no compulsive classical wishers – no Danaids, for instance – take their place alongside Oedipus and Narcissus.

My second example is Baudelaire's poem 'Le tonneau de la haine' ('The Barrel of Hatred'). Here the Danaids in their Hades phase are linked to a hating whose primary and appalling quality is its inexhaustibility, that of the barrel that can never be filled: 'La haine est le tonneau des pâles Danaïdes' – 'Hate is the barrel of the pale Danaids'.[38] Punishment and crime are tied relentlessly together; the endlessness of the Danaidan task is matched by endless murders, as corpses are resurrected by Vengeance only to be once again put down. But then in mid-poem the personifications and the mythology give way to a pub drunk, 'un ivrogne au fond d'un taverne' (9), whose thirst keeps popping up again like the hundred-headed Hydra that won't be killed; the difference is that drinkers, in this sense 'happy', eventually fall asleep, whereas hate never ever lets up:

> – Mais les buveurs heureux connaissent leur vainqueur,
> Et la Haine est vouée à ce sort lamentable
> De ne pouvoir jamais s'endormir sous la table. (12–14)

> But happy drinkers know their conqueror,/And Hate is condemned to this wretched fate/Of never being able to fall sleep under the table.

Ultimately Baudelaire's poem ends in bathos – with the slumbering drunk displacing the pale Danaids, the man the women, the unviolent layabout the murderers, the happy the hating, and the everyday the mythological. The drunk's sleep is the rest and respite that never come for the hatred that is here identified with the Danaids – punishment and crime, out of time, without end.

Finally, the Danaids really were taken up as mythological analogues for the troubled lives of modern feminists – and in English too. Mona Caird's New Woman novel, *The Daughters of Danaus*, was published in 1894, exactly contemporary with Freud and Breuer's *Studien über Hysterie*. Caird explains her allusions to the myth of the Danaids throughout; she does not assume that her readers will know the story. But she uses it, nonetheless, to elaborate her feminist critique. Youthful Danaid rebelliousness is initially seen in the form of wild Celtic dancing and animated debating of modern ideas, those of Emerson especially. Then, like the migration from Egypt to Greece, the scene moves from Scotland to the 'home' counties of southern England. The protest against marriage, first resisted and then reluctantly accepted, does not go as far as murder, but the heroine does run off, post-maritally, to Paris, there to cultivate her musical genius and (almost) have an affair. She leaves behind two small sons as well as a husband but takes with her, in proto-twenty-first-century mode, an adopted daughter (and a nanny). And then, faithful to the final phase of the myth, the Danaid returns and submits herself once more to a life of eternal domestic dullness, varied only by her relationships with various mentor figures, mostly men (with one of whom she has an unsatisfying affair). Lumberingly, the prose spells out the collective conventional dullness and stress:

> And the same savage story was written, once more, on the faces of the better dressed women: worry, weariness, apathy, strain; these were marked unmistakeably, after the first freshness of youth had been driven away, and the features began to take the mould of the habitual thoughts and the habitual impressions.[39]

Caird's description of the visible effects of the well-off women's weary existences reads like a forerunner of Freud's sad picture, in one of his later writings, of the typical woman of about thirty. Her 'psychical rigidity' makes it seem that 'there are no paths open to further development', as though 'the difficult development to femininity had exhausted the possibilities of the person concerned'.[40] This is the miserable anti-parable of the Danaids, a 'before and after' myth of feminist rage followed by stressed and depressed middle age.

NOTES

1. In 2003, my un-random survey of a handful of (mainly) academics revealed an alarming 100 per cent Danaid-recognition-rate among the French.
2. Freud, 'The Psychotherapy of Hysteria', in *Studies on Hysteria* SE II, 263.
3. Freud, *Studien über Hysterie*, GW I, 262.
4. The first translation of *Studien* into (American) English did away with the mythology and metaphors altogether: neither Sisyphus nor Danaids nor 'Moors' wash' can be discerned in A. A. Brill's version: 'The physician will not be spared the depressing impression of fruitless labor' (*Studies in Hysteria* [Boston: Beacon Press, n.d.], 197).

Not surprisingly in view of readers' likely familiarity with them, French translations of the *Studien* have not abolished the Danaids, having no practical reason to. Just like the English 'Sisyphean task', the expression 'un tonneau des Danaïdes', 'a Danaids' barrel', is commonly used in French to mean useless effort. Anne Berman's translation, like Strachey's from the mid-1950s, renders Freud's sentence: 'Le médecin aura alors l'impression pénible d'accomplir une tâche analogue à celle des Danaïdes ou un "blanchiment de nègre"'; *Études sur l'hystérie* (1956; Paris: PUF, 1992), 212. The transformation of the *Mohrenwäsche* into a 'negro-whitening' maintains the racial element suppressed in the English, although 'blanchiment de nègre' is not an established phrase but an invention for the purpose of the translation, which then makes the change from Moors to 'nègre' a different kind of issue.

5. On the likening of the analytic task to domestic work in *Studies on Hysteria*, see Rachel Bowlby, 'Never Done, Never to Return: Hysteria and After', in *Freudian Mythologies: Greek Tragedy and Modern Identities* (Oxford: Oxford University Press, 2007), 47–74.

6. See Albert Camus, 'Le mythe de Sisyphe', in *Le mythe de Sisyphe* (1942; Paris: Gallimard, 1961), 159–66; 'The Myth of Sisyphus', in *The Myth of Sisyphus*, trans. Justin O'Brien (London: Hamish Hamilton, 1955), 96–9. Camus summarises several very different versions of the story of how Sisyphus came by his punishment. One of these, to which much the most space is allotted, involves a twisted version of marital brutality, possibly on both sides. Sisyphus had decided to test his wife's love by ordering her, after his death, to throw his unburied body into the middle of the public square. He woke up in Hades, was 'annoyed [*irrité*] by an obedience so contrary to human love', and got permission from Pluto to go back to the world to punish his wife. His own violation of the terms and conditions for this – he didn't come back to the underworld of his own accord – then led to the rock punishment. The wife's fate, above or below, is not recorded. Did she willingly or unwillingly obey the (husband's own) demand to transgress the laws of love and religion, thereby making herself into a kind of anti-Antigone?

7. Evelyne Sullerot, *La vie des femmes* (Paris: Gonthier, 1965), 94. Sullerot continues: 'We use things. The important thing for us is not the effort, but this substance that gets used up under our fingers, beneath our eyes, and ends up haunting us. What we think about is no longer the effort begun over again each day, but this trickling away of things we lack, constantly, inescapably, in the shorter or longer term.' Sullerot goes on to give examples of the things whose wearing out prompts this kind of obsessional and futile repair work, often because of poverty: shoes, socks or sheets.

8. Stephen Duck, *The Thresher's Labour*, in *Two Eighteenth Century Poems*, ed. by E. P. Thompson and Marian Sugden (London: Merlin Press, 1989), 12; Mary Collier, *The Woman's Labour*, in ibid., 23.
9. Alluding to Walter Benjamin's essay, 'The Task of the Translator', which discusses translations in relation to the 'afterlife' (*Überleben*) and 'continuing life' (*Fortleben*) of literary works (in *Illuminations*, trans. Harry Zohn (New York: Schocken, 1969), 69–82; 71); 'Die Aufgabe des Übersetzers', in *Illuminationen* (1955; Frankfurt am Main: Suhrkamp, 1977), 50–62; 51.
10. As long ago as 1838, the German scholar P. F. Stuhr argued 'that the water-carrying was to be considered as a symbol of house-work, and that the Danaids' punishment was the pointless, hopeless life of one who had not fulfilled herself as a housewife', A. F. Garvie, *Aeschylus' 'Supplices': Play and Trilogy* (Cambridge: Cambridge University Press, 1969), 235.
11. For those who clung to the theory of an early *Suppliants*, one hypothesis was that the author had somehow had the thing stashed away for later use. Richmond Lattimore nicely debunked this many years ago: 'to postulate that Aeschylus put this one on ice for years and then brought it out seems to me to be a desperate means of defense for a position which may not be worth defending'; *The Poetry of Greek Tragedy* (Baltimore: Johns Hopkins Press, 1958), 12. Another counter-argument claimed that the performance could have been a revival; in the same way D. W. Lucas, again already in the 1950s, characterised this as 'a desperate hypothesis' in *The Greek Tragic Poets* (2nd edn, London: Cohen & West, 1957), 64.
12. See Janet Lembke, 'Introduction' to her translation of Aeschylus, *Suppliants* (New York: Oxford University Press, 1975), 3–20; Froma I. Zeitlin, 'The Politics of Eros in the Danaid Trilogy of Aeschylus', in *Playing the Other: Gender and Society in Classical Greek Literature* (Chicago: Chicago University Press, 1996), 123–71. Most enthusiastic of all in his claims for the interest and complexity of the play is Michael Ewans: 'For me . . . *Suppliants* is Aischylos' greatest surviving drama outside the *Oresteia*', 'Introduction', Aischylos, *Suppliants and Other Dramas*, ed. and trans. Ewans (London: J. M. Dent, Everyman), p. xxxix).
13. In *Mutterrecht* (1861), J. J. Bachofen said that in all versions of the legend, 'right' is on the side of the Danaids – the right to murder as well as the right to reject the men – and 'freche gottverhaßte Gewalt', 'insolent odious power' is on the side of the Aegyptoi. '[W]hich is patently untrue', comments Garvie in parentheses after citing this (Aeschylus' *'Suppliants'*, 213); yet Bachofen's radical view of the play (and myth) in the categorical terms of sexual conflict and justice is interesting in its own right.
14. The word occurs as a noun or adjective nine times in the play (at lines 31, 80, 103, 426, 487, 528, 817, 845, 880); in all but one of these cases it

is used by the Chorus in reference to the Aegyptoi. The exception is line 487, when King Pelasgos tells Danaus that the people of Argos will hate the *hubris* of the 'male band' (*arsenos stolou*) when they see the signs of the women's supplication.

15. At one point (lines 854–7), there may be the hint of a refusal of maternity, too. Arguing with the Egyptian herald who has now arrived, the chorus say (in one conjecture) that they wish never again to see the fertilising, life-engendering waters of the Nile; see Eschyle, *Les Suppliantes*, ed. and trans. Paul Mazon (Paris: Les Belles Lettres, 2003), 63–4. (Other texts make the Aegyptoi the subject: the negative wish is that *they* ('you') may never again see the Nile.) On the *Suppliants*' use of the regular Greek association of the Nile with male fertility, see Phiroze Vasunia, *The Gift of the Nile: Hellenizing Egypt from Aeschylus to Alexander* (Berkeley: University of California Press, 2001), 43–7.
16. Aeschylus, *Suppliants*, trans. Lembke, 39–40.
17. See Claude Lévi-Strauss, *Structures élémentaires de la parenté* (1949); trans. James Harle Bell and John Richardson Sturmer, *The Elementary Structures of Kinship* (Boston: Beacon Press, 1969).
18. See Richard Seaford, 'The Tragic Wedding', *Journal of Hellenic Studies*, cvii (1987), 106–30, esp. 110–19.
19. Zeitlin gives a comprehensive account of interpretations of the Danaids' sexual predicament in *Playing the Other*, 153–60.
20. In strikingly contemporary language, Ewans refers to a history of 'pre-feminist male indifference to a woman's right to dispose of her own body' in relation to this play; he notes that 'A remarkable number of male interpreters have diagnosed the Danaides as suffering from a pathological aversion to marriage, because they assert their right not to marry men they do not want' ('Introduction', Aischylos, *Suppliants and Other Dramas*, p. xlii).
21. Vasunia pursues this question in *The Gift of the Nile*, 40–3.
22. Robert Graves, drawing on several sources, says that both the Danaids and Aegyptus's sons were 'born of various mothers': 'Libyans, Arabians, Phoenicians, and the like' in the case of the Aegyptoi, 'Naiads, Hamadryads, Egyptian princesses of Elephantis and Memphis, Ethiopians, and the like' in the Danaids' (*The Greek Myths*, 2 vols. (1955; 2nd edn, Harmondsworth; Penguin, 1960), i. 200. Campbell Bonner, on the other hand, in his compendious study of the Danaid myth, does not actually bring up the issue of mothers but says: 'There are also varying statements about the wives of the two brothers. Each had only one wife, according to Hippostratus' ('A Study of the Danaid Myth', *Harvard Studies in Classical Philology*, 3 (1902), 130).

23. Edith Hall points out Aeschylus' linguistic indication of the Egyptians' barbarity by the use of 'cries, repetition, and alliteration'; *Inventing the Barbarian: Greek Self-Definition through Tragedy* (Oxford: Clarendon Press, 1989), 118. Like *stolos* (band), *barbaros* is used in relation to both the foreign men *and* the foreign women: The word occurs a number of times, e.g. at line 235, when King Pelasgos, arriving on the scene for the first time, asks: 'Where has this crowd come from, with such un-Greek-looking clothes, luxuriously clad in barbarian robes and headgear, to whom I'm speaking?' (234–7). As well as neatly identifying the barbarian and the non-Greek, the king's opening question is an elaborately ornate version of the customary identity check on foreign arrivals, *tís kai pothen*; – 'Who are you and where do you come from?'
24. On the ethnicity of the Danaids in relation to that of the Aegyptoi, see further Vasunia, *The Gift of the Nile*, 41, 47–53.
25. One fragment that does survive from the further tragedies is part of a speech by Aphrodite in praise of love. It is thought that this could have been spoken at the trial undergone by the one defecting sister, Hypermestra, who refused to murder her man. While the other sisters do eventually receive the water-pouring punishment in hell, it may be that the situation evoked here initially was such that Hypermestra could be prosecuted for her non-murder, perhaps because it involved breaking a vow to her father, perhaps now the king.
26. Pindar, *Olympian Odes, Pythian Odes*, ed. and trans. William H. Race (Cambridge: Harvard University Press, Loeb, 1997), 352–3.
27. Bonner, 'A Study', 134.
28. Bonner, 'A Study', 134, 144.
29. On Bachofen's interpretation of the Danaid myth see above, n14, and see Bonner, 'A Study', 145. It is interesting too that the Danaids' water-carrying punishment (as opposed to their crime or any other of the stories attributed to them) inspired a number of English paintings at this time – several, in particular, by J. W. Waterhouse, and a 'Labour of the Danaids' of around 1878 by John R. Weguelin.
30. Jane Ellen Harrison, *Prolegomena to the Study of Greek Religion* (1908; 3rd edn, Cambridge: Cambridge University Press, 1922), 620. More recent commentators have followed Harrison in discussing the ambiguity of myth in relation to a female body either intact or else 'uninitiated' in relation to marriage, identifying the Danaids' situation as 'between' virginity and womanhood; their punishment perpetually repeats the filling and the leaking of the resisted event. See Giulia Sissa, *Le corps virginal* (Paris: Vrin, 1987), 147–94; Jean Alaux, 'Introduction', Eschyle, *Les Suppliantes* (Paris: Les Belles Lettres, 2003), pp. xxv–xxvi.

31. The *splendide mendax* Hypermestra is exemplary in a quite different way as well. In his edition of Book III of Horace's *Odes* (London: Macmillan, 1952), T. E. Page's note on the phrase ignores the woman and the ethics but describes the phrase as '[p]robably the best-known instance in Latin of oxymoron' (84).
32. See Oscar Wilde, *The Picture of Dorian Gray* (1891). In developing his theory of narcissism, Freud does not refer to Ovid, the principal source for the Narcissus myth; instead, he takes up and characteristically universalises a category that had been proposed in the late nineteenth century to describe specific perversions involving sexual attraction to one's own body. The French psychologist Alfred Binet and the British sexologist Havelock Ellis had used the term before it was introduced into German in 1899 by the criminologist Paul Näcke; see Elisabeth Roudinesco and Michel Plon, *Dictionnaire de la psychanalyse* (Paris: Fayard, 1997), 707. Regarding their origins, then, Narcissus and Oedipus are not classical brothers in the psychical pantheon. Freud himself engendered Oedipal Oedipus on the basis of his knowledge and experience of Sophocles' tragedy; the Narcissus of narcissism was already a sexualised young man – Binet's first use of the term was in 1887 – at the time when Freud adopted him around 1910.
33. On women's 'recognition' of sexual difference in the Freudian account, see Bowlby, *Freudian Mythologies*, ch. 5, ch. 6.
34. See e.g. Teresa Brennan (ed.), *Between Feminism and Psychoanalysis* (London: Routledge, 1989).
35. Fifty-strong single-sex groups are not unusual in classical mythology. Speaking of female monsters in folktales, in which 'the qualities of bloodthirstiness and lasciviousness are frequently conjoined', Campbell Bonner darkly suggests that 'Similar ideas may underlie the account of Heracles' relation to the fifty daughters of Thespius' ('A Study of the Danaid Myth', 153). The fifty Nereids (the daughters of Nereus) appear for instance in Euripides' *Ion* (line 1081) and Sophocles' *Oedipus at Colonus* (line 718), where they are 'hundred-footed' (*hekatompodôn*). As with the Danaids plus the Aegyptoi, fifty always seems to suggest its double – and in fact the Nereids themselves sometimes number a hundred (see R. C. Jebb, ed., *Sophocles: Plays: Oedipus Coloneus* (1900; London: Bristol Classical Press, 2004), 123). Nor are the Danaids and the Aegyptoi the only example of a fifty-fifty match of young men and women. The *Iliad* mentions the fifty sons and fifty daughters of Priam and Hecuba, and Virgil refers (*Aeneid* II, 501) to the ensuing 'centumque nurus' or 'hundred brides' – the fifty daughters plus fifty daughters-in-law. Maternal capacity is an unspoken problem, since Hecuba is the acknowledged mother of all the hundred sons and daughters in this story.

The scholiast Servius 'has a worried note, and speculates upon polygamy', R. G. Austin tells us in his own note to the line; Virgil, *Aeneid II*, ed. Austin (Oxford: Clarendon Press, 1964), 194.

36. Arthur Schopenhauer, *The World as Will and Representation* (1819), trans. E. F. J. Payne, 2 vols. (New York: Dover, 1969), i. 318. Other references to the Danaids in this connection occur at i. 196 and i. 362; in the first of these, Ixion and Tantalus join them as symbols of the ever-unsatisfied subject.
37. Schopenhauer is close to two classical philosophical personifications of endlessly unsatisfied desire which all but name the Danaids. In the 'mythologising' passage of Plato's *Gorgias* (493a-b), a leaky jar appears as an image for the desiring part of the mind in stupid (*anoêtoi*) or 'uninitiated' people; in Hades this doubles into an image of fruitless labour as they carry water in a perforated sieve to pour into a leaky jar. Lucretius (*De rerum natura*, Book III) has a catalogue of the characters from hell, wittily demythologising – and remythologising – them one at a time by declaring that Tantalus or Sisyphus or Ixion do not exist; rather these people are to be found as particular types in the real world. Sisyphus is a stressed-out workaholic, who never achieves what he is aiming for. Right after him come those who are always feeding up their ungrateful natures with good things but are never satisfied ('*satiareque numquam*', 1004); these suggest the story of those 'girls in the flower of their youth' ('*aevo florente puellas*', 1008) forever pouring liquid into a perforated vessel. Those girls are not named.
38. Charles Baudelaire, 'Le tonneau de la haine' (1851), *in Œuvres complètes*, ed. Claude Pichois (Paris: Gallimard, Pléiade, 1975), i. 71, line 1.
39. Mona Caird, *The Daughters of Danaus* (1894), ed. with an Afterword by Margaret Morganroth Gullette (New York: Feminist Press, 1989), 465. Ann Heilmann sees the novel primarily as a version of the Medea story rather than that of the Danaids; Caird is shifting the emphasis 'from Medea's violent transgression [in killing her children] to her artistic aspirations' (*New Woman Strategies: Sarah Grand, Olive Schreiner, Mona Caird* (Manchester: Manchester University Press, 2004, 223). The novel mentions Euripides' *Medea* just once (95). Heilmann's downplaying of the title's Danaids reflects and reinforces their obscurity, both a century ago and now.
40. Freud, 'Femininity' (1933), SE XXII, 135; GW XV, 144.

11

Domestication*

In collections of essays on topics of current theoretical interest it's becoming quite common, if not yet a fully established part of the genre, to start off the piece with a little story about the final stages of its genesis. Such a story typically mentions the last-minute influence of a suggestion or critique by someone whose position, in terms of their gender or race or sexual orientation, might be thought to give their opinion legitimacy of a kind that the writer, by their own position, might be thought to lack. 'I was discussing this article over breakfast with a lesbian friend, and she said . . .', writes someone who thereby identifies themselves as either a man, or straight, or both.

This type of gesture serves a number of functions. It seems to apologise for writers' disqualifications to speak about what they are going to speak about, marking an awareness that what they say will be open to modification. And it also does the opposite, making up for the disqualifications through the medium of the qualified friend who puts things right, and supplying the text with a provisional certificate of political or even general correctness: with an input from every possible position, the chances are that you can add up all the elements into a complete account.

A third element is the setting of the little story, which is regularly given a context of domestic intimacy: this is the sort of friend I have breakfast with. This aspect contributes to the legitimation effect ('some of my best friends . . .'), but it also provides a bit of human interest and narrative enigma by hinting, through the provision of the homely detail, at the possibility of a personal story. In this instance, domestication functions in an odd kind of way. It supplements

---

* First published in Diane Elam and Robyn Wiegman (eds), *Feminism Beside Itself*, Routledge, 1995.

and disrupts the abstract theoretical scenario, taking us somewhere else. Yet it also harmonises, calming down the possible disjunctions between the positions, theoretical and social, of writer and interlocutor over the soothing influence of the shared bagels and cream cheese.

In these instances, an image of domestication serves as a hidden support to a theoretical argument that appears to come from a would-be neutral, overview position which, for purposes of narrative and political plausibility, needs to be brought down to earth – into the kitchen. And this, it seems to me, is one of many diverse ways in which domestication, as a concept or a theme, may function in relation to contemporary theoretical arguments, deconstructive and feminist ones in particular. In a minute, this essay will look at some of these; but first, let me just throw in one or two autobiographical nuggets, which you can believe or not. They have something to do with the writing of this paper, though I'm probably in no subject-position to say what.

In the summer of 1992, I was invited by Gillian Beer to give a lecture in a series being organised at Cambridge in the wake of a controversy there over Derrida's election to an honorary doctorate. [This, with a tweak or two, is it.] I suggested the topic of domestication, and then noticed that this had happened in the week when I unexpectedly acquired a kitchen table, having thought that the room wasn't big enough to take one. My pleasure at the transformation of this domestic space was both mitigated and reinforced by events soon after, when I went to Paris – a place where I like to think I feel at home – and had my wallet snatched twice. I huddled inside the cosy, familiar interior of the place where I was staying – and wondered how I was ever going write this paper on, of all things, domestication.

The other story goes back a bit further, to earlier that year, when I woke up one morning to the sounds of two voices that turned out to be those of Gillian Beer and George Steiner soundly and roundly in their different ways defending the importance of Derrida's work on the BBC Radio 4 *Today* programme. As I drank my coffee and started to wake up, I reflected that thanks to the Cambridge controversy, here was deconstruction apparently reaching, or being pushed, beyond the books and the seminar rooms, out onto the airwaves and the headlines and into the kitchens and bedrooms of the daily life of the supposed British nation – an ambivalent passage between hypothetical insides and outsides, crossing, erasing and reinforcing innumerable imaginary and symbolic borders. In some sense, it all seemed to suggest that Derrida was beginning to personify a particularly curious specimen of the proper noun: he was becoming a 'household name'.

It seemed to me that this process was at the very least a strange and unpredictable one, aligning Derrida with a hitherto unfamiliar and probably unwelcome peer-group. Not so much Heidegger, Kant, Descartes and the rest; or, in another connection, not so much Lacan and Kristeva and Foucault. Instead, this new grouping would include, I suppose – if you are British [and if it is 1992!] – the likes of Brian Redhead, Domestos, Bruce Forsyth, Boot's, Fergie, Chanel No. 5 and Jeffrey Archer. (On the other side of the Atlantic, perhaps this near-meaningless Anglo-domestic list should be rewritten to something like David Letterman, Mr Clean, Hillary Clinton, Chanel No. 5, Tylenol and Judith Krantz.) It can't be an easy or straightforward transition to find yourself sharing the household name status and facilities with such a heterogeneous community, one whose capacities for comfortable cohabitation, whether with each other or with their new associate, might seem anything but assured.

And yet the related notion of domestication is generally regarded as being the most obvious thing in the world – so obvious, in fact, that once someone or some idea is deemed to have been sent home in this public way, it is as if there were no more to be said: the front door closes definitively on a place removed and retired from the open air of its previous existence – and even though the movement implied is also one of extension, moving out. If a theory gets domesticated, that's the end of it: it becomes like everything else.

The term domestication is used in this way all the time in relation to deconstruction, and to 'theory' in general, including feminist theory. But it does not usually feature the specificity or concreteness of any recognisably domestic location, 'Dunroamin'' or wherever. Instead, 'domestication' is used to signal something unproblematically negative that happens to a theory, when – what? Well, when it loses its radical edge, gets tamed, is co-opted or institutionalised (these last two words are often used virtually as synonyms of domestication). The 'domestication' of deconstruction or other theories implies something which may include the kind of mediatisation that occurred with the 'Cambridge and Derrida' story, but refers generally to processes of simplification, assimilation and distortion – any or all of these – to which the theory in question falls victim, or which it is powerless to resist. Domestication, in this sense, involves a very un-deconstructive story: of a wild and natural identity, a full presence, subsequently, and only subsequently, succumbing to forces that deprive it of an original wholeness.

Here is one particularly clear example of how the term is invoked, from Judith Butler's *Gender Trouble*, one of the most significant deployments of deconstruction in a feminist context:

> The complexity of gender requires an interdisciplinary and postdisciplinary set of discourses in order to resist the domestication of gender studies or women's studies within the academy and to radicalize the notion of feminist critique.

And later on, she says:

> Parody by itself is not subversive, and there must be a way to understand what makes certain kinds of parodic repetitions effectively disruptive, truly troubling, and which repetitions become domesticated and recirculated as instruments of cultural hegemony.[1]

What gets domesticated – in this case, a form of feminist theory – is something defined as being subversive of what will thereby attempt to take it over, settle it down, suppress its difference.

What interests me in this use of domestication in connection with theory as something radical and subversive is the way in which the word itself, and the implied narrative that it brings with it, can go unexamined within an argument which is deconstructively on the look-out all the time for the subtle simplifications and assumptions that discourses of every kind install and seek to maintain. In the opposition played out between radical critique and domesticating cultural hegemony, the qualifications of the two forces are not at issue: the first gets its value from the very fact that it is a challenge to the second, which is identified largely in terms of its superior force. In an inevitable movement, the latter then brings the former under its sway.

Butler's argument does not attribute anything inherently good or natural to the radical theory that succumbs to domestication: this is not a case of a hypothetical full presence or genuine content then becoming contaminated by something else. Rather, the narrative proceeds in terms of power, with the oppositional positive force inevitably succumbing to the stronger, negative one that prompted its protesting existence in the first place. Implicitly, then, there are three stages to the story: initial homogeneity or harmony of the hegemonising force, then the breakaway of the wild radical critique, to be followed by its reintegration or reassimilation into the dominant culture, accompanied by the loss of its critical impetus.

At this point, we might take a first step back indoors to look at one of the stories implied by the word domestication in its more homely, extra-theoretical, everyday existence. Within the word itself, home does not appear as the first place or the natural place: it is a secondary development, *becoming* domestic. In one French usage, *domestiquer* means quite simply the subjugation of a tribe to a colonising power. To 'domesticate' is to bring the foreign or primitive or alien into line with the 'domestic' civilisation and power, just as a 'domesticated' animal is one that has been tamed into home life. Something wild, pre-civilised and verging on the non-human is brought into line with an existing order represented in this case as more complex and sophisticated, but also as less natural.

In anthropology, too, the concept of domestication has had an unexpectedly dynamic, if less imperialistic, existence. The word is used to mark a turning point that is supposed to represent not so much a takeover, a 'home' civilisation absorbing and thereby abolishing the difference of one that lies outside its own domain, as a transition from what are thereby recognisable as two distinct states of culture. 'The domestication of the savage mind', in Jack Goody's recapitulation of a categorisation adopted for instance by Lévi-Strauss in *The Savage Mind* [*La Pensée sauvage*], links together a whole series of two-term oppositions that have been deployed in accounts of the history of humanity in general, and also in relation to the changes affecting what came to be called 'developing' countries in the later twentieth century. Domestication in these connections is associated with a move from oral to literate culture; from collective life to individualism and private families; from myth to history; and from concrete to abstract thinking.[2]

The reliance on the two-term division and the set order of events – or rather the set position of the one event, which can somehow only be pointed to retrospectively as a boundary that a collectivity is seen to have passed – is of a type which deconstruction, even garden-variety or kitchen-variety deconstruction, would be quick to point out. Goody implicitly answers in another way: yes, there are narratable changes, but historically and culturally they by no means fall into these easily superimposable parallels. This line is different from, but not I think necessarily incompatible with deconstruction, despite what kitsch deconstruction might think or be thought to think. To say that this is a pre-deconstructive mode of argument would be to restore just that narrative logic of identifiable progressions and demarcations that deconstruction seeks to make problematic: it is to operate, in fact, with an already 'domesticated' version of deconstruction that would assert its own logics as superior to and clearly distinguishable from the others.

But there is still a further layer to this, which is indicated by the concentration on domestication as a process of civilisation or taming. For insofar as domestication has to do with home, it would seem to elide the starting point. Home is the place of origin, the place that has always been left; domestication, then, would be a return to or reinvention of the home that you left or lost. This three-part story has its standard modern forms in relation both to daily life – wake up, go to work, return home – and to the process of growing up: from home, out into the world, and then on or back to some form of domestic 'settling down'. In this narrative of nostalgia, home is imagined as a place of peace, stability and satisfaction that has subsequently ceased to be; but also as a withdrawal or seclusion from a 'real' world envisaged as a source of the energy or the troubles or mobility that are absent from it.

It is in the context of this other kind of story that domesticity is imagined as a first place of wholeness and rest, but a place from which – and in order for it to be retrospectively seen as such – a separation has always taken place. Two books from the late 1950s, one English, one French, illustrate this in very different ways. Richard Hoggart's *The Uses of Literacy* gives a nostalgic portrait of a working-class culture described in terms of concreteness, locality and oral expression, and in the process of being subsumed by a materialistic American mass culture.[3] In numerous vignettes, the home is represented as the focus and epitome of this all but lost world, which is seen as at once authentic and claustrophobic: it is not so much that it should not give place to some other mode, but that it is being taken over by the wrong kinds of force. In place of the false commercial culture, endlessly secondarised through images of superficiality – tinsel, glitter, tawdriness, show – Hoggart would substitute the kind of reflective thinking of which his own argument, by implication, is an example. So the sequence here is not unlike the anthropological schema deployed by Goody, from oral to intellectual and from local to generalised; but here the terms are reversed, so that the domestic figures as the first, and in this case limited, devalorised state, prior and vulnerable to a mutation that may be negatively or positively viewed – in the direction of commercial surface, or in the direction of intellectual generality.

In a different genre, Gaston Bachelard's *The Poetics of Space* lyrically evokes the peace and dreaminess of the home as a place of corners and nests, with its secret and private spaces. Houses are associated with primitiveness and childhood, and thence with a capacity for maintaining throughout life the qualities of stability, habit and restfulness in which it begins. There is a lovely section on chests of drawers, which Bachelard sees as full of imaginative possibilities of a kind that are lost when a philosopher like Henri Bergson uses them as no more than a polemical metaphor against the tidy separation or compartmentalisation of concepts, as though into drawers. Bachelard, for his part, wants to bring out the full poetic suggestiveness of such seemingly insignificant domestic things: 'When Bergson speaks of a drawer, what disdain!'[4]

Nestlingly benign as Bachelard's enclosure is, it maintains itself nonetheless partly in its firm distance from two other related schools or homes of thought. First, there are the twentieth-century philosophers with their hyphen-crazy abstractions: a being-in-the-world that is always already split up. And second, there is the psychoanalysis of negativity, refusing a primary sense of oneness and always finding evidence of a threatening sexuality.[5]

Bachelard's distinction from Freudian psychoanalysis appears most clearly in his tranquil hymn to homeliness as a source of poetic inspiration: 'In its freshness, in its specific activity, the imagination makes something strange out of something familiar. With a poetic detail, the imagination places us before a new world.'[6] This version of strange familiarity is a far cry from the covertly menacing reversibility of Freud's analysis of the uncanny, the homely *heimlich* that is also, within the same word, the unhomely, marking that unwelcome presence within what is most apparently reassuring in its familiarity and familiality. The house of Freudian psychoanalysis is irredeemably riven by the presence of ghosts, its comforting appearance of womblike oneness doubled from the start by intruding forces, such that human life can never securely make a return to a place untroubled by the untimely and dislocating hauntings of other times and places, and other presences that interfere with the imagined separateness and identifiability of places and people who are known and loved.

I don't want to dwell – if that is the word – too long on Freud's uncanny.[7] But it is obvious that in psychoanalysis, the home is no place of harmony – and all the less for functioning so forcefully as the embodiment of all that has always been lost. The home is where the muddle begins and continues; here, domestication is not a smoothly operating process of adjustment or progress. And Freud in fact is rather specific about possible domestic disturbances, pointing out in *The Interpretation of Dreams* that 'The ugliest as well as the most intimate details of sexual life may be thought and dreamt of in seemingly innocent allusions to activities in the kitchen'.[8] This is, after all, the world of what Freud called 'kettle logic'; and along such multi-tasking paths of connection, we might reflect that if you hear, rather than write, the word 'domestication' – if you return to that famous pre-civilised primitiveness of an oral culture – what you get, out of sight but not out of earshot, and none too neatly tidied away into this capaciously polysyllabic word, is 'mess' and 'stickiness': an Anglo-Saxon sprawl that screeches for attention out of the nicely abstracted Latinate term. As every housewife knows.[9]

Which is perhaps the point at which to turn to look at the ways in which domestication has been treated as a theme in feminist writing. At first sight, the situation would seem to be quite straightforward, as with the deployment of the word in a figurative sense: just as feminists are sure that the 'domestication' of feminist theories is to be regretted, so the rejection of domesticity has seemed a principal tenet of feminist demands for freedom, if not the very first. The home figures as the place where the woman is confined, and from which she must be emancipated in order for her to gain access to a world outside that is masculine, but only contingently so, and that offers possibilities of personal and social achievement that are not available within its limited sphere.

In various forms, this representation could be said to run right through the Western tradition of feminist writing from the past two hundred years – including in different ways Mary Wollstonecraft, Simone de Beauvoir, Betty

Friedan and Virginia Woolf, for whom the 'Angel in the House', with her Victorian insistence on domestic virtues, must be violently abolished before the freer twentieth-century woman can emerge.[10] Before going into more detail about some of these versions, it's worth noticing some of the strong common denominators.

These representations literalise the imagery of inside and outside in such a way that the home is figured as something close to a prison, walled off against a 'real' world of events, which is elsewhere. The condition of femininity, inseparable from women's domestication, is artificially imposed by social and/or masculine forces that women have been powerless or unwilling to resist, or have not recognised as limitations at all. True selfhood is attainable only by moving beyond domestic, local, private boundaries. Though presently allowed chiefly or only to men, this status is not inherently gendered: it is rather a right, or a nature, of which the present organisation of things has unjustly deprived women.

In the second volume of *The Second Sex* (1949), Beauvoir's chapter on marriage delivers a resounding critique of that estate's effect on the woman insofar as it 'confines her to immanence'.[11] As so often, the metaphor of confinement is given a naturalised foundation, a home base, in that it turns out to refer to a life contained within the domestic space. Beauvoir does begin by quoting some passages – from none other than Bachelard and Woolf (*The Waves*) – on the positive symbolic associations of the *foyer*, of being indoors and sheltered. But the critique is for the most part relentless. The housewife with her 'days leading nowhere'[12] is deprived of the capacity to form and carry out projects; her work is mere repetition with no product at the end or in the future, and this automatically casts it into a secondary, devalorised mode:

> She simply perpetuates the present; she does not have the sense of conquering a positive Good but of struggling indefinitely against Evil. It is a struggle renewed every day . . . Eating, sleeping, cleaning . . . the years no longer mount upwards to the sky, they stretch out identical and grey in a horizontal sheet; every day imitates the one that preceded it; it is an eternal present, pointless and without hope.[13]

There is a combination of, on the one hand, temporal and spatial stasis – no progression as no movement outwards, outdoors – and on the other no building up towards the accomplishment of a lasting work. But this stasis is sustained by the need for it to be constantly, daily, reproduced – by the routine that is deplored for being always identical, and by the endless cleaning and cooking for an immediate consumption that leaves neither record nor surplus.

A woman's work, proverbially, is never done, to the point that this never-doneness can come to define it: an interminable task without lasting result or addition. Beauvoir's account in some ways resembles the Marxist theory of the home as the site of the reproduction of labour power. No measurable value is produced there; instead, its 'reproductive' function is an essential condition for the production of surplus value to take place elsewhere. 'Reproduction' operates here in a curiously devious way. On the one hand it is the day-to-day servicing of the workers as one of the elements of production. They need to be fed, cleaned and rested in order to be physically capable of going out again and doing another day's work. On the other hand, it is the reproduction of the species, maintaining the supply of workers. In this second implication, the term moves covertly from the biological to the economic, as the teleology of embryo development in the first of these discourses is latched to the parallel but quite different teleology of the needs of capitalism (workers as a supply to be kept up).

In Marxist theory, then, 'reproduction' evidently does a lot of work for all its apparently secondary status. As in Beauvoir's version, the domestic sphere figures as the place that both makes possible and reinforces a difference attributed to the sphere of real projects or production. This difference is represented both spatially – in the respective 'spheres' or sites – and temporally, in the demarcation of the linear, cumulative time of production and projects from the repetitive, cyclical time of reproduction and housework.

In Friedrich Engels's *The Origin of the Family, Private Property, and the State* (1884), an anthropological narrative of the development of human societies to their modern capitalist forms of organisation draws out the interdependence of the terms of this division in an especially sharp form. Engels's story is derived from the latest anthropological researches of the time, in particular the hypothesis that the present patrilineal, patriarchal order of things is not universal, but was preceded by forms of matrilineal (though not matri*archal*) organisation called 'mother right' (*Mutterrecht*). The changeover from one to the other is glossed in unequivocally dramatic terms:

> The overthrow of mother right was the *world-historical defeat of the female sex*. The man seized the reins in the house also; the woman was degraded, enthralled, the slave of man's lust, a mere instrument for breeding children. This lowered position of women, especially manifest among the Greeks of the Heroic and still more of the Classical Age, has become gradually embellished and dissembled, and, in part, clothed in a milder form, but by no means abolished.[14]

But the precipitating circumstances of the change are nothing other than the process of domestication itself. Previously, according to Engels's anthropological sources, societies were more or less polygamous, and they were communal: there was no private property, and extended households were not based on the nucleus of a single set of parents. The transition to patriarchy accompanies a whole series of other changes: the beginnings of monogamy, the one-couple family, the private home, privately owned property, competitiveness between men, surplus value in production, and the strict demarcation of male from female labour as between the household and what now becomes a separate site of work accorded a superior value.

At one fell swoop, one irrevocable crash and fall, this mythical moment resumes all the standard separations of the domestic from its outside, marking off the domestic as an enclave or 'separate' sphere within a wider world that excludes it but needs it. Crucially, domestication indicates the definitive division of masculine and feminine as operating in and governed according to spaces and times that are irreducible to one another, but mutually dependent. Engels, bless his nineteenth-century feminist heart, is unequivocal about the specific implications of all this:

> The woman's housework lost its significance compared with the man's work in obtaining a livelihood; the latter was everything, the former an insignificant contribution. Here we see already that the emancipation of women and their equality with men are impossible and must remain so as long as women are excluded from socially productive work and restricted to housework, which is private. The emancipation of women becomes possible only when women are enabled to take part in production on a large, social scale, and when domestic duties require their attention only to a minor degree.[15]

(It's worth noting in passing that Engels's emancipatory vision does not include the possibility that it might not be only women's attention directed towards 'domestic duties'; in a similar fashion, his discussions of marriage and sexuality regularly assume that there is a natural desire for monogamy or 'individual sex-love' on the part of women, and an equally natural desire for promiscuity on the part of men.)

In Engels' myth of origins, the overthrow of mother right brings in its train not only the three estates designated by the book's title but also, implicitly, the beginnings of various temporal lines – of history, of accumulation, of production (it is a classic instance of domestication in the sense described by Goody). Not only is the time before patriarchy a kind of pre-time or non-time in relation to the forward directions that are now installed, but the private household comes to represent something like a residue or throwback in the midst of the modern world.

It is in this sense that home can figure too as a refuge from the batterings and struggles of what is variously described as the 'real' world or the 'outside' world. Not long before Engels's manifesto, in a very different mode, John Ruskin's lecture, 'Of Queens' Gardens', from *Sesame and Lilies* (1865), set in place an extraordinary celebration-cum-damnation of the domestic sphere. Ruskin sees this as the site on which to fight out and lay claim to a proper division of the sexes in terms of their respective natures, which he takes to be at once different and complementary.

Ostensibly, the argument is asserting all the well-known virtues of a peaceful, innocent Victorian womanhood – unencumbered by work, and simply blossoming forth with a natural spontaneity that balances the rather more turbulent nature of the man. But the context for the assertion of what Ruskin calls the 'harmonious idea' – glossed somewhat insecurely as 'it must be harmonious if it is true'[16] – is the opposite, a situation of antagonism. Ruskin has opened his question as having to do with what he calls women's 'queenly power', their 'royal or gracious influence', which should be exercised 'not in their households merely, but over all within their sphere'. The domestic space moves out effortlessly to comprise a set of individual 'territories': to each woman her own private colony for domestication.[17] At the same time, there is a specific contemporary background of disorder, which Ruskin explains in this way:

> And there never was a time when wilder words were spoken, or more vain imagination permitted, respecting this question – quite vital to all social happiness. The relations of the womanly to the manly nature, their different capacities of intellect or of virtue, seem never to have been yet measured with entire consent. We hear of the mission and of the rights of Woman, as if these could ever be separate from the mission and the rights of Man; – as if she and her lord were creatures of independent kind and of irreconcileable claim.[18]

It is a verbal unruliness – wild words – which needs to be tamed, civilised and constituted into its prescribed place. Unlike his contemporary John Stuart Mill, Ruskin's starting point has to do with a difference, not a relative sameness, between the sexes. Ruskin both acknowledges that this difference is somehow a tense one, productive of dissent and disturbance, and at the same time asserts almost by fiat that to that very extent – because it is not harmonious – it must be deemed and made so. 'Vain imagination' has been reprehensibly 'permitted': the issue is one of legislation, such that a disruptive or distracting element must be arbitrarily forbidden, or put out of the way.

Ruskin then sets up his ideal social arrangements on the basis of a clearly distinguished difference of sexual natures:

> Now their separate characters are briefly these. The man's power is active, progressive, defensive. He is eminently the doer, the creator, the discoverer, the defender. His intellect is for speculation and invention; his energy for adventure, for war, and for conquest, wherever war is just, wherever conquest is necessary. But the woman's power is for rule, not battle, – and her intellect is not for invention or creation, but for sweet ordering, arrangement, and decision. She sees the qualities of things, their claims, and their places.[19]

Wars and strife are taken to be inevitable, though not valued in themselves: they are subject to considerations of justice and necessity. And it is worth noticing too that in attempting to harmonise – to sweetly reorder, arrange and adjudicate the dissensions – Ruskin himself is 'eminently' less 'a doer' than a woman.

The full expansion of this social arrangement then takes us swiftly away from all the worldly strife to the place of feminine security:

> This is the true nature of home – it is the place of Peace; the shelter, not only from all injury, but from all terror, doubt, and division. In so far as it is not this, it is not home; so far as the anxieties of the outer life penetrate into it, and the inconsistently-minded, unknown, unloved, or hostile society of the outer world is allowed by either husband or wife to cross the threshold, it ceases to be home; it is then only a part of that outer world which you have roofed over, and lighted fire in. But so far as it is a sacred place, a vestal temple, a temple of the hearth watched over by Household Gods . . . so far it vindicates the name, and fulfils the praise, of Home.[20]

Home must thus be constructed against, not in continuity with, the 'outer life' of 'anxieties' that must at all cost be kept out; it is defined not so much by its capacity to provide the basic needs of shelter and warmth, as by its exclusion of the outer, its standing against what is always trying to force or 'penetrate' its way in. Consecrated against the secular troubles of the outside, home has become the haven in an aggressive world; it is where the heart is, but a heart constructed desperately as a defence against an intolerable and ineradicable pressure from what is thereby rejected as an indefinite external source of disturbance.

Here, domestication runs its complete course. Home is set up as a response to and bulwark against something perceived as a threat; it makes an interior separate from and set off against external dangers or anxieties, and its differentiation must be constantly re-established with the risk of every questionable foot across the threshold. But despite this order of things, home is also represented as the place that has always been there, the original temple of the Household Gods, something that pre-dates and will by implication outlive the incursions from the outside, which in this light appear as no more than contingent and ephemeral.

A little excursion at this point – without straying too far from the front door – on the history of home. Witold Rybczynski's charming book *Home: A Short History of an Idea* documents this in loving detail, through developments in bourgeois forms of living accommodation and their accompanying notions of family intimacy and comfort. It is a reassuringly developmental history: the home and its pleasures were just waiting placidly to be found, at the end of a smooth historical path leading straight to the modern armchair and all the rest – all the rest you could ever want. So Rybczynski begins one of his central chapters like this:

> Privacy and domesticity, the two great discoveries of the Bourgeois Age, appeared, naturally enough, in the bourgeois Netherlands. By the eighteenth century they had spread to the rest of northern Europe – England, France, and the German states. . . . The house was no longer only a shelter against the elements, a protection against the intruder – although these remained important functions – it had become the setting for a new, compact social unit: the family. With the family came isolation, but also family life and domesticity. The house was becoming a home, and following privacy and domesticity the stage was set for the third discovery: the idea of comfort.[21]

Slowly and surely, in Rybczynski's story, things have been getting cosier and cosier: domestication is certainly a lengthy process (it took a while for people to discover how nice it is), but it is one that does no more and no less than fulfil wishes that are natural: 'Domestic well-being is a fundamental human need that is deeply rooted in us, and that must be satisfied.'[22] But there can be difficulties in the way of its attainment, as with the mistaken austerity of modernist functionalism, or the postmodern *bric-à-brac* of decors vaguely alluding to heterogeneous styles from the past. Rybczynski is clear this is a mistake: 'It is not watered-down historical references that are missing from people's homes. What is needed is a sense of domesticity, not more dadoes; a feeling of privacy, not neo-Palladian windows; an atmosphere of coziness, not plaster capitals.'[23]

The book ends with an argument that simply sets the natural home in relation to, and usually against, the machine, in the form of either outside experts imposing their views of what it should be, or artificial contrivances, whether decorative or labour-saving. Rybczynski is not straightforwardly opposed to the presence or use of machines in the home, but they have to be kept in their subordinate place: 'We must rediscover for ourselves the mystery of comfort, for without it, our dwellings will indeed be machines instead of homes.'[24] 'We must': as with Ruskin, the true identity of home needs to be constantly reaffirmed.

In Rybczynski's calmer world the incursions from outside are not as formidable in their home-breaking potential as Ruskin's, but they are nonetheless there as a permanent threat, which is also a permanent bolster to the setting up of home as an ideal. In Ruskin, the most sinister aspect of the territorial arrangements is the role ascribed to the woman. We have already come across her vaunted capacities for 'sweet ordering'; more dangerously, she can be held responsible for all that goes wrong:

> There is not a war in the world, no, nor an injustice, but you women are answerable for it; not in that you have provoked, but in that you have not hindered. Men, by their nature, are prone to fight.[25]

So the inside/outside opposition between home and world is now directly transposed onto the difference of male and female natures; now the inside, previously secondary and reactive to the troubles of the world, is allotted a dominant, controlling power whereby the healing sympathies of the feminine home are to spread their influence outwards, taking over the uncontrolled masculine spaces of strife. In this way Ruskin argues against the present situation, in which '[y]ou shut yourselves within your park walls and garden gates; and you are content to know that there is beyond them a whole world in wilderness – a world of secrets which you dare not penetrate; and of suffering which you dare not conceive'.[26] The movement of domestication thus ultimately reverses itself again, with a feminine force called upon to penetrate outwards to overcome the wilderness: sweet ordering through the exertion of a counter-power that repeats in the other direction the invasion from the troubled outside.

Returning now briefly to Beauvoir, who has no doubt been resentfully and repeatedly darning the Sartrean socks all this while, I would like to highlight one moment in her section on the domestic life of the married woman. For the most part, Beauvoir considers both oppression and emancipation from an individual perspective: it is an affliction of single and separate consciousnesses, not – as in Engels's analysis, for instance – the effect of a structure bearing upon women collectively.[27] But here in Beauvoir is a moment of break-out from the confinements of domesticity – within the text, and for the woman it describes – and it is when the housewife goes shopping:

> While they are doing their shopping, women exchange remarks in the shops, on the street corners, through which they affirm 'housewifely values', where each one derives a sense of her importance: they feel they are members of a community which – for a moment – is opposed to the society of men as the essential to the inessential. But above all, buying is a profound pleasure: it is a discovery, almost an invention. . . . Between seller and buyer a relationship of tussling and ruses is set up: the point of the game for her is to procure herself the best buys at the lowest price; the great importance attached to the smallest of economies could not be explained merely by the concern to balance a difficult budget: the thing is to win a round. For the time she is suspiciously examining the stalls, the housewife is queen; the world is at her feet with its riches and its traps, for her to grab herself some loot. She tastes a fleeting triumph when she empties the bag of provisions onto her table.[28]

In this interlude daily life becomes something other than the stifling repetition of itself in solitude, as the housewives move outdoors to take a breath of collective fresh air and to enjoy what is practically the only pleasure that Beauvoir recognises for them. Where Ruskin's woman is enjoined to be a perpetual moral 'queen', Beauvoir's is granted this – 'the housewife is queen' – as a momentary release and a 'fleeting triumph'.

The interval of relative emancipation involves a reversal of the normal hierarchy between the feminine-domestic and the worldly. A later French feminism would pause on this moment of reversal, and hold it out as a possibility of serious philosophical mutation. So Luce Irigaray, eminently Derridean in this strategy, would in effect pick up Beauvoir's denigration of the feminine condition in its absence of forward direction, its lack of an individual project, by classifying such values not as the neutral destination of the human individual, but as specifically masculine. The hitherto subordinated terms – repetition, non-unity, otherness – come forward in Irigaray's account to disrupt and break into what is thereby both identified and challenged as a monolithic but potentially mutable phallogocentric order.[29]

Though the argument and its implications are not the same, Julia Kristeva's essay 'Women's Time' operates upon some comparable reversals. It identifies a quasi-tyrannical linear temporality – the time required for the teleologies of Western history and capitalist accumulation – with masculinity in the psychical sense, and suggests that other structures of time associated with femininity may now be coming to take a less subordinate place, alongside if not instead of the linearity that has dominated modern Western thinking and experience.³⁰ None of the contemporary feminists, however, takes back the abstract temporal questions into the daily life of the kitchen, which is where Beauvoir's disgruntlements begin. In fact, insofar as domestication gets a thematic mention in these more recent theories, it is to perpetuate the assumption that of course women would and should want to leave home and enter the workforce; or at least, not to be spending their days solely as housewives, a situation still implicitly marked by the imagery of confinement within a space that excludes participation in a real world elsewhere.

But in the age of postmodern technology, such straightforward separations are open to rethinking in a way that they never were before. All sorts of technical innovations – faxes, computer networks, and so on – have altered the terms on which one hypothetically private space is related to another. Telephones and radios can now be seen as historically first in this series of instruments that abolish the communicational boundaries of interior spaces from each other, or from the 'world outside' in general. They have made possible, for better or for worse, a sharing of space between home and work, the reproductive and the productive spheres, in a way that has been excluded since the industrial revolution definitively divided the two for all but a few eccentric professions. But this is to put it too simply. For the new potential for blurring and overlap also shows how the division of the domestic from its outside was previously sustained only through a literalisation of the figure of the house within, but separate from, a surrounding world. Those four walls marked out a boundary supposed to keep the domestic clearly apart from its other side, whether defined as the real world, the outside world or the productive sphere.

Finally, a trip to the shops before we bring it all back home. For almost as long as the middle-class ideology of domesticity has existed, consumption has provided a connection between the home and the outside world. From nineteenth-century department stores to twentieth-century supermarkets, via the development at the turn of the century of brand-name goods and the vast expansion of advertising in all the media that enter the home – newspapers and magazines, and later radio and television – consumer culture has been intimately bound up with the changing forms of domestication. So much so that at various times it has been identified as the key to a female oppression now associated with a false, commodified form of home life, implicitly differentiated from something more authentic that either preceded the present situation or might be available in the future, if women could rid themselves of their subjection to the lures of commodities.

Betty Friedan's *The Feminine Mystique* (1963), the book that was so influential for the 'second wave' of feminism on both sides of the Atlantic, is probably the best, as well as the first, example of this type of argument. It is also one of the quirkiest. For Friedan in effect claims that women won their emancipation – votes, professional rights – and then let it go, foolishly seduced by the determined operations of the men of Madison Avenue and their avatars in other areas of life who wanted to ensure their return to that homely place that Friedan uncomfortably names 'the comfortable concentration camp'. Here, consumption figures not as momentary freedom, but as a forceful social pressure driving women, against what are nonetheless their potentially better judgements, back to the 'feminine' home.[31]

But the deeper accusation of Friedan's polemic is the fear that this creeping and artificial domestication is also affecting men, who are sinking into the ghastly 'togetherness' of conjugally shared household activities–and the pattern is being perpetuated through a lack of paternal discipline and an excess of mother-love. Women's renunciation of real-world achievement values – 'human' values, in Friedan's terms – in favour of the circumscribed and secondary values of the home seems to be leading inexorably to a corresponding domestication of the men, who are going soft in the head. Domestication implies for both sexes an alienation from a true, whole self whose field of operation is out there, somewhere else.

It will be clear that there are common elements between this argument and Beauvoir's. In both cases, domestication represents a deprivation of full human potential, and domestication is associated with a false version of femininity. Women should be allowed access – out of the home, into the wide world – to the prospects and projects of an authentic subjectivity that is not in itself gendered: the feminine exclusion is contingent, not structural. Because of their individualistic frameworks, both Friedan and Beauvoir see women's liberation as their own responsibility: resistance is up to each one on her own.

We have considered different constructions of domestication in relation to its outsides, seen diversely as either a wilderness waiting to be tamed, or a neutral space of social reality and opportunity. The home itself may function as a residual sanctuary and as a source of moral values seen to be absent from the outside world. It is a place of rest, with its dailiness and removal seen as complementary to, rather than subversive of, the dominant external order. In feminist versions, this becomes a stagnantly artificial prison or cage for a woman whose fulfilment can only be 'outside'.

How then might we think of the domestication of deconstruction or the domestication of feminism? As for deconstruction – well, in one sense, of course, deconstruction is always already domesticated, or never not yet domesticated, to the extent that it does not pretend to set itself up as something outside, radically separable from, the structures and logics it comes to analyse. There is no such thing as a pure deconstruction; instead, it can only be seen insofar as it works in and through certain texts or structures. However, this is not much use in thinking about the more dismissive use of domestication that I began with: always-already structures tend all too easily to slip into 'it's-all-the-same' structures, as though there were then no distinctions to be made between uses or adaptations of deconstructive methods. But I would like to say something about one of the processes that get damned as domestication: the transmission or presentation of deconstructive ideas.

The metaphor of accessibility is regularly used in this context, with a connotation of diminishment and simplification: insofar as you make a theory accessible, you automatically simplify it, abolishing a complexity that is seen as the virtue of the original. This characterisation operates with special force in conjunction with the idea of translation and importation, in a weakening that is assumed to occur in the movement from French to English. Associated with this is an implicit devaluation of English as the language of common sense, and behind this again lies the whole history of the development of theory in Britain and other English-speaking countries, where it has been valorised for qualities of Frenchness, complexity and difficulty seen to be absent from domestically English or Anglo-American traditions of thinking. In this context, inaccessibility and obscurity of presentation come to be linked as positive and indissociable terms.

Yet there is nothing inevitable about this state of affairs, no reason to assume that complexity has to go with obscurity, or accessibility with simplification. Deconstruction is assuredly finding some homes in English-speaking intellectual culture, but such domestications need not necessarily follow a pattern of decline and distortion. There are doubtless more domestications, there and elsewhere, than are dreamt of in any common or kitchen philosophy of domestication as meaning the moment that marks the end of the interesting story.

A different, though related argument applies in the case of feminist domestication (though I don't mean to imply a necessary separation between feminism and deconstruction: there are many points of overlap between the two, in practice and in theory, and most of those who bring them together would claim that they are inseparable). The use of 'domestication' as a straightforwardly negative metaphor, in need of no further analysis, implies simple binary oppositions and two-stage stories, whereby something initially natural, spontaneous or subversive gets pushed into a conformity or homogeneity that deprives it of whatever made it different. This much would apply to any deployment of domestication; but in feminist contexts, there is an added irony because the would-be abstract term is rich in thematic ambiguities and histories which, from the point of view of feminist demands and aims, could hardly be closer to home. Feminism cannot just get away from domestication, whether by sweeping it under the carpet as a dusty old error, or by identifying it with an uncomplicated and inevitable process of assimilation.

Domestication is not such a settled concept in the first place, as the various examples of this essay have shown. Like feminism, it's full of surprises.

NOTES

1. Judith Butler, *Gender Trouble: Feminism and the Subversion of Identity* (New York: Routledge, 1990), pp. xiii, 139.
2. See Jack Goody, *The Domestication of the Savage Mind* (Cambridge: Cambridge University Press, 1977).
3. See Richard Hoggart, *The Uses of Literacy: Aspects of Working-Class Life* (London: Chatto & Windus 1957).
4. Gaston Bachelard, *La Poétique de l'espace* (1957; Paris: PUF, Quadrige, 2001), 79.
5. On hyphenating philosophy, see Bachelard, 128,192; for the critique of a negative version of psychoanalysis, see e.g.112–13, 155–7.
6. Bachelard, 129.
7. But I must add a domestic detail from the last half hour: as I was typing this, to the reassuring dim backing of the radio, the voice of Dave Lee Travis (a household name on British radio until he faded ignominiously from the airwaves in the summer of 1993) filtered itself across, asking some quiz question to some pub team somewhere in East Anglia, about – as I subsequently reconstructed it – the total weight in tonnes of the quantity of cargo shifted through Heathrow Airport every year. A few moments later the reply came back, as it turned out just one or two off the correct answer, somewhere in the hundred thousands. With what sounded to me like genuine disturbance, DLT returns: 'That's a little too close for comfort, that's a very uncanny guess.' To me, about to start a paragraph on the uncanny, this too was a little too close for comfort, as if the radio, habitually used in some nebulous way to be soothing or enlivening, just *there* in an unremarkable, domestically familiar way, had suddenly jumped out to take on a quite different role, unsettling in its direct reinforcement of the main direction of my attention.
8. Freud, *The Interpretation of Dreams* (1900), SE V, 346, GW II/III, 352.
9. In which connection, there is the following searing passage from the end of Upton Sinclair's novel *The Jungle* (1906; Harmondsworth: Penguin, 1986), spoken by an advocate of cooperative communities:

> Surely it is moderate to say that the dish-washing for a family of five takes half an hour a day; with ten hours as a day's work, it takes, therefore, half a million able-bodied persons – mostly women – to do the dish-washing of the country. And note that this is most filthy and deadening and brutalizing work; that it is a cause of anaemia, nervousness,

ugliness, and ill temper; of prostitution, suicide, and insanity; of drunken husbands and degenerate children. (406)

Sinclair goes on to imagine the hygienic twentieth-century wonders of a communally owned 'machine that would wash and dry the dishes, and do it, not merely to the eye and the touch, but scientifically – sterilizing them' (406–7).

10. See Virginia Woolf, 'Professions for Women', *The Crowded Dance of Modern Life: Selected Essays*, vol. 2, ed. Rachel Bowlby (Harmondsworth: Penguin, 1993).
11. Simone de Beauvoir, *Le deuxième sexe* (1949; Paris: Gallimard, Folio essais series, 1986), vol. II, 259.
12. Beauvoir, 259.
13. Beauvoir, 267.
14. Friedrich Engels, *The Origin of the Family, Private Property, and the State* (1884; trans. New York: Pathfinder Press, 1972), 68.
15. Engels, 152.
16. John Ruskin, 'Of Queens' Gardens', in *Sesame and Lilies* (1865; London: J. M. Dent, Everyman Library, 1970), 50.
17. Ruskin, 49.
18. Ruskin, 49–50.
19. Ruskin, 59.
20. Ruskin, 59.
21. Witold Rybczynski, *Home: A Short History of an Idea* (London: Heinemann, 1988), 77.
22. Rybczynski, 217.
23. Rybczynski, 220–1.
24. Rybczynski, 232.
25. Ruskin, 75.
26. Ruskin, 75.
27. This is a point eloquently made by Michèle Le Dœuff in *L'étude et le rouet* (Paris: Seuil, 1989).
28. Beauvoir, 272.
29. See Luce Irigaray, *Speculum: de l'autre femme* (Paris: Seuil, 1974).
30. See Julia Kristeva, 'Women's Time' (1979), trans. Alice Jardine and Harry Blake, in Catherine Belsey and Jane Moore (eds), *The Feminist Reader* (London: Macmillan, 1989).
31. See Rachel Bowlby, '"The Problem with No Name": Rereading Friedan's *The Feminine Mystique*', in *Still Crazy After All These Years: Women, Writing and Psychoanalysis* (London: Routledge, 1992), 76–94.

12

'We're Getting There'

Woolf, Trains and the Destinations of Feminist Criticism*

Trains, like women, are never on time. This is a truism of which it seems only fair to remind the reader, realising that not everyone necessarily falls into the category of British Rail traveller or spectator of British television commercials. 'We're getting there' has been an advertising slogan utilised by British Rail to promise possible future efficiency in the form of timely arrivals at a destination; and the slogan derives any efficacy it might itself have in getting through to its destined audience by going against what it takes as a prevailing assumption on the public's part that British Rail doesn't, or won't, get there.

Given a question of trains, some of that public might perhaps be moved to make a connection with Saussure's example, renowned on certain academic networks, of the 8.45 pm express from Paris to Geneva and the issues of identity and difference that it raises.[1] In what sense might today's train, and the line it follows, be different from yesterday's? Others – or perhaps the same people – might go in the direction of Melanie Klein's pedagogical playing of trains with her young patient Dick, invited or pushed to identify the train with 'Daddy' and the station with his mother.[2] And at these points, 'We're getting there' arrives at or returns to the similarities or differences between trains and women, and the possible ends or destinations implied in speaking of 'feminist' writing and criticism. Where is feminism, or feminist theory going, and what would constitute its 'arrival', the end of the women's 'movement'? Is the very idea of getting from A to B – or indeed from A to Z – necessarily bound up with masculine fantasies of linear progression that feminism should have no truck with?

---

* First published in *Virginia Woolf: Feminist Destinations*, Basil Blackwell, 1988; the present revised version in *Feminist Destinations and Further Essays on Virginia Woolf*, Edinburgh: Edinburgh University Press, 1997.

Virginia Woolf's 1924 essay 'Mr Bennett and Mrs Brown' is a kind of literary Clapham Junction for the crossing and potential collision of questions of representation, history and sexual difference. Taking as its starting point the subject of 'modern fiction', the essay is cast in narrative form. It tells the story of an unfinished third-class railway journey from the periphery to the centre of London involving a 'Mrs Brown' whose key, if marginal, position is well enough indicated: 'I believe', declares Woolf, 'that all novels begin with an old lady in the corner opposite.'[3] Also present is a man called Mr Smith; the narrator, who represents herself as one of the passengers, uses the scene as a vehicle for discussing 'what novelists mean when they talk about character, what the impulse is that urges them so powerfully every now and then to embody their view in writing' (422). Woolf stresses the 'infinite variety of ways' in which Mrs Brown could be represented or 'treated', 'according to the age, country, and temperament of the writer' (426).

Such differences are further signalled by the train's ambiguous status as a form of communication between two points, whether they be historical moments, novelistic conventions, the two sexes, the two ladies (who never speak to one another), or the writer and the readers to whom the communication of Mrs Brown is no straightforward matter. By the end of the journey, this question of forms of communication has coupled itself with that of historical change and how to represent it. What does it mean to travel from A to B, from Richmond to Waterloo, from the Edwardians to the Georgians, and perhaps from 'realism' to 'modernism'? And might it have something to do with a movement from Mr Bennett to Mrs Brown, or indeed to Mrs Woolf? A third type of issue breaks in here, as the passage from one literary or historical phase to the next seems to become inextricably involved with a contention about injustices and reparations to the old lady.

Within the context of the essay, the scene is set up to dislocate the tedious compilations of data associated, for Woolf, with the pre-war Edwardian novelists. H. G. Wells, Arnold Bennett and John Galsworthy are parodied via sardonic paraphrases of their likely narrative versions of the encounter on the train with the 'old lady in the corner opposite' (425) who hypothetically begins every novel. In this dispute, the old lady is up for grabs, caught between opposing constructions of her likely story or background, all of which, apparently, claim to have fixed her once and for all.

But much more is going on in the train than this initial retelling of Woolf's story would suggest. In addition to the problem of identifying the woman there is another line running through it, which is a thesis about the historical development and contemporary situation of the English novel. The infinite number of stories to which Mrs Brown might give rise would in this light appear to depend not so much on the static personal or national predilections of novelists as on the changing 'code' (434) or 'conventions' (430) of literary representation. In this framework, the Edwardians figure as a point of transition between nineteenth-century literature and whatever will supersede it. That something else is on the way is suggested both by 'the smashing and the crashing' (433) of the subsequent Georgian generation, and by the allegedly self-evident obsoleteness of the Edwardian conventions or 'tools' (430) of factual realism.

It is surely no accident that the encounter with Mrs Brown takes place on a train. By this time, the imagery of public transport had become literally a commonplace for suggesting the repetitive and banal 'types' of realist fiction, as with the standardised 'man on the Clapham omnibus'. Woolf, on the contrary, alters the terms – by putting the novelist into the carriage with her subject, and by using the public space as a sign of strangeness rather than predictability. She also suggests, as we shall see, that the genders of the participants are by no means a matter of indifference. Writers, characters, readers, and the linguistic means of bringing about an interchange between them are radically shaken around in this suburban railway journey, which is at first sight such an unlikely setting for an argument against realism. Here, the theme of transport and movement makes way for the contrast with the stationary quality of the Edwardian writers' preoccupation with houses. The compartment does have some of the qualities of the domestic sitting room, but this only adds to its curiously ambivalent suspension halfway between two states, in this respect as in others. This is a public space superficially identical to a private one, so that the anonymity of the limited number of passengers is all the more significant from its contrast to the scene of intimacy it resembles.

Following another line, the train indicates a mobile, rather than a static or external position for the narrator. In fact, the train suggests several possible relations between observer and subject. There is the train passing, seen from elsewhere; there is what is seen from the train through the window, like a picture in motion; and there is the scene inside the railway compartment. All these positions prove to be important in looking at Woolf's narratives; and it is also worth recalling here that trains at this period had no corridors, so that passengers were completely confined to their carriage while the train was between stations.[4]

In terms of literary history, Woolf's piece links the movement beyond Edwardian realism to a shift in consciousness that is hypothetically, if not arbitrarily, marked at a specific date. This is the famous and enigmatic pronouncement that 'in or about December, 1910, human character changed' (421).[5] Here Woolf takes the line of historical determination as far as it will go, to a point where chronological precision practically becomes a caricature of this type of explanation. Her formula is an exasperated transposition of the blandness of factual records to the shock effect of a sensational headline or slogan. In the very form of the quasi-ludicrous specification, Woolf questions the possibility of anything like the confident ordering, listing and chronicling that she associates with the Edwardians. It can never be more than provisional and retrospective, at least for the post-1910 mind, to posit a fixed position from which to view or analyse what might be seen as an event or a change in human society or consciousness.

But Woolf's provocatively sloganising style could itself be linked to the alleged change in forms of communication and understanding: it could be compared to the 'sky-writing' aeroplane advertisement in Mrs Dalloway; or to the need to mark a distinction between what she calls later in the essay the 'myriads of irrelevant and incongruous ideas' (425), which are constantly vying to make an impression.

Woolf continues, then, by stressing that her claim marks serious questions about historical change and its representation:

> I am not saying that one went out, as one might into a garden, and there saw that a rose had flowered, or that a hen had laid an egg. The change was not sudden and definite like that. But a change there was, nevertheless, and, since one must be arbitrary, let us date it about the year 1910. (421–2)

It is a matter neither of the repeated cycles of nature – hens and flowers – nor of simple chronology – 1910, 1911, 1912. But the demarcation of an 'event', 'arbitrary' and approximate though it must be, is still an issue of some consequence. In this case – both a seemingly random 'example' and a test case on which all of history and history-writing will hang – it will not be a matter of discovering and then instantly transmitting the true nature of a transhistorical and eternal Mrs Brown, the natural woman hitherto unrepresented or distorted in fiction and now to be seen at last blooming in her corner. Nor will it be a matter of Mrs Brown's presence on the train simply being noted, *à la* Bennett, as evidence of progressive female emancipation: before the war, Mrs Brown would have needed a protector and now she travels alone. Mrs Brown is neither a natural phenomenon nor a social statistic, and it is not yet clear what difference the fact of her being a woman might make.

To some extent, as the ambivalence of her use of the concept of 'convention' shows, the terminus *ad quem* for novel-writing is presupposed in the way the story is set up. Edwardian realism is considered by Woolf to be at once historically necessary and necessarily to be overtaken as only a first stop on the line: its 'conventions' are also said to be like those of a hostess 'bridging the gulf' with her 'unknown guest' (431), and never getting beyond what should be only preliminary chat about the weather. The objection to this as too simple is the starting point for Woolf's expository journey when she introduces Mrs Brown as standing for the problem she claims to be common to novelists at all times, of how to represent 'that overwhelming and peculiar impression' (425) produced by the unknown potential character: 'Myriads of irrelevant and incongruous ideas crowd into one's head on such occasions; one sees the person, one sees Mrs Brown, in the centre of all sorts of different scenes' (425). The prospective author does not sit in a neutral position surveying a knowable scene; rather, she is afflicted from outside by the 'myriads' of ideas which 'crowd' in without any principle of order or coherence, 'irrelevant and incongruous'. The language here can be related to the modernist 'stream' of consciousness – or perhaps it should rather be called a 'train' of thought – with the 'fragments' and 'chaotic condition' of current literature then corresponding to or emanating from a chaotic, fragmented state of mind that has now taken over from the clearly marked boundaries and certainties of Edwardian stability. But such a change cannot be simply narrated as a movement from outer to inner; instead, as this sentence shows, it is a question of a different relationship between inside and outside in which the chaotic incoherence of mental 'ideas' is identified with the social 'crowd', and where the disturbing effect of the whole crowd is produced by 'that overwhelming and peculiar impression' (425) of the single old lady seen in the railway carriage.

The issue, then, is not so much one of ebbs and flows in the vitality of artistic conventions, despite Woolf's implicit use of an Arnoldian alternation between 'critical' and 'creative' periods of literary history. Rather, it involves a completely new representation of social and subjective experience. In terms of writing, it is only the striking claim that will jolt the reader amid such a barrage of chaotic impressions. At the end of her lecture, Woolf makes an explicit identification between writer and reader as fellow observers of the mysterious Mrs Brown:

> For she is just as visible to you who remain silent as to us who tell stories about her. In the course of your daily life this past week you have had far stranger and more interesting experiences than the one I have tried to describe. You have overheard scraps of talk that filled you with amazement. You have gone to bed at night bewildered by the complexity of your feelings. In one day thousands of ideas have coursed through your brains; thousands of emotions have met, collided, and disappeared in astonishing disorder. (436)

Mrs Brown now moves on from being just a symbol of literary character. Here she becomes a figure for the confusion and 'complexity' of a 'daily life' represented as the source of the internal 'disorder' of the 'thousands of ideas' to which, like her, it gives rise. There is 'amazement' and unfamiliarity in the most everyday experiences, in the fragmentary, anonymous quality of the 'overheard scraps of talk'. Inner and outer, seer and seen, psychic and social, can in no way be represented apart.

Despite this engagement with the representation of personal experience as a social and historical question, Woolf has often been criticised or dismissed for a presumed elitism in her linguistic complexity, or a snobbish indifference to or ignorance of the details of ordinary life to which the novelists from which she distinguishes herself devoted such minute attention. In this kind of argument, she is set up as the lady whose leisure and income enabled her to retreat into a private, self-contained haven whence to expatiate on the beauties of Art and the delicate contents of her self-absorbed mind. There are, certainly, many moments in Woolf's writing where it is not difficult to understand the possible grounds for such a case. In this essay, for instance, the reader is encouraged to seek substantiation for the alleged change in human character by reference to the case of 'one's cook' (422). There are assumptions in that word 'one's' that grate now in the same way as most uses of the masculine as a general pronoun by someone writing after the mid-1970s.

If the problem is granted to be one involving changing conventions of writing and changing expectations of readership, then the objection can only be sustained if the writer is imagined to be some transcendentally omni-egalitarian consciousness, not only ahead of her time but outside time altogether. But it is usually the consciously 'historical' critic who makes this type of criticism, ironically working from idealist, ahistorical assumptions about the practice of authorship that would be rejected immediately in other contexts. In this particular example, in fact, not only is the question of historical change the actual theme of Woolf's argument, but the rise of the cook-upstairs from the 'lower depths' of the Victorian cellar to the reading of newspapers and the borrowing of hats, which is given as a 'homely illustration' of 'the power of the human race to change' (422).[6]

It is precisely around this question of the changing place of women that Woolf's objections to the Edwardian writers become most insistent. 'How shall I begin to describe this woman's character?' she asks:

> And they said: 'Begin by saying that her father kept a shop in Harrogate. Ascertain the rent. Ascertain the wages of shop assistants in the year 1878. Discover what her mother died of. Describe cancer. Describe calico. Describe—' But I cried, 'Stop! Stop!' And I regret to say that I threw that ugly, that clumsy, that incongruous tool out of the window. (432)

As Woolf in desperation calls a halt to the train, the over-extended conversational formalities of the Edwardian novelist-as-hostess have taken on the far less genteel appearance of an ugly, clumsy 'tool'.[7] Like the 'man's sentence' in *A Room of One's Own*, it is clearly 'unsuited for a woman's use', and like the 'awkward break' Woolf there identifies in the text of *Jane Eyre*, and then herself repeats by cutting off the quotation, 'Stop! Stop!' is an angry refusal of any continuity between the men's way of approaching Mrs Brown and her own.[8]

Woolf pulls the communication cord on Edwardian certainties in no uncertain terms, exposing the masculine force that lies behind the seemingly neutral Edwardian equipment. The overtones here of rape are foregrounded even more strongly within the main line of the story, where the narrator who enters the compartment comes upon what appears to be a violent scene between Mr Smith and Mrs Brown: 'It was plain . . . that he had some power over her which he was exerting disagreeably . . . Obviously against her will she was in Mr Smith's hands' (424). And then, following the man's abrupt departure at Clapham Junction: 'He had got what he wanted, but he was ashamed of himself' (424).

Given the title of the essay, which would not lead the reader to expect a story about a Mr Smith, it is not hard to see in this 'bullying, menacing' Mr Smith (424) a reference to Mr Bennett.[9] As Mrs Brown also represents novelistic characters in general, Woolf's narrating of her own entry into the train becomes all the more significant: 'I had the strange and uncomfortable feeling that I was interrupting' (423). What she turns out to imagine herself interrupting is this spectacle of suppressed violence, perpetrated by a man against a woman, over a matter having to do with the signing away of property. This situation is then plotted onto the running question about the transition or break between one literary period and the next, when the old lady starts later on to complain at her own misrepresentation: 'There was Mrs Brown protesting that she was different, quite different, from what people made out, and luring the novelist to her rescue' (433). Mrs Brown's protest, echoing Woolf's own 'Stop! Stop!' then leads to an explicit connection between the inadequacy of literary tools and the rescue of the woman:

> At whatever cost of life, limb, and damage to valuable property Mrs Brown must be rescued, expressed, and set in her high relations to the world before the train stopped and she disappeared for ever. And so the smashing and the crashing began. (433)

It might seem that Mrs Woolf's fortunate interruption will suffice to secure the reappraisal and rise of the maligned and molested Mrs Brown, as the two ladies settle down comfortably at last, with Mr Smith and his tools safely out of the way, reading and writing in a railway carriage of their own. But things do not advance so rapidly. The pressing need for Mrs Brown's rescue has so far produced only 'the smashing and the crashing' of the Georgians, which sounds no different from the earlier antics of Mr Smith's incursions: 'He banged. He slammed. His dripping umbrella made a pool in the hall' (425). With a certain matronly disapproval, Woolf likens the behaviour of the new writers to the rebelliousness of little boys rolling in the mud as a resistance to genteel constraints (434).

Woolf's suspicions here lead her to mark the present time as only a station *en route* to a prospective arrival at new conventions where Mrs Brown will be decently treated. But in discussing why change should proceed so slowly, she raises another question, wheeling on yet another 'strange travelling companion' in the form of that 'suggestible and docile creature', the public (432). And here, once again, her illustration has to do with the representation of sexual difference:

> If you say to the public with sufficient conviction, 'All women have tails, and all men humps', it will actually learn to see women with tails and men with humps, and will think it very revolutionary and probably improper if you say 'Nonsense. Monkeys have tails and camels humps. But men and women have brains, and they have hearts; they think and they feel,' – that will seem to it a bad joke, and an improper one into the bargain. (432–3)

In this full-blown send-up of conventional representations, what the 'docile' public finds unacceptable is the alteration of what is already a reversal of the symbolic norm, that women have humps and men tails. But this parody is reinforced by a parody of symbolic significance itself, in the literalising of the humps and tails; and the whole question of the difference of the sexes is deflected onto the distinction of power and intelligence that supposedly operates between the meaning-making writers and their obtuse but potentially stubborn public, a neutral 'creature' or 'it'.

Sexual difference may, then, mean nothing, or something 'quite different', in the end or the future; but in the meantime it is the source both of the gravest injustice, in the mistaking of Mrs Brown, and of the greatest resistance to change on the part of a convention-bound public. Mrs Brown's claim to be 'different, quite different from what people made out' suspends the conclusion of her story by withholding a positive identification of what she might be, and establishing the issue as having to do with representational conventions. Her difference is not necessarily that of absolute uniqueness or that of

Woman from Man in some universal sense; it is difference from the way she is presently dealt with.

As the train makes its way from Richmond to Waterloo, this question of sexual difference has come, at least in this interested reconstruction of the journey, to occupy a place of privilege. It seems clear that by or about the 1920s, questions of possible modifications in 'human character' have come to formulate themselves in male and female characters and their different lines of development. While at one level the conventions of Edwardian realism are mocked as merely anachronistic or meaningless, like the superficialities of polite hostesses, at another their tools are associated with a violence that borders on the threat of rape. The 'illustrations' in this essay – Mrs Brown herself; 'one's cook' and 'the power of the human race to change'; women with humps instead of tails – all turn out to have to do with women or sexual difference, and to link themselves into a miniature narrative or series of questions about the representation of woman and her place: from traditional representations of the fictitious old lady, through protestations of equal rights and difference from 'what they made out', to a parody of the social implications of male and female.

Woolf's third-class railway compartment has maintained its place as a *locus classicus* for discussions of the journey from realism and modernism as hypothetical stops on the line of literary history, or as general labels for alternative types of literary representation. Recently, this debate has become linked with feminist questions, with the possible move from Mr Bennett to Mrs Brown as writers and with demands that the real Mrs Brown stand up, or sit down, not so much as 'character' or 'human life' in general, but as a woman. Pinning her down as a textual or sexual being, getting her to show the valid ticket of her twentieth-century identity, has become a major preoccupation. And the venerable old lady in the corner has come to look not a little like the figure of Mrs Woolf herself.

For it would seem that Woolf, like Mrs Brown, has become an 'exemplary' character – and exemplary in paradoxical ways. Woolf is the only twentieth-century British woman writer who is taken seriously by critics of all casts. Whether she is seen to fit in with or to subvert what the critic identifies as established literary standards, and depending on whether subversion or conformity is the criterion of value, Woolf is vehemently celebrated or denounced from all sides. Among feminist critics who approve her work, she is seen as exemplary both in the sense of exceptional – a unique heroine, a foremother, a figurehead – and as an example, in some way representative or typical of something called 'women's writing'. Among those who dislike her work, it is taken as not matching up to the criteria of women's writing, but fitting in all too well with the patriarchal norms, literary or social, to which authentic women's writing should by definition be opposed.

The issues in feminist criticism are related to the overt concerns of 'Mr Bennett and Mrs Brown': in particular, to what is at stake in the privileging of modernism because it brings into the foreground questions of language and representation. One strand of feminist criticism takes its cue from this model, positing women's writing as the principal locus of the undermining of realist conventions identified as masculine. Another strand, working with broadly realist assumptions, takes 'women's writing' to describe a female experience hitherto devalorised, if not wholly banished, by the institutional or more general constraints implied by a patriarchal society. In the 'exemplary' case of Virginia Woolf – the woman writer *par excellence* and, at the same time, a test case for women's writing in general – this has led to various different types of criticism. She is celebrated as a modernist breaking with formal literary conventions, and thereby also with the normative structures of patriarchal – or phallocentric – language; she is also celebrated as a realist, by appeal to her authentic description of women's lives and experiences, and her commitment to the end of patriarchal society. At the same time, Woolf is also attacked from both these standpoints: as not realist enough (too much Bloomsbury aestheticism) or as not modernist enough (always falling back into a nostalgic desire for unities rather than radical breaks). Woolf has been confidently situated in all four categories, which then signals that what goes on in her writing, and in particular what goes on in the famous railway carriage, is strikingly amenable to compartmentalisation; but also that it doesn't easily stay put.

There is also the question of biography. On the one hand there are the legends of Bloomsbury and the privileged upbringing in a family where genial Victorian men of letters were always dropping in for tea. On the other hand there is the work with women's organisations, the lecturing to working-class audiences, the membership of a Sussex village Labour Party. Bloomsbury snob versus socialist feminist, by an easy enough transposition. Apart from the public persona, there is Woolf's personal legend, which leaves little to be desired or dreaded in the way of striking characterisation. Childhood seduction, madness, confinement, frigidity, anorexia, lesbianism, suicide: in the very extremity of its outlines, the tale can become either a demonstration of common female oppression – the norm revealed at its outer edges – or proof of exceptional status. In her oddness or in her representativeness, Virginia Woolf is always treated as a 'case'. Here again, with the woman as with her writing – and the two are rarely separated – it is the problem of the 'exemplary'. For her advocates, either the extraordinary nature of Woolf's life is what makes her distinctive, or its typicality is what makes her writing a woman's. For her detractors, Woolf's peculiarities mar her work and disqualify her from writing as a woman, or else her all too normal experiences confine her work within 'womanly' limits that cannot achieve the status of art.

It will be apparent from all this not only that is Woolf considered worthy of a formidable quantity of critical attention, but that the criticism frequently takes the form of violent attack or defence – of Virginia Woolf herself, of what she wrote or (most often) of some nebulous fusion of the two. And somehow the question of identifying the real nature of Woolf gets bound up with identifying the real nature of woman, or literature, or feminism, or feminist literature. Like the Bible, Woolf's texts provide ample support for almost any position: she is taken to hold the key to the meaning of life and the proper nature of woman; she is the object of both veneration and vehement hatred; and like the Bible too, she is sometimes merely treated as 'literature'.

Uncannily enough, the 'Mr Bennett and Mrs Brown' essay seems to prefigure the fate of Woolf herself. 'I shall never know what became of her', Woolf says of Mrs Brown (425); but it is as if Woolf herself has since become nothing else than the all-purpose 'exemplary' figure of Mrs Brown, source of an endless variety of treatments and mistreatments, and calling forth the most diverse and zealous critics and defenders, all eager to put her in her place, high or low, and to save her from those who have put her somewhere else.

To take one example, Toril Moi's influential book *Sexual/Textual Politics*, on the present state of feminist criticism, opens with a chapter on Woolf as a natural starting point for any discussion of this issue. Arguing against the realist assumptions of Woolf's feminist critics, who object that she does not provide enough images of strong women, Moi goes on to say that 'the major drawback of this approach is that it proves incapable of appropriating for feminism the work of the greatest British woman writer of this century'.[10] There is a possible tension here between the given absolute status of the greatest writer, and the criterion of utility, 'for feminism'; while 'appropriating' could sound not unlike what Mr Bennett *et al.* did to Mrs Brown – all the more ironically given that this section of the chapter is entitled 'Rescuing Woolf for feminist politics'.

Clearly, the Mrs Brown question does not easily go away. But I am not suggesting that it is possible or desirable to stop 'appropriating', 'rescuing' or even mildly mistreating Virginia Woolf, who says herself at the end of her essay 'Modern Fiction': 'If we can imagine the art of fiction come alive and standing in our midst, she would undoubtedly bid us break her and bully her, as well as honour and love her, for so her youth is renewed and her sovereignty assured.'[11] In saying that the (inconclusive) answers to almost all generalising questions about 'woman', 'literature' and the rest are already anticipated by Woolf – in the 'Mrs Brown' essay and others, and above all in *A Room of One's Own*, where she moves through just about all the positions that have subsequently been attributed to her as definite stances – I am, of course, only repeating the gesture of deification; but then it is not so easy to step out of this particular railway carriage.

To appropriate Toril Moi's suggestive link in my turn: it seems to me that the interest in Woolf's writing is to be found precisely in the juxtaposition Moi proposes between Woolf's literary achievement and her feminist questions. As in 'Mr Bennett and Mrs Brown', issues of literary representation, historical narrative and sexual difference are inseparable throughout Woolf's work. She insists upon the difficulty of distinguishing the question of what constitutes a plausible story, historical or biographical, from the question of what constitutes the difference of men and women. Sometimes her concern is more to dissect the presuppositions of received forms of representation, and sometimes it is more to argue from the given state of those forms, taking them as 'read'. Sometimes, that is, she analyses the railway compartment in all its contingency, showing the unfounded nature of its claim to normality; and at other times, she considers the compartment as it is, recognising but disputing the sexually differentiated terms of travel it imposes, and asking where it may go from here.

It is precisely in her insistence on the sexual inflection of all questions of historical understanding and literary representation that Woolf is a feminist writer. She constantly associates certainty and conventionality with a complacent masculinity, which she sees as setting the norms for models of individual and historical development. It makes sense, then, that it will be from the woman in the corner of the railway compartment – or the woman not synchronised with the time of the train – that the most fruitful and troubling questions will be posed, and that new lines may emerge. But given that Woolf is engaged in questioning the very notion of straightforward directions and known destinations, it is not clear what those lines will be, or where they will go; or what a woman may look like, 'if and when' she has succeeded in changing the conditions of travel and the present timetable.

NOTES

1. Ferdinand de Saussure, *Cours de linguistique générale*, ed. Tullio de Mauro (Paris: Payot, 1984), 151. As if to emphasise the question, the English version features the same (or a different) train as not the 8.45, but the 8.25 (*Course in General Linguistics*, trans. Wade Baskin, revised edition with an introduction by Jonathan Culler (London: Fontana, 1974), 108).
2. See Melanie Klein, 'The Importance of Symbol Formation in the Development of the Ego' (1930), in *The Selected Melanie Klein*, ed. Juliet Mitchell (Harmondsworth: Penguin, 1986), 102–03.

3. *The Collected Essays of Virginia Woolf*, vol. 3, ed. Andrew McNeillie (London: Hogarth Press, 1988), 425; further references will be included within the main text. In McNeillie's edition, in part to avoid confusion with a short version that appears in the same volume, the essay appears under its first published name of 'Character in Fiction'.
    Andrew McNeillie's edition includes 'Byron and Mr Briggs', an unpublished text from the early 1920s, which likewise uses the railway compartment as a setting for a discussion of modern scenes of writing and reading (473–500). 'An Unwritten Novel' (1920; rpt. in Susan Dick, ed., *The Complete Shorter Fiction of Virginia Woolf* [London: Hogarth Press, 1985], 106–15) further confirms the power of this setting as an image for Woolf's thinking about the sources of the novelist's urge to make up stories. In this story, the narrator sees enough of the post-train life of her subject to find out that she has got her Mrs Brown equivalent wrong. This raises questions different from those of the essay, in which Mrs Brown does not dislodge the narrator from her place of open speculation or invention by the inclusion of counter-fictional evidence.
4. Michel Foucault describes the multiple implications of a more modern arrangement of the train: 'It's an extraordinary bunch of relationships, the train, since it's something along which you go, it's something too by which you can go from one place to another, and it's also something which goes past' ('Des espaces autres', in *AMC (Architecture Mouvement Continuité)*, 5 (octobre 1984), 47). The isolation of the compartment before the introduction of corridors gave rise to the often-sensationalised interest in 'railway rapes', and to the fears and fantasies of passengers, as becomes apparent in the context of Woolf's novel *Jacob's Room*; see Rachel Bowlby, *Feminist Destinations and Further Essays on Virginia Woolf* (Edinburgh: Edinburgh University Press, 1997), ch. 6. For further details on this and every other aspect of the early sociology of the train, see Wolfgang Schivelbusch, *The Railway Journey: Trains and Travel in the Nineteenth Century* (1977), trans. Anselm Hollo (Oxford: Basil Blackwell, 1979). Those interested in investigating the rich topic of the relations between railways and art forms are referred to Karen Bowie and Marie-Noële Poilino, *Arts et chemins de fer*, a special issue of the *Revue d'Histoire des Chemins de Fer*, nos. 10–11 (Printemps–Automne 1994).
5. 'December, 1910' was the month after the first exhibition of post-Impressionist paintings opened in London, organised by Roger Fry, and this event itself conceals a further parable of the retrospective marking of an event or a historical break. It was Fry who invented the label 'Post-Impressionist' – an English naming of a French artistic movement, which was then retranslated into French. Further, the 'post' of 'Post-Impressionism' now seems to anticipate (or rehearses), *avant la lettre*, the 1980s discussion of the significance of

the 'post' in the terms 'post-structuralism' and (especially) 'postmodernism'. The postmodern was theorised by the French philosopher Jean-François Lyotard not as what comes after modernity, but as the experimentation or lack of fixity that turns out, retrospectively, to have preceded the establishment of rules and norms of representation in any given period of the history of art. See Lyotard, 'Answering the Question: What is Postmodernism?' (1982), trans. Régis Durand, appended to *The Postmodern Condition* (Manchester: Manchester University Press, 1984), 71–84.

6. A second instance given is that of 'the married life of the Carlyles' (*Essays*, 3, 422): 'Bewail the waste, the futility, for him and for her, of the horrible domestic tradition which made it seemly for a woman of genius to spend her time chasing beetles, scouring saucepans, instead of writing books. All human relations have shifted – those between masters and servants, husbands and wives, parents and children.' Woolf doesn't consider here the possible 'waste' of the 'genius' of a cook, or whether saucepan-scouring and literature are compatible. This is perhaps the point behind Q. D. Leavis's somewhat self-congratulatory remark in her much later response to Woolf's *Three Guineas*: 'myself . . . have generally had to produce contributions for this review with one hand while actually stirring the pot, or something of that kind, with the other'; *Scrutiny*, 7, 2 (September 1938), 210; rpt in *Virginia Woolf: The Critical Heritage*, eds Robin Majumdar and Allen McLaurin (London: Routledge & Kegan Paul, 1975), 409–19.

7. In 'Modern Fiction', Woolf hints more strongly that the third-class railway carriage may indicate a more serious engagement with novel-writing than that of the men, who in fact are cosseted rather than challenged by the 'material' facts they describe: 'More and more they seem to us, deserting even the well-built villa in the Five Towns, to spend their time in some softly padded first-class railway carriage, pressing bells and buttons innumerable; and the destiny to which they travel so luxuriously becomes more and more unquestionably an eternity of bliss spent in the very best hotel in Brighton'; *Collected Essays*, ed. McNeillie, 4 (London: Hogarth Press, 1994), 159.

8. Woolf, *A Room of One's Own* (1929; London: Granada, 1984), 73, 66.

9. Woolf quotes directly from Arnold Bennett's novel *Hilda Lessways* (1911; Harmondsworth: Penguin, 1976), choosing a passage that is meant to illustrate the author's preoccupation with external information rather than with the woman herself. But she seems unable to call a halt to her own exasperated reiteration of Bennett's allegedly irrelevant details about the socio-geography of real estate in Hilda's town, which extends over two whole pages. And in a sense, her own narrative repeats elements of Bennett's, but turns them round to make a criticism that is more hidden than that of the main line

of her argument against him. For *Hilda Lessways*, just like 'Mr Bennett and Mrs Brown', includes a memorable scene involving a man and a woman in a railway carriage (Book III, ch. 2). In it, the adventurous Hilda, who despises her mother's domesticity and has made herself into the local queen of shorthand, is titillatingly represented as more excited than fearful of the unbuttoned storytelling of her male companion, who has been filling her in on the professional grievances from which he is getting away:

> Hilda was afraid of his tempestuous mood. But she enjoyed her fear, as she might have enjoyed exposure to a dangerous storm, She enjoyed the sensation of her fragility and helplessness there, cooped up with him in the close intimacy of the compartment. She was glad that he did not apologise for his lack of restraint, nor foolishly pretend that he was boring her.
> 'It does seem a shame!' she murmured, her eyes candidly admitting that she felt enormously flattered. (183)

Thus in Bennett's novel too there is a fragile and helpless woman, and a man showing a lack of restraint. But in the man's text she enjoys it, and is glad that he does not say sorry. Woolf says that *Hilda Lessways* was randomly selected as her example, 'the first book that chance puts in my way' (429). Be it chance or forgetfulness, disingenuousness or design, Bennett's scene looks like the exact equivalent of the one recounted in Woolf's essay, with the sexual roles the same – vulnerable woman, pushy man – but the responses altered to show up a gendered difference of view.

10. Toril Moi, *Sexual/Textual Politics: Feminist Literary Theory* (London: Methuen, 'New Accents', 1985), 8.
11. Woolf, 'Modern Fiction', *Collected Essays* 4, 164.

13

Untold Stories in *Mrs Dalloway**

For some time now, it has been common to separate modernist from realist writing, both historically and formally. Either way, realism is the loser: whether it is seen as the lumbering nineteenth-century precursor of modernism (what else is the nineteenth century there for, but to give way to the twentieth?), or whether instead it is seen as based on the sort of simplistic narrative assumptions that modernist texts undermine. Such demarcations simplify in their turn; and the underlying argument of this chapter is that Woolf – without ceasing to be a modernist – is much more of a realist than she has been given credit (or discredit) for. She assumes, that is, that writers try, and rightly so, to represent that elusive thing that in her critical essays she calls 'life' or 'reality'. But this life is not non-verbal or even non-narrative: it is a reality that is already made up of stories. Life is sustained by being perpetually represented and retold.

To show how this works, I will approach Woolf's realism mainly through *Mrs Dalloway*, and mainly through minor characters – or rather, through minor minor characters: the obscure, the outsiders, those who appear to have only a passing significance. Subordinate to the principal figures, they enter the novel briefly and their departure from it, quite often, is unrecorded. Such figures both generate and reinforce what are always active questions for Woolf about visibility and representation, about who gets to have or to tell a story. The semi-presence, half-written or half-noticed, of the characters who exist to one side, or in the corner, then opens onto issues about the recognition and imagining of other people in the storytelling and story-making of everyday life.

In Woolf's essay 'The Lives of the Obscure', the opening scene is in an eccentric library. It is a nineteenth-century backwater where neglected, dust-gathering biographies forlornly wait to be momentarily raised from the dead

---

* First published in *Textual Practice* 25:3 (2011).

by the life-giving attention of a real contemporary reader.[1] Like the ghosts of the Homeric or Virgilian underworld, these 'Lives' may enjoy or suffer the temporary resurrection accorded them by a visitor from the present; and at the close of her first paragraph, faithful to the numerical conventions of epic limbo, Woolf duly chooses three of them: three shelf-mark numbers that will come to stand for crowds of buried lives, all awaiting release within the memoirs of their individual authors.

Woolf has fun with the trivialities and minor turbulences of the reported lives that she then represents in her turn. The garrulousness of their authors is seen as a substitute for a lack of real substance or significance in the doings and persons they honour.[2] But apart from the particular lives that Woolf reprieves, it is crucial to note that the 'lives' of the obscure are books, not people. As long as they remain unopened, these books consolidate the non-existence of their subjects (in another way, their obscurity): to be dead is to be unread. But by the same token the book in the library harbours a potential for a kind of third life, after the lived life and the life set down in the memoir. That third life is when someone picks up the biography, and reads it, and perhaps (as Woolf does here) writes about it. There is even a fourth life when (as now) another reader then reads or writes about the reader writing about the life – and so it goes on. (If it ever begins or continues: of course, the majority of lives cease to be remembered not too many years after their death; and the majority of published 'lives', in the same way, are unopened, unread or discarded.) This multiplication of distance – not just one life, one remove, or one representation – has the effect of exaggerating and emphasising the normal structure whereby any person – any life – is at once superseded and kept alive, kept going, by the stories that represent them. Lives are also, inevitably, distorted; or rather, they take their second and subsequent existences only in the altering medium of the representation into which they are translated. There is no going back: this is the life that was.

Mrs Dalloway has an exceptionally large population of characters whose existence is marked as minor: characters who teeter on the verge of representational death, but live a small novelistic life all the same in their subordinate, half-hidden ways. We could think for instance about the ones who have walk-on parts, with no influence on the plot or the other characters, but are nonetheless known to the narrator, and named as such, without further amplification. Scrope Purvis is one such. You may not remember him, unless for his extraordinary name, and if so, that is part of my point. He is the character, if that is not too grand a word, who turns up at the start of the novel as someone who recognises Clarissa Dalloway when she is waiting to cross the street, and mentally deems her 'a charming woman'.[3] We learn nothing about him except, indirectly, that he is a neighbour of Clarissa's; and we never hear of him again. After his moment, the narrative turns to Clarissa's own thoughts, just as it moved into Scrope's after a direct statement of narrative fact. His thoughts give us some information about Clarissa (that she has been ill), and they also give us the first instance of what will become a persistent use of bird metaphors to describe both Clarissa and another of the principal characters, Septimus Smith.

As is the way with any novel at its beginning, we don't yet know how much we should make of these points; but perhaps the most unexpected sequel, or non-sequel, to the mini-scene is that Scrope himself – if we can take the liberty of calling him by that very peculiar appellation – never returns. He's a sort of hapax, a one-off like his first name itself.[4] He has his moment, then off he goes – away he flies. This is all the more surprising in terms of conventional narrative expectations when we consider that he is introduced on the very first page of the novel, and also that he is a neighbour of the Dalloways and even a kind of counterpoint to Clarissa (the narrative viewpoint switches between them in such a way that we cannot be sure, until halfway through the paragraph that follows his appearance, that we are back with the thoughts of Clarissa herself and not still with the thoughts of Scrope Purvis).

If we keep in mind neighbours of the Dalloways, we will inevitably be drawn, in the light of our knowledge of the whole novel, to compare Scrope Purvis with a second character who makes a passing appearance – noticed, in her case, by Clarissa, as Scrope is not. This is the old lady in the window opposite Clarissa's: the old lady whom Clarissa twice stops to watch, the second time during her party when she has withdrawn after hearing of the suicide of Sir William Bradshaw's patient, Septimus Smith. Scrope Purvis knows Mrs Dalloway by name, just as the novel knows *him* by name; the old lady, for all she is as close to Clarissa as can be – she inhabits an adjacent house and she can be seen going to bed – has no name; or rather no name that either Clarissa or the novel knows. Yet with the old lady, there is a kind of momentary projected intimacy on Clarissa's side:

> She parted the curtains, she looked. Oh, but how surprising! – in the room opposite the old lady stared straight at her! She was going to bed. . . . She was going to bed, in the room opposite. It was fascinating to watch her, moving about, that old lady, crossing the room, coming to the window. Could she see her? It was fascinating, with people still laughing and shouting in the drawing-room, to watch that old woman, quite quietly, going to bed alone. (158)

The passage is full of repetitions: 'It was fascinating' (twice), 'going to bed' (three times), and three variations on 'the old lady'; one effect of this is to suggest the almost ritualistic sense of the scene, both as a spectacle that Clarissa is watching and as a regular routine that the old lady goes through daily. Clarissa quite clearly sees what she sees – she does indeed look in and 'watch that old woman' as she is – but she does not know whether in reality, and as it appears, 'the old lady stared straight at her!' Because in fact, of course, it is she who is staring straight at the old lady and imagining the possible but unascertainable return of the look. The effect is one of mutual mirroring, potentially.

But Clarissa also sees and respects the distance and difference of the old woman over there, so near and so far, whom she does not 'know' in any social sense but whose private world she sees. After hearing about what has happened to 'the young man' whom she does not know as Septimus (and whom she has never seen), the old lady 'going to bed' is for Clarissa at once a reassurance of life continuing, life repeating in its daily actions, and also, at the same time, another death, as the woman lays herself to rest (and the window is a reminder of the way that Septimus died). The anonymity and the familiarity, the alter ego and the stranger, are all intimations, I think, of the suspended state that this scene evokes between life and death, and without any simple distinction between them. And the simultaneous knowing and not knowing – or neither knowing nor not knowing – of the other (the other who is also the double) is integral to this ambiguous location.

If we return to Scrope Purvis, that neighbour or passer-by to whom the novel does not return, and to whom Clarissa Dalloway gives not even a subordinate clause's semi-attention, we find once again that the issue of knowing the other person is raised, but with a very different resonance. Here, in its entirety, is Purvis's brief paragraph, his minimal novelistic life:

> She stiffened a little on the kerb, waiting for Durtnall's van to pass. A charming woman, Scrope Purvis thought her (knowing her as one does know people who live next door to one in Westminster); a touch of the bird about her, of the jay, blue-green, light, vivacious, though she was over fifty, and grown very white since her illness. There she perched, never seeing him, waiting to cross, very upright. (3)

'A charming woman' is about as generic and impersonal a description as could be – as much of a cliché, a typical phrase for a lady, as the phrase Peter Walsh is said to have used of Clarissa when they were young, which so hurt and hurts her: 'the perfect hostess' (6, 53). 'A charming woman' implies neither intimacy nor any particular personal interest, though Purvis does pause to give voice in his thoughts to rather a colourful literary simile and he evidently knows that she has had some sort of illness that has left its mark. But then what is the force of the parenthetical 'knowing her'? At one level, it may simply mean that they are on speaking terms, they have been introduced, they know each other's names and some basic informational minimum about each other's lives, as then appears from the reference to the illness. But living next door is neither inherently a barrier to better or closer knowing nor, on the contrary, a guarantee of even such entry-level acquaintance. Later on, as I have described, we do meet, or rather see, the old lady in the window who is perhaps the neighbour on the other side from Scrope Purvis (or more likely, if this is a terrace, in the house behind); and she and Clarissa do not 'know' each other in Purvis's sense here at all.

Thus at the beginning and the end, with these differently known or unknown neighbours, the novel seems to plant a question about the degrees and forms of human connection and, concomitantly, of people's knowledge or knowing of one another. Without ever having met or spoken to her, Clarissa takes something from a woman to whom she feels a real attachment: the relationship may be (literally) one-sided – although that is not known – but it is nonetheless real to her. Scrope Purvis knows Clarissa in an almost entirely general or socialised way: sufficiently or insufficiently so as to characterise her with a conventional formula and for even his mode or degree of acquaintance to be stated in terms of social typicality: 'knowing her *as one does* know people who . . .'. In this first universe of knowing people there are only types (or Forsterian flat characters, perhaps); but in the other, between Clarissa and the old lady, there is little resemblance at all to the ordinary signs of social character and social interchange.

E. M. Forster's round and flat characters have enjoyed a lively existence ever since he created them in the late 1920s.[5] Ironically the flats have probably had far more attention than their sibling rounds, being always available for ready disparagement in critical discussions of all kinds. In fact, Forster did not make the distinction as a matter of authorial skill (where it would be a fault to be unable to bulk out your characters beyond the two-dimensional). Instead, he was talking about the degree of complexity that characters might have in relation to their relative significance in the story. Big part, more features; small part, basic type (or stereotype). That broad-brush distinction, flat in its own simple way, is what *Mrs Dalloway* dissolves. In that novel, you never know where you are with a character, because all the usual guidelines for distinguishing the major and the minor in the context of a given narrative have been withdrawn.

Looked at from this point of view, *Mrs Dalloway* appears much concerned with the question of ways of knowing other people and likely stories about them. There is even, on the part of some of the characters, an articulation of the difficulty – or the opportunity – that the inherent unknownness of people presents. Again there is an indication of this right at the beginning. Clarissa has been thinking (for no particular reason) about Peter Walsh who, in her mind, is interested, among many other things, in 'people's characters eternally' (6); and she has been going through her own eternal comparison of Peter with Richard Dalloway, re-convincing herself, as she will endeavour to do throughout the day, and has implicitly been doing throughout her life, that she had been right to marry one and not the other. Now she is watching the buses in Piccadilly and a new paragraph begins: 'She would not say of anyone in the world now that they were this or were that'; it ends, 'she would not say of Peter, she would not say of herself, I am this, I am that' (7). We should note that the uncertainty is linked to being older ('now'). It amounts to nothing less than a universal ('anyone in the world') refusal to categorise or fix.

This programmatic unknowing seems to suggest two doubts at once: about the quality of the knowing (of oneself or of others), and about the object of knowledge. In other words, without this being quite spelt out, the fact that I cannot know you is somehow the same proposition as you being essentially and inevitably not 'this or that', not fixed or definite and definable. From this it is only a small step to the notion that insofar as we do (and must) maintain relatively fixed and specifiable ideas about who we are or who others are, that is a necessary fiction, a realistic story. For convenience and for sheer survival: as Woolf puts it in 'Mr Bennett and Mrs Brown', 'it would be impossible to live for a year without disaster unless one practised character-reading and had some skill in the art'.[6] That is to say, ordinary living depends on treating people as characters to be read or interpreted, according to previously learned criteria ('some skill in the art'); and this practice is not some superfluous literary luxury, but vital ('without disaster').

The fictionality of selves and others can be, at times, a source of pleasure. There is the episode in *Mrs Dalloway* when Peter Walsh unthreateningly stalks a young woman who then turns the tables on him by disappearing through her front door and putting an end to the game. He ruefully but resignedly concludes:

> And it was smashed to atoms – his fun, for it was half made up, as he knew very well; invented, this escapade with the girl; made up, as one makes up the better part of life, he thought – making oneself up; making her up; creating an exquisite amusement, and something more. But odd it was, and quite true; all this one could never share – it smashed to atoms. (46)

'Making oneself up; making her up' is 'fun' and 'exquisite amusement', all acknowledged as conscious fantasy. And it is also 'the better part of life', not dismissed as secondary or false. Making up has many other suggestive associations too. It is one possible counterpart of losing, which is Peter Walsh's other habitual psychological mode: he is endlessly trying to make up for not getting Clarissa all those years ago, endlessly repeating to himself that he is 'not' in love. It can also refer to consolation and to reconciliation. You make up for a disappointment or any kind of negative experience by the compensation of putting something else in its place. You can even, linguistically at least, make up for lost time.[7] In Peter's pursuit of the girl, the making up is just pure fun because he doesn't in any sense 'know' her: they have no history or future and are simply playing a game without consequences on the spur of the moment. (In this respect, this miniature seduction drama contrasts radically with the story of Peter and Daisy, the young married woman in India with two small children whose divorce Peter is in London to initiate, and with whom, though he realises he never thinks about her, he is supposed to be going to begin a future life.)

The language of smashed atoms in the post-fun passage also recalls Woolf's essay 'Modern Fiction' in which experience is represented as a hail of atoms, too many to take in:

> The mind receives a myriad impressions – trivial, fantastic, evanescent, or engraved with the sharpness of steel. From all sides they come, an incessant shower of innumerable atoms, and as they fall, as they shape themselves into the life of Monday or Tuesday, the accent falls differently from of old; the moment of importance came not here but there; so that, if a writer were a free man and not a slave, if he could write what he chose, not what he must, if he could base his work upon his own feeling and not upon convention, there would be no plot, no comedy, no tragedy, no love interest or catastrophe in the accepted style, and perhaps not a single button sewn on as the Bond Street tailors would have it. Life is not a series of gig lamps symmetrically arranged; life is a luminous halo, a semi-transparent envelope surrounding us from the beginning of consciousness to the end.[8]

Woolf goes on to protest against the 'conventions' that writers are subject to in shaping the atomic stories according to recognisable genres; instead, the novelist's 'task' is to try to represent the 'luminous halo' that is 'life', 'a semi-transparent envelope surrounding us from the beginning of consciousness to the end'. This is then, in a stylistic tilt from the mystical to the polemical, restated as: 'the proper stuff of fiction is a little other than custom would have us believe it.'[9]

Let us note that for all her promotion of a quasi-mystical philosophy of 'life', Woolf nonetheless follows the most familiar – and conventional – of programmes in taking it for granted that the job of the writer is to represent life (and indeed that the job of the writer is a job at all: a worthwhile 'task'). If this has been taken as one of the key statements of a new modernistic paradigm, it is also, no less, a manifesto for realism: literature should convey real life.

There is another point to bring out about this passage in relation to Peter Walsh's 'made up' fantasy and made-up life. Woolf's author in 'Modern Fiction' is a receptacle for the falling atoms: he (or she) does not choose them, even though he may be active in what he does with them ('if he could write what he chose . . .'). Peter Walsh, on the other hand, is making up what he wants. He does not wait for the impressions, he actually contrives his own beautiful experience ('creating an exquisite amusement'). He is thus in one sense more actively a maker (up), playing and playing up a story from moment to moment and reading what he chooses into the real girl he is following.

What Peter's made-up scene then suggests is that there is no simple contrast between 'life' and the telling of it, whether life is seen as more like a series of gig lamps or more like a semi-transparent envelope. In Peter's case, life is itself already, and in yet another sense of the phrase, made up – put together, constructed – of stories: that is part of its substance or its mode of being. The stories may well be perfectly conventional or formulaic, as indeed is Peter's particular fantasy about the *passante* or passing woman, the classic dream girl spotted on the street. In this view of things, we make our daily lives in the ways that we find and tell stories about them; there is not first 'life' and then the representation of it.

It is a commonplace of criticism to denounce the mistake of treating fictional characters as if they were real people. But this objection harbours what I think is a mistaken assumption of its own: that real people are real people – prior to how they are imagined, including by themselves, or to the stories that are told about them. It seems to me that we are always, all the time, making people up, inventing them, reading them, and we do this to a large extent in line with plausible or likely paradigms of character and action and plot: of the kinds of things that people do, the kinds of ways that people act and think.[10] Conversely, these same paradigms make up a provisional – and always changing – basis for our own actions and responses and our own (limited) understanding of 'who we are'. Real life is already, in this small sense, literary: it's already to do with a play of likely and less likely stories and roles.

Developing Woolf's image, then, it could be said that in 'real life' as in novels, the stories that are experienced and the selves that figure in them, first, second and third persons, require a process of selection that inevitably takes in – admits – only a tiny fraction of all the possible events and people. But the selection is neither arbitrary nor automatic, and perhaps the filtering model that Woolf deploys for the author trimming down their mental inbox of 'impressions' is somewhat disingenuous. Woolf's argument suggests that the conventions – the suit buttons or the standard generic plotlines – can be discarded as simply inadequate for conveying the reality of life, which is not itself in question.

It is worth noticing, too, that Woolf is dismissive about fashion and clothing, mocking the masculine pretentiousness of the Bond Street tailors, and in this she perhaps herself shows up in moderately old-fashioned, anti-modern colours. In Baudelaire's *The Painter of Modern Life* (1863), there is a comparable emphasis on the multitude of 'impressions' marking the artist at every moment during the day. And as for Woolf, it is the artist's job to get this down, to re-present it. Yet for Baudelaire the detail of dressing seen on the street is not a sign of predictability or convention, but just the opposite: as *la mode*, as fashion, it is the paradigmatic instance of the ever-changing and exhilarating daily movement and moment of the present.[11]

If we confine ourselves to *Mrs Dalloway* alone, we can readily see that Woolf does seek to break the mould, to snap off the buttons of the established narrative patterns and the expected kinds of character. Keeping only to the big picture, her great innovation is to write a novel of courtship and marriage that is chronologically situated a full generation – thirty years – after the decisive events. But actually, nothing is fixed – nothing was fixed. These people did what people in novels do (and what the related assumptions of everyday life stories would suggest): that is, they fell in and out of love when they were young, and eventually settled on one of their possible candidates for marriage. And they settled down too – or Clarissa and Richard Dalloway and Sally Seton did, at least. For even more radically than if all the marriages had been unhappy, Woolf suggests that behind or within the settled life, a life without large regrets, much of the passionate instability and openness of the first moment, before the choice, may remain. Clarissa is still questioning her feelings for both Richard and Peter, decades after the decision between them, and even though she considers herself married to the right man. The radical gesture here is to undermine the conventional plot by keeping it, but putting it into a different frame. Woolf shows it to mask a whole subterranean field of different experience – unexplored, and unrepresented. The temporal distance achieves the same effect in another way, by focusing on a cast of characters who are not beautiful or eligible young people, but in their early to mid-fifties (incidentally, this is a novel that is extremely precise about ages).[12] Clarissa and Richard's daughter, Elizabeth, the only possible 'bright young thing' in the novel, is not one of the central characters.

In *Mrs Dalloway* Woolf does not only change the plot. As I began to indicate in the discussions of Scrope Purvis and the old lady in the house opposite, she also modifies the forms of representation for the novel's minor characters. Of these Doris Kilman is, so to speak, the dominant one: Miss Kilman has attracted plenty of critical attention because of her in-your-face poaching of Clarissa's daughter, and Clarissa's conscious resentment of her. There is also the memorable episode in the Army and Navy Stores, where Miss Kilman ungracefully buys a petticoat, stuffs herself with cakes in the restaurant, and is then humiliatingly abandoned by an Elizabeth dashing for freedom. But perhaps this character who herself protests at the way that the world has pushed her back has had her share of the critical foreground; and I want instead to turn attention to two other 'minor' female characters of the novel, both of them women so seemingly insignificant in its pages, and in the world in which they figure, that they may well escape our attention altogether.

My principal unheroine features in just a single scene, the lunch party given by Lady Bruton, attended by Richard Dalloway and Hugh Whitbread. Initially, a long sardonic description highlights the daily 'illusion' provided by the ritual serving of beautiful meals, as if without the involvement of money or work: the servants appear in the passive as 'a soundless and exquisite passing to and fro through swing doors of aproned, white-capped maids, handmaidens . . . adepts in a mystery or grand deception practised by hostesses in Mayfair from one-thirty to two' (88). But there is also a second woman at the table, and that is Lady Bruton's secretary, Milly Brush. Miss Brush, unlike the maids, is exempt from manual or 'handmaiden' labour, but although she has her place with the privileged, she is visible neither as one of them nor as part of the servants' performance. The novel gives her a name and a couple more sentences here and there across the six or seven pages that the luncheon takes up; but she is not accorded anything approaching a story or history of her own. There is no marked enigma about her and little to rouse curiosity on the part of either readers or other characters.

Here is Miss Brush's introduction, parenthetically on the end of a very long sentence that begins as a series of reflections on the character of Hugh Whitbread:

> for he would never lunch, for example, with Lady Bruton, whom he had known these twenty years, without bringing her in his outstretched hand a bunch of carnations, and asking Miss Brush, Lady Bruton's secretary, after her brother in South Africa, which, for some reason, Miss Brush, deficient though she was in every attribute of female charm, so much resented that she said 'Thank you, he's doing very well in South Africa', when for half-a-dozen years, he had been doing badly in Portsmouth. (88)

The crisp assurance of 'deficient as she was in every attribute of female charm' mocks both the generalising tendencies of narrators and, more particularly, their claims to 'know' or to read character and to have a language for it; the bite here comes from Miss Brush's allegedly uncharacteristic compliance on this occasion with social and feminine convention. Normally – 'deficient' as she is – she might have protested against the inaccuracy and told Hugh Whitbread what the narrator tells us, that in fact the brother (there is at least a brother) is in the south of England rather than in South Africa. To be charming and feminine is to preserve the polite surface.

Later, the charmlessness is expressly restated. We are given Miss Brush's musings about Hugh's appetite: 'one of the greediest men she had ever known, Milly Brush thought, who observed men with unflinching rectitude, and was capable of everlasting devotion, to her own sex in particular, being knobbed, scraped, angular, and entirely without feminine charm' (90). Notice that Miss Brush is herself a judge of character, a kind of surrogate for the narrator himself (or herself): she gets it right too, according to this one, observing men with 'unflinching rectitude'; and again, 'entirely without feminine charm' is on the cusp of being a backhanded compliment, delivered at once with some sympathy for the 'knobbed, scraped, angular' woman who has no physical or social attractions to assist her, and also with some disdain for the sorts of 'this or that' judgement that simply take up the clichés of conventional categories. An uncharming woman, the narrator thinks her.

Miss Brush's general capacity for 'everlasting devotion', narrowed down 'to her own sex in particular', is later further specified in her being said to be 'devoted' (92) to her employer. The closeness of the attachment sometimes appears in a near-identification. Lady Bruton, too, is 'angular' (the word is used twice of her), and she is anything but an embodiment of feminine charm. Her very name, Millicent Bruton, seems to suggest aggressively masculine qualities of militancy and brutality. She is awkward in her handling of the flowers Hugh has brought her, and she doesn't like small talk, what she calls 'trifling' (92) – wanting instead to get on to what is for her the main business of the lunch, the composition of a letter to the *Times*. Most revealingly of all, the two women have almost identical names: Milly is presumably short for Millicent, and the first three letters of their surnames are the same. This cannot be accidental, and yet it is easy to pass by, or brush off, just as Milly herself fades into insignificance beside the dominant Lady Bruton. At the end of the lunch, this could not be more explicit: 'Miss Brush disappeared into the background', we are told, while Lady Bruton stands on the doorstep with her dog, 'handsome; very erect' (94). It is also Lady Bruton's half-asleep dreams that the narrative then follows as she snoozes on her sofa after her guests have left – while Milly Brush has gone from the novel for good.[13]

What, if anything, can be imagined of Milly Brush's life, of her inner or her outward history before her settling down with Lady Bruton? There is, as we shall see in a moment, one solitary paragraph in which we gain a glimpse of something like a possible personal past. This occurs after the lunch conversation has turned to Peter Walsh being back in London, and Milly Brush is both inside and outside the compass of the characters' thoughts:

> They all smiled. Peter Walsh! And Mr Dalloway was genuinely glad, Milly Brush thought; and Mr Whitbread thought only of his chicken.
>   Peter Walsh! All three, Lady Bruton, Hugh Whitbread, and Richard Dalloway, remembered the same thing – how passionately Peter had been in love; been rejected; gone to India; come a cropper; made a mess of things; and Richard Dalloway had a very great liking for the dear old fellow too. Milly Brush saw that; saw a depth in the brown of his eyes; saw him hesitate; consider; which interested her, as Mr Dalloway always interested her, for what was he thinking, she wondered, about Peter Walsh? (90–1)

Milly is positioned, once again, as an observer: she interprets 'Mr Dalloway' as being 'genuinely glad' when 'They all smiled', a trio to which she doesn't belong; the disparaging thought about Hugh and his food is also Milly's, because only she (not the narrator) would think of him as 'Mr Whitbread'. The separation of Milly from her companions is even clearer in what follows, when 'All three, Lady Bruton, Hugh Whitbread, and Richard Dalloway, remembered the same thing', which is stated from narrative authority, not from the perspective of Milly's speculations. At this point the to and fro between the narrator and Milly as co-respondents to the scene becomes more and more difficult to disentangle. It is as though Milly really is a surrogate for or equivalent of an observing though not an omniscient narrator, and as though, too, her drive to consider and guess at the meanings of what she sees and hears might itself be prompted by her lack of inclusion in what is going on – and in what went on all those years ago. Her position, in other words, is halfway between the presumed detachment of a general narrator and the interested participation of a full character.

Then, following a first move back to Milly, as personally curious about Richard – 'what was he thinking, she wondered?' – we enter a short new paragraph which answers that question but not, it turns out, for Milly herself:

> That Peter Walsh had been in love with Clarissa; that he would go back directly after lunch and find Clarissa; that he would tell her, in so many words, that he loved her. Yes, he would say that. (91)

The narrator is giving what has to be taken as the truth about what Richard is presently thinking and planning; it is as if she (or he) is directly responding to her co-narrator, Milly, in a conversation they are having over the heads, as it were, of the principal three round the table. The narrator is someone for Milly to talk to, someone to whom she offers her own readings or questions about the others' thoughts. Yet of course, this conversation is not two-way, as the official narrator sees or divines what Milly can only 'wonder' about; and she does not or cannot communicate to Milly what she (or he) communicates to the novel's readers, as here. Moreover, the narrator knows everything about Milly (however little is told), and now, following the expression of the answer to Milly's question, attention returns to her. This is the beginning of the paragraph mentioned before, when Milly has her tiny romantic moment:

> Milly Brush once might almost have fallen in love with these silences; and Mr Dalloway was always so dependable; such a gentleman too. (91)

There it is, in the most plangently conditional form, the declaration of a long ago possible passion. *Might almost* have fallen in love is desperately poor. She didn't; it wasn't even that she 'might have', but that she 'almost' might have – and not so much with Mr Dalloway himself as with 'these silences', these gaps when there is the space for making a mystery of him, for wondering what he is thinking. That what he actually *is* thinking, at this moment, is how much he loves Clarissa – not Milly – only adds to the poignancy of the semi-admission.

Milly Brush's falling in love is thus declared only in the form of its never even having happened. In some ways this resembles the missed passion of Baudelaire's speaker in the poem 'A une passante' – 'To a Passing Woman' – where the woman seen on the street is adored in her very disappearance, in the impossibility of their love. Past unfulfilled conditional: 'O toi que j'eusse aimée, ô toi qui le savais!'[14] – 'Oh you whom I would have loved, oh you who knew it!' But this is stronger or closer than Milly Brush's situation in at least two ways. In the poem, there is a question of possible reciprocity or complicity, whereas Milly does not go so far as to imagine feelings being returned to her from the 'gentleman' with the silences whose thoughts, whatever else they might be, are not, and she knows it, of her. And Milly *knows* Richard – she graces him with the solid labels of 'dependable' and 'gentleman' – whereas the attraction of the *passante* is that she could be anyone, she is open to every fantasy and projection on the part of the speaker. Milly's loss is therefore more personal, which in turn is reinforced by her never having been an object of special interest for Richard, despite their social relations over many years (as 'once' implies).

In the context of the novel as a whole, the pathos of Milly's moment of almost loving comes from its being a distant mirror of the erotic attachments of the principal characters. Even Hugh Whitbread belongs here, because there is an ancient rumour that he may once have kissed Sally Seton in 'the smoking-room' (62, 161) – a putative incident whose status as almost absurd seems to heighten the difference of Sally's kiss back then with the as yet undetermined Clarissa. All these characters – Clarissa, Richard, Peter, Sally and Hugh – had and have their loves; and for some of them those possibilities 'once' that were not fulfilled, or not settled into a marital future, are still active now as part of their live day-to-day experience. Such possibilities were also of interest – passionate interest – both to the objects of love and to their friends: witness, just now, the immediate collective response when 'All three . . . remembered the same thing', the familiar story of Peter having been in love with Clarissa. For Milly, there is no shared history of that kind.

After its extraordinary – but only passing – reference to what might, just almost might have been for Milly Brush, the narrative turns to the present moment and generalises it to Milly's quotidian way of being in the world:

> Now, being forty, Lady Bruton had only to nod, or turn her head a little abruptly, and Milly Brush took the signal, however deeply she might be sunk in these reflections of a detached spirit, of an uncorrupted soul whom life could not bamboozle, because life had not offered her a trinket of the slightest value; not a curl, smile, lip, cheek, nose; nothing whatever; Lady Bruton had only to nod, and Perkins was instructed to quicken the coffee. (91)

The first sentence has the effect of merging Milly and Lady Bruton – since it must be Milly who is forty (Lady Bruton's age is given precisely as sixty-two, and she was involved in the planning of military action some time in the 1880s).[15] The hanging participle, however, leaves the question of who is who momentarily suspended: it is as if there is no real separation, grammatically or psychologically, between the two women, whose communication is automatic ('Milly Brush took the signal') and overrides all other considerations ('however deeply she might be sunk . . .'). This is how Milly Brush has ended up, 'being forty', as an extension of the older, more powerful woman who yet retains or has acquired an almost otherworldly apartness – the 'detached spirit' and 'uncorrupted soul' – through her very abandonment by 'life'. Like the negation of a love poem, her missing of curl, smile, lip, cheek, nose – of any 'trinket' or charm – has condemned her to this half-existence as Millicent Bruton's faded lackey. Somewhere too here there lurks a contrast with Hugh Whitbread's wife, for whom he uxoriously seeks to buy jewellery shortly after the lunch and to whom, dull and ever-ailing as she is understood to be, 'life' has offered rather more than it has to Milly Brush.

The one-sidedness and assumed unrequitedness of Milly's potential wishful attachment to Richard Dalloway is bound up with a class difference that is all the more forceful for never being explicitly declared. Along with her lack of feminine charm, Milly's relative subordination – seen but not seen, there but not there, part of the upper-class group round the table but also an employee – has evidently disqualified her for the kinds of attraction and attachment that have been the norm for most of her dining companions.[16] The novel itself appears to replicate this half-and-half situation by making Milly Brush into a sort of semi-character, with very few sentences given her individually, very little in the way of a narratable private history, and a compensatory role as a secondary partner to the narrator.

Finally, and at the end of the novel itself, let us consider a second neglected middle-class woman: another obscure lady who has a there-and-not-there position among the novel's main people. Ellie Henderson is one of several figures from the distant past who reappear at Clarissa's party. The most striking of these is Miss Helena Parry, Clarissa's aunt, because she had earlier been mentioned, in Peter's thoughts, as no more: 'She was dead now' (138). As a result, her presence partly operates as a kind of resurrection in the face of the announcement, also at the party, of the death of Septimus Smith. But this contingent rescue – here she is! – also suggests that a person who is out of sight and out of mind is in effect non-existent, for those for whom he or she fails to figure as a topic of story and speculation. This, I have been trying to show, is the situation of someone like Milly Brush, who barely even has a name of her own, and who musters a sort of half-life in her faithful service and her private, 'detached' reflections on the people around her, for whom she herself hardly exists. And in a posthumous sphere of existence, it resembles the situations of those dead library Lives that no reader ever looks into.

Ellie Henderson is such another half-character. She is in fact a 'cousin' of Clarissa's, a connection that has the effect of highlighting the social distance between them. Ellie features for a moment prior to the party when Richard Dalloway persuades his wife to invite her (Clarissa thinks her too dowdy).[17] She duly and dully turns up as one of the first arrivals, and is among the last to leave, having spoken to no one apart from Richard, momentarily. As with Milly Brush, the narrative gives Ellie Henderson a certain amount of attention, certainly more attention than she gets from any of Mrs Dalloway's guests. This includes a summary of the course of her life so far, and also, again as with Miss Brush, an imperceptibly close modulation between her thoughts and the narrator's judgements. At the party, Miss Henderson is worrying about the draughts from open windows now that young women wear more exposing clothes:

> It was the girls she thought of, the young girls with their bare shoulders, she herself always having been a wisp of a creature, with her thin hair and meagre profile; though now, past fifty, there was beginning to shine through

some mild beam, something purified into distinction by years of self-abnegation but obscured again, perpetually, by her distressing gentility, her panic fear, which arose from three hundred pounds income, and her weaponless state (she could not earn a penny) and it made her timid, and more and more disqualified year by year to meet well-dressed people who did this sort of thing every night of the season, merely telling their maid 'I'll wear so and so,' whereas Ellie Henderson ran out nervously and bought cheap pink flowers, half-a-dozen, and then threw a shawl over her old black dress. (143)

The ramshackle sentence moves from Ellie's concern for the girls, to a thought (which could be either her own or the narrator's) about her youthful wispiness, to what is definitely only the narrator's reflection on her 'mild beam' and its perpetual extinction, 'obscured again'. There are numerous points of comparison with that other half-lit character, Milly Brush, not least in that both are compared, implicitly and explicitly, with more affluent women: Milly with the one she works for, and Ellie with Clarissa, who is the same age, who is her cousin and who buys the flowers 'herself', in the novel's very first sentence, because she chooses to, not because she has no servant to do it for her. For both these women, the narrator ventures a social critique of their obscure position, in Ellie's case economically detailed (her income, her lack of earning power, her gradual loss, through ageing – 'disqualified year by year' – of the only (non-)occupation for which her class and sex have fitted her). Unlike Milly Brush, Ellie Henderson has anxious emotions – timidity, 'panic fear' and nervousness; these are attributed to her straitened material situation. But in a comparable way, Milly's lack of 'charm' comes, according to the sympathetic narrator, from life not having offered her 'a single trinket' – not beauty, but also not money or status. And both women are observers of the social scenes of which they are on the margins: even though there is no one for her to talk to, Ellie 'felt that they were all such interesting people to watch' (144).

With Ellie, it turns out, the watching goes one stage further. At first this is put with perfect parenthetical understatement: '(She must remember everything to tell Edith)' (143). The promise of future recounting is repeated a little later when the party's celebrity guest appears and Ellie gets a tiny paragraph of her own:

The Prime Minister? Was it really? Ellie Henderson marvelled. What a thing to tell Edith! (146)

Later, in the very last paragraph of the novel, the same thought is expanded:

Even Ellie Henderson was going, nearly last of all, though no one had spoken to her, but she had wanted to see everything, to tell Edith. (165)

Insignificant Ellie Henderson is there at the very end, 'nearly last of all' in the novel as at the party. Not only is she an observer, but she is going to tell the story. Having an Edith to tell, for whom to remember everything, gives Ellie a role; story-making gives her a life. The party will have been what she makes of it, what she makes it up to have been; and it will have a continued existence in the sharing of the subsequent account. At the same time, Ellie's narrative will be another version of the same story of the party that has just been told in the novel now reaching its end; and we readers, in turn, are thus in the position of Edith. On its tiny scale, this little drama of Ellie's recounting is an everyday echo of the novel's own grander narrative of the scene, with its juxtaposition of Septimus's death and Clarissa's life-affirming party:

> The young man had killed himself; but she did not pity him; with the clock striking the hour, one, two, three, she did not pity him, with all this going on. There! The old lady had put out her light! the whole house was dark now with this going on, she repeated. (158)

Repetition and continuation work alongside and against the death that Clarissa acknowledges. 'All this going on . . . this going on' is itself repeated, just like the routines of the old lady going down for the night and the chiming of the clock; even the words – 'she repeated' – enact the process that keeps things ticking on by doing and saying them over and over; by continuing the story. 'All this going on' is the party, but also life, in both its banality and its eventfulness. The phrase encapsulates the combination of occurrence and extension that is also signified by Ellie's projected story of the evening; but it also implies the surprise of the unanticipated.

In ordinary usage, 'What's going on?' suggests something unexpected or unusual, something that calls for special explanation. But it also suggests that whatever's happening is worth turning into a story. The capacity or curiosity to talk about what's going on perhaps indicates a fundamental narrative urge: in another common turn of phrase, 'going on about it' is explicitly representational, an excess of storytelling. That is why readers are all in the place of Edith, and why *Mrs Dalloway*, in its way, is Woolf's own complex affirmation of life that 'goes on' – life in which we seek and make stories in order to survive, to keep going on, and keep going on about it. It is shadowed, with their obscure late beams, by the just-glimpsed other stories of the women who lack the means of staging a special event, but who keep going all the same with the life that they too observe and narrate. *Mrs Dalloway* tells, obliquely, obscurely, the story of these other smaller stories that keep life going: these everyday stories that sustain their subordinate tellers in the midst of the larger realities where they themselves fade into the background.

AFTERSTORY

Time passes. In the middle of Mrs Ramsay's dinner party in *To the Lighthouse*, she is taken back to a day twenty years before that she spent with some people called the Mannings, with whom she is no longer in touch. One of her guests, William Bankes, has received a letter:

> So he had actually heard from her this evening! And was Carrie still living at Marlow, and was everything still the same? Oh she could remember it as if it were yesterday – going on the river, feeling very cold. But if the Mannings made a plan they stuck to it. Never should she forget Herbert killing a wasp with a teaspoon on the bank! And it was still going on, Mrs Ramsay mused, gliding like a ghost among the chairs and tables of that drawing-room on the banks of the Thames where she had been so very, very cold twenty years ago; but now she went among them like a ghost; and it fascinated her, as if, while she had changed, that particular day, now become very still and beautiful, had remained there, all those years.[18]

A trivial event, William Bankes getting this letter, has triggered not only the memory of 'that particular day', but a sense of its fixing outside a continuing sequence, 'very still and beautiful'. That long-past day is no longer itself; or rather, it is what it is, now, by appearing as a moveless object of contemplation that 'fascinated her'. Gone time and present time are interchanged as Mrs Ramsay (who is simultaneously eating her dinner and talking to Mr Bankes) smoothly 'glides like a ghost', as if the old day were the living reality. Her gliding gives a new gloss to the simpler philosophical demarcations of 'Think of a kitchen table . . . when you're not there'.[19] Small and specific events and explanations – the feeling of cold, the tale of the teaspoon-killed wasp – come precisely back, 'as if it were yesterday': back in the telling image of perfect recall, and the cliché that fixes the characters once and for all: 'if the Mannings made a plan they stuck to it.' That very description is now what sticks to them. These Mannings, like the ghost of Mrs Ramsay, are imaginary characters, come from another time; with their limited, set-piece performance, they have flitted into the present moment of the dinner party in the image of a changeless past.

Once upon a time, this decades-old day of Mrs Ramsay's memory was not the start of a marvellous story; like most days, it was neither a beginning nor a culmination of anything in particular. It has just happened to come back, for a moment; or Mrs Ramsay has happened to go back to it. For most readers of *To the Lighthouse*, too, it is not a passage that remains in the mind – and in this it follows the experience of Mrs Ramsay, for whom these Mannings are forgotten from one year to the next until suddenly Mr Bankes's letter has brought them back (and brought back, for her, a vision of herself in another, younger and long-ago life).

In their transitory, equivocal existence at this point in the novel, the Mannings are not, novelistically, alone. Woolf enjoys popping in characters of this curious type who have no consequence within the ongoing present story of a narrated day or time. The outlandishly named Scrope Purvis at the start of *Mrs Dalloway* is one of these, and the Mannings also belong to a teasing Woolfian class of otherwise insignificant characters who reappear or are resurrected, at least in name, from one novel to another. In *Mrs Dalloway*, they are there again (or before) as the possible hosts for the occasion when Clarissa met Sally (again, many years before the present time):

> Take Sally Seton; her relation in the old days with Sally Seton. Had not that, after all, been love?
> She sat on the floor – that was her first impression of Sally – she sat on the floor with her arm round her knees, smoking a cigarette. Where could it have been? The Mannings? The Kinloch-Joneses? Some party (where she could not be certain). (28)

Here the capsule memory blurs the Mannings, who may have been the Kinloch-Joneses in any case (and for all we know, may not be 'the' Mannings of Mrs Ramsay's abandoned acquaintance). 'Some party', no more, as a setting for Sally so casually sitting on the floor. Some story, one day, back then.

NOTES

1. See Virginia Woolf, 'The Lives of the Obscure' (1925), in *The Essays of Virginia Woolf*, vol. 4, ed. Andrew McNeillie (London: Hogarth Press, 1994), 118.
2. These include, ironically, Richard Edgeworth and Thomas Day, two of the eighteenth-century scientists, inventors, and entrepreneurs now revived and celebrated through Jenny Uglow's collective biography of them, *The Lunar Men: The Friends Who Made the Future* (London: Faber & Faber, 2002).
3. Woolf, *Mrs Dalloway* (1925), ed. David Bradshaw (Oxford: Oxford University Press, 2000), 3. Further references will be given within the main text.
4. As a surname, however, 'Scrope' does have a history, and one that may well have impinged upon Woolf through her reading for 'The Pastons and Chaucer' (1925), an essay she wrote for *The Common Reader* at the same time as she was working on *Mrs Dalloway*. In the fifteenth-century Paston

letters, Scrope appears as a determined but unsuccessful suitor for the hand of Elizabeth Paston (who subsequently marries someone else). See Diane Watt (ed. and trans.), *The Paston Women: Selected Letters* (Cambridge: D. S. Brewer, 2004), especially 116–17, letter of Elizabeth Clere to John Paston I, 29 June[?] 1449. In the order of the narrative of *Mrs Dalloway*, Scrope Purvis appears (and disappears) before either Peter Walsh or Richard Dalloway, who were both Clarissa's suitors, are brought into literary existence: so he is indeed a sort of fleeting and initially prominent candidate for a close acquaintance who never quite makes it across the threshold into the main structure of the novel.

5. See E. M. Forster, *Aspects of the Novel* (1927), ed. Oliver Stallybrass (London: Penguin, 1990).
6. Woolf, 'Character in Fiction' (1924), in *The Essays of Virginia Woolf*, vol. 3, ed. Andrew McNeillie (London: Hogarth Press, 1988), 421. 'Character in Fiction' is one version of the essay better known as 'Mr Bennett and Mrs Brown'; see further Chapter 12, 'We're Getting There'.
7. For more on the multiple meanings of making up see Chapter 6, above.
8. Woolf, 'Modern Fiction' (1925), *Essays*, vol. 3, 160–1.
9. Woolf, 'Modern Fiction', 161.
10. Woolf herself makes the point about real-life reading directly: 'I have said that people have to acquire a good deal of skill in character-reading' (*Essays*, vol. 3, 421), and in the sentence quoted above: 'it would be impossible to live for a year without disaster unless one practised character-reading and had some skill in the art'.
11. See Charles Baudelaire, *Le Peintre de la vie moderne* (1863), in *Œuvres complètes*, ed. Marcel A. Ruff (Paris, Seuil, 1968), esp. 553: 'Si une mode, une coupe de vêtement a été légèrement transformée, si les nœuds de rubans, les boucles ont été détrônés par les cocardes, . . . croyez qu'à une distance énorme *son œil d'aigle* l'a déjà deviné'; 'If a fashion, the cut of a garment, has been slightly altered in form, if ribbon ties or buckles have been dethroned by rosettes, . . . you can be sure that *his eagle eye* has already guessed it at an enormous distance.'
12. Clarissa herself is fifty-one: 'She had just broken into her fifty-second year' (31).
13. Although she is not present, Milly is subsequently mentioned, by Lady Bruton, at Clarissa's party, when she has a brief conversation with Peter Walsh: 'But her house, her servants, her good friend Milly Brush – did he remember her? – were all there only asking to be used if – if they could be of help, in short' (155). As with Hugh Whitbread, the remembering of Milly, the employee euphemistically described as a 'good friend', does not go without saying.

14. Baudelaire, 'À une passante', line 14, *Œuvres complètes*, 101.
15. At forty, Milly is closer in age to Woolf (born in 1882) when she wrote the novel in the early 1920s than are the main characters.
16. Nothing is said of marital or amorous inclinations for Lady Bruton (either towards her or on her part) at any point in her life. At most, the picture of her tomboy childhood with her brothers in Devon functions as a retrospectively confirming prelude to her commanding, quasi-masculine identity.
17. On a June day in 1923 – the month when *Mrs Dalloway* is set – Woolf records in her diary how Mrs Asquith ('I was impressed'), at a party given by Lady Ottoline Morrell 'was very affable with "people" when she had to be; sat on the window sill talking to a black shabby embroideress, to whom Ott. is being kind. Thats one of her horrors – she's always being kind in order to say to herself at night & then Ottoline invites the poor little embroideress to her party, & so to round off her own picture of herself'; *The Diary of Virginia Woolf*, ed. Anne Olivier Bell, vol. 2, 1920–24 (1978; Harmondsworth: Penguin, 1981), Monday 4 June (describing a party on the previous Saturday), 244–5. The point in common between the reported scene and the novel is that in both there is a needy woman who is charitably invited. Interestingly, it is the *Diary* episode that is consciously about the elaboration of a persona by both narrator and character. Woolf imagines Lady Ottoline approving the self-image she has confirmed through her patronage of the Ellie-like figure, 'to round off her own picture of herself'; and then immediately upbraids herself for her own construction of Ottoline: 'To sneer like this has a physical discomfort in it.'
18. Woolf, *To the Lighthouse* (1927), ed. Margaret Drabble (Oxford: Oxford University Press, 1992), 118–19.
19. Woolf, *To the Lighthouse*, 22.

14

'I Had Barbara'

Women's Ties and Wharton's 'Roman Fever'*

The setting of Edith Wharton's short story 'Roman Fever' (1934) is consciously casual. Two wealthy American widows with 'time to kill' sit chatting through the afternoon, on the terrace of a restaurant in Rome, overlooking the ruins of the ancient city.[1] They have known each other off and on all their lives. Both have daughters who are at present out together, as they speak, with two eligible young Italian men; and the women recall their own courting days, also together, also in Rome. There is a risky edge to this talk because they had both been in love with the same man, and knew it at the time. One of the women had been engaged to him, and duly married him, yet it is she, Mrs Slade, who now asks herself, in relation to the other one, 'Would she never cure herself of envying her?' (17) – and who pushes the conversation forwards with further questions.

In its final pages, the story moves into high gear with the production, one after another, of three interlocking secrets from that earlier time. Mrs Ansley had received a letter from Delphin Slade inviting her to meet him one night at the Colosseum. The first thrust comes from Mrs Slade declaring that it was she, out of jealousy, who wrote that letter, in an attempt to trick her rival into a dangerous adventure. (Behind the stratagem lay the now repeated story of an old great-aunt who, by sending her out one cold night to the Forum 'because they were in love with the same man' (18), had caused her sister's death.) For Grace Ansley, this admission ruins the memory of 'the only letter I ever had from him' (21), and Mrs Slade's triumph seems to be confirmed. But then – return blow – Mrs Ansley reveals that the date did in fact take place (she replied to the letter). Mrs Slade recovers from this with difficulty:

---

* First published in *Differences* 17:3 (Fall 2006).

'I oughtn't to begrudge it to you, I suppose. After all, I had everything; I had him for twenty-five years. And you had nothing but that one letter he didn't write.' (24)

With perfect pacing, Wharton then completes the series of revelations and reversals, ending the story like this:

Mrs Ansley was again silent. At length she turned toward the door of the terrace. She took a step, and turned back, facing her companion.

'I had Barbara,' she said, and began to move ahead of Mrs Slade toward the stairway. (24)

'I had Barbara' is the clinching shock announcement. We take it to mean, as must Mrs Slade, that Delphin Slade was the father of Barbara Ansley, conceived that night of the meeting at the Colosseum. The scandalous information then appears to sort out several doubts and suspicions that Wharton has carefully planted during the course of the narrative. Mrs Slade envies Mrs Ansley her bright, 'dynamic' daughter Barbara and cannot understand how two such 'exemplary characters' as Grace and Horace Ansley could have produced her (16–17); she, meanwhile, is disappointed in her own too perfect Jenny. Grace had been ill after her late-night 'sight-seeing' (19) all those years ago, and she was 'married to Horace Ansley two months afterward' (22). If Barbara is now shown to be Delphin's daughter, then these anomalies seem to be cleared up: Grace was quickly married because she was pregnant, and Barbara is after all the daughter of the dynamic Delphin Slade.

Grace Ansley's punchline – 'I had Barbara' – rounds off the series of blows initiated by her ancient rival. A final detail appears to confirm that the relations between the two women have shifted, as Mrs Ansley, previously seen as the more timid and passive of the two, 'began to move ahead'. Thus the battle that has taken place this present afternoon seems both to repeat and complete the one that occurred a generation before. Then, Alida had taken the initiative in attempting to punish Grace for her interest in her fiancé. She had sent the fake letter that was meant to lead to a long, lonely wait at the entrance to the Colosseum, but in fact her action had the effect of bringing about exactly what she was seeking to avoid, a rendezvous between the two potential lovers. Today, unaware of what happened between Grace and Delphin as a result of her letter, Mrs Slade has been continuing to attempt to control the future. Her renewed jealousy of Grace is prompted by a 'prophetic flight' (17) in which she imagines Grace settled in grandmotherly contentment near her sparkling daughter's family. It is this fantasy – 'Would she never cure herself of envying her?' – that sets off the conversational prod that is meant to humiliate Grace once more, but instead – and again as before – has the opposite result.

When the story is reread in the knowledge of what is revealed at the end, many phrases seem to take on a second, confirming meaning that did not appear the first time. One of the girls is described as a 'rare accident' (14). The two women are 'old lovers of Rome' (11). Grace's knitting collapses in 'a panic-stricken heap' (20); 'one, two, three – slip' (16) seems to point to a fall, not a pattern. Violence is everywhere: in 'so purposeless a wound' (21), verbally inflicted, or in the 'time to kill', where the leisurely cliché now sounds openly murderous – time *to kill*. On the second reading, we see significance in the 'mutual confession' (13) that at first seemed only to refer to middle-aged women's regret at the dullness of their lives in comparison with their daughters'. Great-aunt Harriet, who had sent her sister out to her death, 'confessed it years afterwards' (18), just as Mrs Slade owns up to her own attempt to follow the great-aunt's example. Long ago, when she was the Ansleys' neighbour in New York, Mrs Slade had joked that 'I'd rather live opposite a speak-easy for a change' (12): belatedly, the speak-easy's double suggestion of transgression and confession has now turned the joke against her.

In going over the story again and finding hitherto unnoticed indications of what happened – the old story that the current story brings out – we are in the same position as the two women characters. They find themselves engaged in a process of reinterpretation and reconstruction as they go back over the events of twenty-five years before, as well as over their subsequent views of the other: 'So these two ladies visualized each other, each through the wrong end of her little telescope' (14). Each has partial and sometimes mistaken knowledge, and the present conversation causes the emergence of what had previously been hidden from both. Seemingly tangential elements in the narrative also suggest, the second time, the need for this kind of reappraisal of the situation, by readers and protagonists alike. Grace Ansley concurs with her companion's remark about the 'beautiful' view of the Palatine from where they are seated:

> 'It always will be, to me,' assented her friend Mrs Ansley, with so slight a stress on the 'me' that Mrs Slade, though she noticed it, wondered if it were not merely accidental, like the random underlinings of old-fashioned letter-writers. (10)

On the second reading we know, as Mrs Slade has also found out, that there is more of a 'me' in Grace Ansley than had been imagined. She did not initiate, but she did go along with, the illicit tryst with Delphin Slade. Also, the very idea of the 'merely accidental' is discredited in this story: accidents happen not by chance, but in relation to particular designs and purposes that go wrong – both those in the past, and those in the present conversation. 'Like the random underlinings of old-fashioned letter-writers'? After the first reading, we know that in this story there need be nothing random or simply decorative about an old-time letter like the one that Alida Slade once signed with the initials 'D.S.'; nor are old-fashioned ladies, like Great-aunt Harriet, as innocent or haphazard in their ways as might be thought. Whatever the truth of the 'tradition' (18) of Harriet's youthful misdemeanour, as a tale it was effective both as a deterrent – 'Mother used to frighten us with the story', says Grace – and as an example to follow, as Alida then did when 'you frightened *me* with it' (19): Mrs Slade's characteristically conscious 'stress on the "me"'.

If the interpretation and use of stories is an issue within this one, there is also overt reference, by both characters and narrator, to confusions between different levels of language, making it difficult to know which elements are to be taken as central to a main story, and which as 'merely' metaphorical or accidental. 'Well, I mean figuratively' (9), Barbara is heard to say to Jenny as the two girls depart; 'figuratively' here refers to metaphorical knitting, which in fact is what Grace will literally be doing on the next page, though with additions of emotion and opulence that immediately detract from the bare fact: 'Half guiltily' – one more phrase that resonates differently on the second reading – 'she drew from her handsomely mounted black handbag a twist of crimson silk run through by two fine knitting needles' (10). Sliding into suggestion, literal knitting itself becomes ominous once more – 'one, two, three – slip.'[2] In New York, when their husbands were alive, Grace and Alida 'had lived opposite each other – actually as well as figuratively – for years' (12), the two would-be contrasting adverbs thrust into the middle of an otherwise innocuous clause, and raising a question about how, exactly, their meanings are to be understood. At one point Mrs Ansley takes up her knitting 'almost furtively' and Mrs Slade takes 'sideway note of this activity' – as though furtive or almost furtive herself, but also, in this story, as a matter of marginal uncertainty: only in light of the later revelations is it clear which gestures and which words need to be actively noted or interpreted. And at almost the end, when 'A stout lady in a dust-coat suddenly appeared, asking in broken Italian if any one had seen the elastic band which held together her tattered Baedecker' (23), she seems to be both a crazy diversion, a trivial distraction from the suspended drama, and also, equally, a comically allegorical sideshow that embodies the unravelling – 'broken' language, broken guidebook – of previously settled stories of the ladies' youthful past.

Whether trivially touristic or highly serious – as always, in this story, both and either are possible – allusions to classical culture are scattered throughout

'Roman Fever'. The letter from 'Delphin' proves oracular in its production of a future event. The story's setting above the ruins of Rome provides the backdrop for the emergence of long-buried stories, and for the gladiatorial violence of Mrs Slade/'slayed'. As in a Greek tragedy, Mrs Ansley's face shows a 'mask' (20); at one point she 'looked straight out at the great accumulated wreckage of passion and splendour at her feet' (17). In its own minor key, the story could even be taken as a modern version of *Oedipus*. As in Sophocles' drama, what happens is not so much a new action as a conversation which, driving to its painful denouement, goes over ancient events, showing their significance to be quite different from what participants had imagined. Oedipus finds that a man he once murdered was his own father; that Polybus, the man he thought was his father, was not; and that Jocasta, the woman he married, was his birth mother. In 'Roman Fever', too, there is a revelation involving both illicit sexuality and mistaken paternity. The two families that 'actually, as well as figuratively' 'lived opposite each other' are in one sense the same family – more actually than 'actually' first suggested – conjoined by girls who turn out to have the same father. In 'Roman Fever', the attempt to ward off a feared event precipitates its happening; and so for Oedipus the fulfilment of the oracle that he will murder his father and marry and have children with his mother is enabled by the successive attempts, by his birth parents and later himself, to avert it (the newborn baby is exposed, and does not know his first parents; the young man flees those he wrongly thinks are his parents, and thereby encounters first Laius, his father, and then Jocasta).

To make such a grand comparison is perhaps to do an injustice to 'Roman Fever', a story without such classical or universal affiliations – or destinies – as Sophocles' *Oedipus*. For one thing, there is nothing at stake in the modern tale beyond the private concerns of two well-off, unoccupied women. In *Oedipus*, on the other hand, the inquiry that leads eventually to the discovery of Oedipus' other history, his 'true' identity, is initiated – by Oedipus himself – as a matter of social urgency: the city is suffering from a plague and the oracle has said that the person responsible for the pollution, Laius' murderer years ago, must be tracked down. The strong point of likeness between the ancient drama and the modern story is that in each, the action consists only of conversation and its accompanying emotions; words alone have the effect of changing the sense of the past and, thereby, of changing the characters' understanding of themselves and their place in the present time.

It would also be possible, in different ways, to look at 'Roman Fever' as a female version of the Oedipal paradigm. Freud adopted Sophocles' drama as his literary template for thinking about children's – essentially, boys' – development to adulthood, from early years of incestuous longings and rivalrous hatred, out into the wider world of the cultural community in which the loss of their princely uniqueness – 'His Majesty the Baby' – was compensated by the adult privileges of a life beyond the confines of the first family.³ The girl had no comparable story; rather, in Freud's attempts to consider her different development, she ended up only – at best – a misfit, forever unconsciously seeking the masculinity of which she was deprived. Feminists since Freud's own time have regularly protested against this overt secondarisation of femininity, but many too have understood the theory as a useful allegory of the complexities of women's psychological placement in a patriarchal society. In this context 'Roman Fever', written quite literally from the women's point of view, as Grace and Alida sit overlooking the valued remains of a violent masculine civilisation, might seem to lend support to two different perspectives on women's lives in a modern but age-old patriarchal culture.

From the first point of view, Mrs Ansley and Mrs Slade have both lived the conventional feminine lives of girl, wife, mother and widow; their identities have been primarily in relation to husbands secured, then lived with, then lost. Mrs Slade was proud to see herself admired as '*the* Slade's wife' (13). After the death of her husband and, prior to that, of their son, 'There was nothing left but to mother her daughter' (13), presented less as compensation for her losses (Jenny's, too) than as a poor third choice. '[N]othing left but . . .' also seems to echo the *ennui* that has led to the two ladies' spending the afternoon talking – the equivalent, on this particular day, of the third-choice outlet for unused energies. '[S]ometimes I get tired just looking – even at this', says Grace; 'Her gesture was now addressed to the stupendous scene at their feet' (10). With nothing going on in their own lives – no one to tend – the women are jaded sightseers, and conversation is tediously time-filling, time-killing, before – and alongside – its secret violence.

The differences she thinks she sees from her 'opposite' side cause Mrs Slade to rank herself and her marriage far above that of Grace and Horace Ansley, whom she dubs 'two nullities' (12); but it is also stressed that the two women's life stories have been virtually identical. They married, they had children, they 'lived opposite each other', their husbands died; now, 'The similarity of their lot' (13) has brought them back together. Their daughters are repeating or continuing the same old story of girls, in each generation, finding husbands. Within it, there are minor historical variations to do with local conditions and the degree of restraint placed upon the young ladies, but essentially the same one narrative, which is likely to involve rivalry between two girls for the same man. Great-aunt Harriet is the most ancient version of this, and Alida takes it for granted that the same thing is going on between her daughter and Grace's right now.⁴

The lack of individuality that this entails is specified by Grace, in response to Alida's reaction to the mockery of the disappearing daughters:

> 'That's what our daughters think of us!'
> Her companion replied by a deprecating gesture. 'Not of us individually. We must remember that. It's just the collective modern idea of Mothers.' (10)

Later, this suggestion of historical determinations is elaborated and corroborated in Mrs Slade's version of maternal Roman history:

> 'I was just thinking,' she said slowly, 'what different things Rome stands for to each generation of travellers. To our grandmothers, Roman fever; to our mothers, sentimental dangers – how we used to be guarded! – to our daughters, no more dangers than the middle of Main Street.' (15)

What looks like a semi-sociological objectivity in this account becomes less striking when it turns out that Mrs Slade is about to home in on 'the spice of attraction' (16) that drew girls out in their own generation. But still it remains true that both women think back through their mothers, and their foremothers' daughters, just as their focus today is on their own daughters' amorous adventures. This could be seen as further evidence of their subordination to the underlying patriarchal arrangements, in which mothers protect, more or less, and daughters escape, more or less, until the point where they settle down ready to repeat the story in a new updated form a generation later. But it also points to the other feminist perspective through which the female relationships of 'Roman Fever' might be considered.

For it could be said that far from being victims of men, collectively or individually, the women of 'Roman Fever' are the drivers of the plots; it is they, not the husbands or boyfriends, who control what happens. No men appear in the present scene of the story, apart from unidentified waiters of another class and nationality than the protagonists, whose role is no more than to let the ladies sit on through the afternoon. The young Italian men with whom the daughters are spending the day feature only as the presumed objects of the girls' predatory desires: 'if Babs Ansley isn't out to catch that young aviator – the one who's a Marchese – then I don't know anything' (16). In the past time that the conversation brings up, Delphin Slade and Horace Ansley are given purely reactive or passive roles. Delphin goes to the assignation with Grace because he receives her reply to the letter sent in his name. Horace appears in several dual situations with his wife – one of 'those two nullities'; 'two such exemplary characters'; 'just the duplicate of his wife' (12). Here he has no distinctive character and no masculinity of his own; they are two of a dull kind, he second ('duplicate') to her. At one crucial point he is engaged in a doubly passive situation, after Grace's unspecified 'illness' when, according to Alida, 'As soon as you could get out of bed your mother rushed you off to Florence and married you' (22–3). Horace is merely the accessory groomed for a mother's swiftly pragmatic arrangement of a daughter's wedding; in fact he is not even mentioned, so that the marriage appears, syntactically, to take place between mother and daughter alone.

In this second view, it is women who call the shots, even if their sphere of influence remains that of the family and marriage.[5] From generation to generation, what takes place is a female negotiation over men. There is also the suggestion that despite appearances, the primary relationships of women are not with men so much as with one another. Babs and Jenny go around as a pair. Alida and Grace 'had been intimate since childhood' (12). They are introduced at the start of the story as a kind of dual subject:

> From the table at which they had been lunching two American ladies of ripe but well-cared-for middle age moved across the lofty terrace of the Roman restaurant and, leaning on its parapet, looked first at each other, and then down on the outspread glories of the Palatine and the Forum, with the same expression of vague but benevolent approval. (9)

They move as one, they lean as one, and their expression is the 'same' one. 'Mrs Slade and Mrs Ansley had lived opposite each other – actually as well as figuratively – for years': a cohabitation, figuratively if not actually, alongside their marriages. When, prior to the final exchange of secrets, the two fall silent, 'Mrs Ansley was slightly embarrassed by what seemed, after so many years, a new stage in their intimacy' (15). It is crucial, too, that the only declaration of love represented in the story is from woman to woman: the letter to Grace, purportedly from Delphin, that was written by Alida.

Division and rivalry are part of this two-in-one, with the facing Upper East Side windows functioning like mirrors that both separate and join the two women as one and as two, self and image 'opposite'. There are also the metaphorical distorting telescopes through which 'these two ladies visualized each other, each through the wrong end'. 'You think me a monster!' Mrs Slade bursts out after confessing to her writing of the precious love letter; but then a few lines further down, reflecting on Grace's treachery in getting together with her fiancé: 'Wasn't it she who was the monster?' (22). Each woman projects onto the other the features dissociated from herself, or exaggerates the assumed differences that make them so conveniently contrastable and comparable, like their supposedly divergent daughters.

There is a further way in which the primacy of woman-to-woman relationships comes through as a buried possibility in this story. The closing 'I had Barbara' appears, initially, to be dramatic and euphemistic shorthand for 'Your husband was the father of my child'; it is a formally symmetrical riposte to 'I had him for twenty-five years' (24). In the context of what has been said about Barbara's unusual and emphasised '*edge*' and the doubt about 'where she got it, with those two nullities as parents' (12), the line's ultimate reference to paternity seems to explain a minor mystery as well as produce a personal scandal. Everything we have heard up to this point would suggest the likelihood of this other parentage, once it is mooted, while the whole argumentative force of the struggle between the two women seems naturally to come to an end with the decisive reversal.

But what Grace Ansley actually, not figuratively, says is that she had Barbara. She does not say she had sex with Delphin on that night – or that Delphin is Barbara's father. The simple meaning of her statement of motherhood escapes notice, is overlooked, because it is what we and they already know: sure, Grace had Barbara, Barbara is Grace's daughter.

Maternity is never in doubt; paternity has been, throughout the history of human storytelling, the question-generating status. This is what leads us as readers, and presumably Alida Slade as well (no reply is actually given), to interpret Grace's announcement as supplying new information, clinching the story with the utterance of an age-old species of female secret. And to all intents and purposes, it makes no difference whether Grace meant to speak more than her words or not, since the dramatic effect is exactly as if she had: 'She began to move ahead of Mrs Slade toward the stairway' (24) – end of story.

Yet if we look again at the evidence that the closing statement seems to support, it turns out that it too involves elisions. For if Barbara is Delphin's daughter, she remains, surely, Grace's as well. So there is still, in Alida's terms, a problem about how one of 'two such exemplary characters as you and Horace had managed to produce anything quite so dynamic'. Even more strikingly, no doubt is raised at all about the equally anomalous quiet daughter of 'the exceptional couple' (13), the Slades. Dull Jenny has not only come from '*the* Slade' (13), but from a mother known for her 'vividness' (14): more than Babs, she has two inexplicable parents, not just one. While we may go with the rhetorical flow of the final sentences, it does not, on closer inspection, sweep away the kinship questions that the story has explicitly raised (in the case of Babs) and, following the same logic, suggested (in the case of Jenny).[6] The story leads us to accept that a daughter should be 'like' her father or 'like' her parents. The missing connection, between her and her mother, could then be seen as the one surreptitiously supplied by 'I had Barbara'.

It turns out, then, that there may be more to the ambiguity of 'I had Barbara' than a formal point about narrative undecidability. 'I had Barbara', in its lovely literalness, says nothing about a father; instead it matches a desirable daughter against Mrs Slade's boast of having had 'him', that husband or father. There is no second parent in view: in the singular, 'I' had Barbara. In this sense the hidden victory of 'Roman Fever' goes to a same-sex bond, and to the connection of mother and daughter elided and downgraded by paternal kinship relations.[7]

Yet the opposition between the known, literal mother and the inferred and doubtful father may seem, from another point of view, too neat an affirmation of what is itself a classically patriarchal division. '*Pater semper incertus est*', as Freud puts it in his essay 'Family Romances', using the Latin legal phrase; and if the father is always necessarily uncertain, then the mother, at the other extreme, is superlatively certain, '*certissima*'.[8] This is the distinction, Freud argues, that comes to enter into every child's understanding of the relations between the sexes; and it is never abandoned, remaining as the basis of adult thinking.

Freud is individualising a theory put forward by nineteenth-century anthropologists, who saw a crucial and progressive turning point in the move made by primitive cultures from matriarchal to patriarchal thinking; this is how he puts it himself, in *Moses and Monotheism*:

> [I]t came about that the matriarchal social order was succeeded by the patriarchal one – which, of course, involved a revolution in the juridical condition that had so far prevailed. An echo of this revolution seems still to be audible in the *Oresteia* of Aeschylus. But this turning from the mother to the father points in addition to a victory of intellectuality over sensuality – that is, an advance in civilization, since maternity is proved by the evidence of the senses while paternity is a hypothesis, based on an inference and a premiss. Taking sides in this way with a thought-process in preference to a sense perception has proved to be a momentous step.[9]

This vaunted cultural progress comes about because bodily evidence is replaced by intellectual evidence, logically consistent ('based on an inference and a premiss') but necessarily fallible (no DNA testing yet). It seems, at best, a shaky shift, confirming rather than cancelling the fragility of fatherhood as a category.

Read in its connotative sense, as we initially take it, 'I had Barbara' succinctly combines a patriarchal logic ('he's the father') with the maternal self-evidence ('I gave birth to her') that allegedly needs no proof. But it subordinates, as culture does, the obvious, 'sensual' side, within the closing logic of the story and the overt rivalry between the two women. In its maternal rather than paternal emphasis, 'I had Barbara' goes without saying and therefore doesn't *figure*: it is what is already known and is the other available meaning.[10] It is ironically apt, in this context, that the name Barbara originates in the feminine form of the ancient Greek word for the non-Greek, non-civilised 'barbarian' or *barbaros*. The barbarian was named for his (rarely her) incomprehensible language, sounding to Greek ears like a meaningless repetition ('bar . . . bar'); he had no place in the community defined by its *logos*: logic, reason, language. What Grace Ansley 'had' was (in both senses) out of order – a wild child, as yet unassimilated to patriarchal civilisation. Like any baby, but especially like any girl.

There are other tensions concealed in the phrase 'I had Barbara'. To begin with, 'I' is apparently 'I as opposed to you': you had him for all those years, but Barbara is what I had. But there is also, obliquely, a claim to maternal autonomy: 'I' not 'we'. Here both 'fathers' – the likely biological one and the one who raised her – are dismissed from having had Barbara. Only 'I' 'had' her, even if an illicit paternity is also being asserted. But what does it really mean, even for a mother alone, to 'have' Barbara, or to have 'had' Barbara? In this connection the simple statement of maternity opens out into more than one possibility. 'Having' a baby is what women do at the point of birth; it is the specific point of separation. But Grace has also implicitly 'had' Barbara for the twenty-five years that Alida 'had' Delphin; the daughter represents a long-term affective tie, begun but not defined by giving birth. 'I had Barbara' all that time: better than having had 'him', boy baby or husband.

When I first read and reread 'Roman Fever', decades ago, the less obvious because so obvious maternal meaning of 'I had Barbara' seemed to me interesting mainly because of the way it could be used to illustrate a narrative instability even in stories that seemed most tightly stitched together – actually as well as figuratively. 'One, two, three – slip': meaning was never as neatly knitted together, nor destinies and pasts so safely patterned or predictable, as they might appear. In this particular development, orderly in its own consciously dis-ordering fashion, a structuralist analysis such as was found in the earlier writings of Roland Barthes must now give way to a more deconstructive openness to the misfit elements in a text. At that time, in the 1980s, the theoretical emphasis was moving on, now allowing for movement and 'give' in the object of study as well.

A generation on from *that* moment, something else has happened to the solely maternal meaning of 'I had Barbara'. In light of developments occurring elsewhere than in theory, the statement has lost its apparent literal simplicity of contrast to an inferred, assumed and disputable father. Today, single parenthood can be seen and experienced as a positive choice, and many women are adopting children – for the most part daughters – on their own. Seeking to have a child of one's own is a quest that may well be separate from and set above the desire for any other kind of attachment, including to possible co-parents. So Grace Ansley's words acquire a different historical resonance, in relation to subsequent possibilities and patterns of parenthood, or of women having daughters. No 'prophetic flight' of Alida Slade's, fearful or fantastic, could have seen these changes on the horizon; today, they may give Mrs Ansley's closing statement about her past the surprising twenty-first-century gloss of an alternative future.

NOTES

1. Edith Wharton, 'Roman Fever' (1934), in *Roman Fever and Other Stories* (London: Virago, 1983), 10. Further page references will be given within the main text.
2. In another way, the description of Grace's luxurious bag opens up metaphorically onto the silky secret of something soft that must have been 'run through' at different times by two penetrative instruments.
3. 'His Majesty the Baby' appears in Freud, 'On Narcissism: An Introduction' (1914), XIV, 91.
4. In *Roman Fever: Domesticity and Nationalism in Nineteenth-Century American Women's Writing* (Columbus: Ohio State University Press, 2004), Annamaria Formichella Elsden argues that there is a distinct progression for each successive generation of women. Mrs Slade's handling of the waiters is Wharton's suggestion of how far (American) women have come since the nineteenth century. Their daughters' repetition of the old story is only in Mrs Slade's projection; today they are flying high above the 'bad air' of the old dangers of 'Roman Fever' (malaria). 'Even more than their mothers, Barbara and Jenny are able to take command of the foreign environment' (123); 'the accuracy with which Mrs Slade reads the situation and the poise with which she manipulates circumstances indicate her independence and efficacy and allow her to get what she wants' (122). It is certainly true that we are told nothing of Babs and Jenny's actual relations, whether with each other, their mothers or their men – which leaves it entirely possible that there may be real differences from the previous generation. But we do know that it is Mrs Slade's own attempts to 'read' then react to situations, to 'take command' or 'manipulate circumstances', both in the past and during the present conversation, that form the story of her failures.
5. It is here that Wharton's perspective differs markedly from that of an earlier text, *Daisy Miller* (1878). Henry James's story focuses on a contemporary American girl whose incautious behaviour in Rome, including a late-night

visit with a man to the Colosseum, ultimately leads to her contracting Roman fever – malaria – and dying. Daisy is filtered through the perceptions of an observing American man who is fascinated, attracted, judgemental and ultimately critical of his own prejudices. Daisy's point of view is never given; the story is rather concerned with the man's responses to a modern girl who assumes a freedom that ignores the conventions of sensible or respectable conduct. Wharton also uses the idea of Roman fever differently. In a previous generation – the Daisy Miller generation – Great-aunt Harriet's sister did die of it, but what Grace Ansley caught from her Roman night out was pregnancy, initially represented as an illness only in order to conceal it. Within the story, it is historically distanced – 'what different things Rome stands for to each generation of travellers. To our grandmothers, Roman fever . . .'. Malaria had, in fact, ceased to be the real danger it had been in nineteenth-century Rome. But Roman fever's title role makes it also function for Wharton's story like a catch-all, semi-euphemistic diagnosis of wayward sexual behaviour in young American women abroad.

6. My argument here is similar to Jonathan Culler's in relation to *Oedipus the King*. Culler points out that the claim more than once in Sophocles' tragedy that there were 'many murderers' of King Laius, not just one, is never disproved; rather, it is forgotten in the face of the compelling convergence of narratives that leads us, like Oedipus himself, to be convinced that the murderer was him; see 'Story and Discourse in the Analysis of Narrative', in *The Pursuit of Signs: Semiotics, Literature, Deconstruction* (London: Routledge & Kegan Paul, 1981), 169–87.

7. Dale M. Bauer sees equally transgressive implications in the primary interpretation of 'I had Barbara': 'Grace threatens the symbolic order of society by exposing the arbitrary assumption Alida makes about Babs's father, not to mention the assumption about Grace's respectability'; *Edith Wharton's Brave New Politics* (Madison: University of Wisconsin Press, 1994), 160.

8. Freud, 'Family Romances' (1909), SE IX, 239.

9. Freud, *Moses and Monotheism* (1939), SE XXIII, 113–14.

10. See Barbara Johnson, 'Is Female to Male as Ground is to Figure?', in *The Feminist Difference: Literature, Psychoanalysis, Race, and Gender* (Cambridge: Harvard University Press, 1998), 17–36.

Index

abortion, 8
Adams, Heney Foster, 89
adoption, 22–8, 31–44, 45–59, 67
Adoption of Children Act (1926), 58n4
adolescence, 151–2
advertising, 7, 73–8, 83–5, 138, 183–4, 188, 191
Aeschylus, 165n25
   Prometheus Bound, 157
   Suppliant Women, 10, 147–53, 157
afterlives, 204
Amymone, 147, 153–4
Antigone, 148, 151, 156–7, 162n6
Aphrodite, 165n25
Are You Being Served?, 125
Argos (Greece), 147–50, 152–3, 164n14
Argos (mythical character), 150, 157
Argos (shop), 109, 113
Arnold, Matthew, 192
artificial insemination, 18; *see also* sperm donation
asylum seeking, 147–9, 152
Austen, Jane, 7, 75
   Emma, 126–30
   Pride and Prejudice, 9, 60–70, 126

babies as commodities, 23, 138
Bachelard, Gaston, *The Poetics of Space*, 173–5
Bachofen, J. J., 154, 163n13, 165n29
barbers, 126
Barthes, Roland, 100n10, 234
   'From Work to Text', 98
   Mythologies, 87–8, 98
Baudelaire, Charles
   The Painter of Modern Life, 211, 222n11
   'Le tonneau de la haine', 160
   'A une passante', 215
Bauer, Dale M., *Edith Wharton's Brave New Politics*, 236n7
Beauvoir, Simone de, *The Second Sex*, 174–5, 181–2
Beer, Gillian, 169
Benjamin, Walter, 163n9
Bennett, Arnold, 189, 194
   Hilda Lessways, 201–2n9
Bergson, Henri, 173
Berman, Anne, 162n4
Binet, Alfred, 166n32
biography, 203–4, 217
Bloomsbury Group, 197

Bon Marché, 6
Bonner, Campbell, 154, 164n22, 166n35
Bowie, Karen, 200n4
Bowie, Malcolm, 60
Bowlby, Rachel
  Back to the Shops, 12n12
  Carried Away, 7
  Freudian Mythologies, 30n20, 162n2, 166n33
  Just Looking, 6, 7
  'Walking, Women and Writing', 130n4
Brennan, Teresa, 166n34
Brill, A. A., 161n4
British Rail, 188
Brontë, Charlotte, *Jane Eyre*, 194
Brown, Louise, 9
Burney, Fanny, *Evelina*, 123–4
Burns, Wilfred, 125–6
Butler, Judith, *Gender Trouble*, 170–1

Caird, Mona, *The Daughters of Danaus*, 160–1
Camus, Albert, *The Myth of Sisyphus*, 145
Carnegie, Dale, *How to Win Friends and Influence People*, 94
childlessness, 24, 26, 30n16, 45, 50–3
china shops, 122–3, 133
Chodorow, Nancy, *The Reproduction of Mothering*, 28–9n4
choice, 7–9, 16–17, 27, 81, 91, 99, 152, 211
Christ's Hospital, 134
Cixous, Hélène, 1
  La jeune née, 11n
class, 4, 16, 27, 28n3, 61, 74, 76, 102–19, 193, 197, 201n6, 201n7, 216–18
Clément, Catherine, *La jeune née*, 11n1
Cobbett, William, *Rural Rides*, 7, 131–9

Coleridge, Samuel Taylor, 91
Collier, Mary, *The Woman's Labour*, 145
colonisation, 3, 89–90, 171
commodification, 131–9
communications, 183, 189, 191
comparative literature, 6
computers, 183
consumer culture, 5–8, 27, 73–141
consumer psychology, 7–8, 73–6, 79–101
Consumer Reports, 83, 96
contraception, 8–9, 16, 18, 21
Courtivron, Isabelle de, *New French Feminisms*, 11n1
Cowper, William, *The Task*, 120–4, 129
Crete, excavations in, 2
Cretney, Stephen, *Family Law in the Twentieth Century*, 58n4
Culler, Jonathan, 236n6

Danaids, 10, 142–67
'dark continent', 2, 3, 12n7
deconstruction, 6, 169–72, 184–5, 234
DeLillo, Don, *White Noise*, 116
'democracy', 149–50
department stores, 6–7, 81–2, 84, 92–4
Derrida, Jacques, 2, 169–70
Dickens, Charles
  Dombey and Son, 44n4
  Great Expectations, 9, 31–44, 45, 47, 48, 55
Dirmeik, Felicity, 28n1
DNA testing, 18, 27, 233
domestication, 10, 152, 168–87
Duck, Stephen, *The Thresher's Labour* 145

egg donation, 18–19, 25–7, 30n18
Electra, 148, 151
Eliot, George, *Silas Marner*, 9, 45–59

Ellis, Havelock, 166n32
Elsden, Annamaria Formichella, *Roman Fever*, 235n4
Engels, Friedrich, *The Family, Private Property and the State*, 176–7, 181
Euripides
 Ion, 166n35
 Medea, 167n39
 Phoenician Women, 156–7
Evans, Tanya, *Sinners? Scroungers? Saints?*, 44n2
everyday life, 192–3, 203, 210
Ewans, Michael, 163n12, 164n20

family forms, 17–30
Farnham, 104, 109, 113
fashion, 211
faxes, 183
feminism and feminist theory, 1–11, 15–16, 19, 29n5, 147–52, 169–71, 174, 181–6, 188, 229
fertility, 20, 22, 24, 164n15
fish and chip shops, 126
food sources, 131–9
Forster, E. M., 207
fostering, 23, 56–7
Foucault, Michel, 2, 76, 200n4
Franklin, Benjamin, 91
Franklin, Sarah, 27
Freud, 1–4, 6, 10, 21–2, 86, 96–8, 157–8, 173–4
 Minoan-Mycenaean civilisation analogy, 2
 'dark continent' of female sexuality, 2–3
 on sexual difference, 158–9, 228–9
 WORKS:
 'Analysis Terminable and Interminable', 144

 'Case of Female Homosexuality', 22, 30n14
 Delusions and Dreams in Jensen's 'Gradiva', 68, 96
 'Family Romances', 18, 23, 67, 233
 'Female Sexuality', 2
 'Femininity', 2, 4
 The Interpretation of Dreams, 24, 160, 174
 Moses and Monotheism, 233
 'The Psychogenesis of a Case of Homosexuality in a Woman', 22, 30n14
 The Question of Lay Analysis, 3
 Studies in Hysteria, 69, 70n8, 143–4, 160, 161n4
 'The Uncanny', 174
 Three Essays on the Theory of Sexuality, 21
Friedan, Betty, *The Feminine Mystique*, 78
Fry, Roger, 200n5
Furneaux, Holly, *Queer Dickens*, 43n1
furniture selling, 102–4, 132–9

Gallop, Jane, 2
Galsworthy, John, 189
Garvie, A. F., 163n3
generations, 15–30, 106, 211, 230, 234, 235n4
gender, 4–5, 15–16
Ginsberg, Allen, 'A Supermarket in California', 112
Goody, Jack, 172–3
Graves, Robert, 164n22

hairdressing, 125
Hall, Edith, 165n23
Harrison, Jane, 154, 165n30
Heidegger, Martin, 170, 173

Heilmann, Ann, 167n39
Hoggart, Richard, 7, 102–19, 173
Homans, Margaret, *The Imprint of Another Life*, 58–9n5
Homer
  Iliad, 166n35
  Odyssey, 204
Horace, 147, 154–5
hospitality, 152
housework, 145–6, 175–7
Hypermestra, 153–7, 165n25

ICSI, 44n5
Io, 148, 150–3, 157–8
Irigaray, Luce, *Speculum*, 11n1
Ismene, 151
IVF, 8–9, 18–19, 26–8, 29n6
Ixion, 143, 154, 167n35, 167n37

James, Henry
  Daisy Miller, 285–6n5
  What Maisie Knew, 19, 21
James, William, 88
Jarrell, Randall, 'A Sad Heart at the Supermarket', 112
Jefferys, James B., *Retail Trading in Briatin*, 132
Jensen, Wilhelm, *Gradiva*, 96
Johnson, Barbara, 236n10

Keating, Jenny, *A Child for. Keeps*, 58n4
Khanna, Ranjana, *Dark Continent*, 12n7
kinship rules, 150
Kitson, Henry Dexter, *The Mind of the Buyer*, 86–9, 91
Klein, Melanie, 188
Kristeva, Julia, 'Women's Time', 182–3

Lacan, Jacques, 1
  Encore 11n1
Lattimore, Richard, 163n11

Leavis, Q. D., 110–11, 201n6
Leavis, F. R., 98, 110
Leclerc, Annie, *Parole de femme*, 11n1
Le Dœuff, Michèle, 187n27
Leigh, Ruth, *The Human Side of Retail Selling*, 81–2, 84, 92–5
Lembke, Janet, 148
Lévi-Strauss, Claude, 150, 172
Lucretius, *De rerum natura*, 167n37
Lyotard, Jean-François, 200–1n5

McNeillie, Andrew, 200n3
mail order, 108
making up, 84–6, 208–10, 219
malaria, 236n5
marketing, 6, 73–8
Marks, Elaine, *New French Feminisms*, 11n1
marriage, 8, 18, 21, 52, 57–8, 60–70, 147–57, 161, 164n20, 175–7, 181, 201n6, 211, 231
Marshall, Alfred, 96
Marxist theory, 16, 74, 76, 175
masculinity, 148, 199, 229
maternity, 17–18, 24, 151, 232–5
matriarchy, 233
Medea, 148, 167n39
menopause, 29n6
Mill, John Stuart, 178
Miller, Michael B., *The Bon Marché*, 6
Minoan-Mycenaean civilisation, 2
minor characters, 203–4, 207
Mitchell, Juliet, 28n1, 29–30n13
modernism, 189, 192, 197, 203, 210
Moi, Toril, 198–9
Montrelay, Michèle, *L'Ombre et le nom*, 11n1
Morrison, Toni, *The Bluest Eye*, 3–4
mother right [*Mutterrecht*], 154, 163n13, 176–7

Näcke, Paul, 166n32
narcissism, 166n32
Narcissus, 157–8, 166n32
newsagents, 126
Nile, 164n15
Novy, Marianne, *Reading Adoption*, 44n2, 58n2

Oedipus, 158–9, 166n32; *see also* Sophocles, *Oedipus the King*
Oldham, 9
Ovid, 5, 166n32
  Heroides, 154–8
  Metamorphoses, 157–8

parenthood, 15–70, 224–36
passante, 210, 215
Paston, Elizabeth, 222n4
paternity, 17–18, 24, 151, 228, 232–4
patriarchy, 1, 3, 176–7, 197, 229–30
Pavlov, Ivan, 96
Penguin Freud, 1, 3, 12n4, 12n5
Perry, Ruth, *Novel Relations*, 70n5
Pindar, 153
Pitkin, Walter B., *The Consumer*, 82–3
Plato, *Gorgias*, 167n37
Poilino, Marie-Noële, 200n4
Post-Impressionism, 200n5
postmodernism, 200–1n5
Pound, Ezra, *ABC of Reading*, 99–100
pregnancy, 8–9, 16, 18–19, 29n9, 236n5
pronouns, 4–5, 193

race and racism, 3–4, 16, 28n3, 76, 152–3, 162, 165n24, 168
radio, 3, 186n7
realism, 189–90, 196–8, 203, 208, 210
reproductive technologies, 8–9, 16, 18, 21, 27, 30n18, 39, 151

Ribczynski, Witold, *Home*, 180–1
Richardson, Samuel, *Pamela*, 9, 60–70
Rochester, NY, 112
Ruskin, John, 'Of Queens' Gardens', 178–81

salesmanship, 79–101, 103–05, 124
Saussure, Ferdinand de, 188
Schopenhauer, Arthur, *The World as Will and Representation*, 159–60
Seaford, Richard, 151
seeklings, 32–3
sexual difference, 4–5, 15–16, 25–6, 97, 158, 195–6, 199, 228–9
sexuality, 21, 173, 177
Shakespeare, William, 91
shops and shopping, 5–8, 102–19, 120–30, 182
Sinclair, Upton, *The Jungle*, 186–7n9
sisters, 151
Sisyphus, 10, 143–5, 162n6, 167n37
smoking and pregnancy, 29n9
Sophocles
  Antigone, 151
  Electra, 151
  Oedipus at Colonus, 151, 166n35
  Oedipus the King, 9, 22–8, 166n32, 228–9, 236n6
The Spectator, 122
sperm donation, 19–20, 25–7, 30n181
Steele, Richard, 130n3
Steiner, George, 169
Strachey, James, 144–5
structuralism, 234
Stuhr, P. F., 163n10
Sullerot, Evelyne, 145, 162n6
supermarkets, 5, 7, 12n11, 104–5
surrogacy, 18–19, 27, 30n18
Sussex, University of, MA in Critical Theory, 1
sweet shops, 126

table, 132–3, 169, 220
Tantalus, 143, 167n35, 167n37
telephone, 183
television, 183, 188
Thane, Pat, *Sinners? Scroungers? Saints?* 44n2
Thatcher, Margaret, 83, 96
Tityus, 154
tourism, 26–7, 115–17, 229
trains, 188–90, 200n4
translation, 3, 143–6, 185, 199n1, 204
Tredell, Nicholas, 111
Twain, Mark, 91
types, 105, 121, 190, 207

Uglow, Jenny, *The Lunar Men*, 221n2
'unexpected items', 5

Vasunia, Phiroze, 164n15, 164n21
Veblen, Thorstein, 96, 136–7
Virgil, *Aeneid*, 166–7n35, 204

Waterhouse, J. W., 165n29
Watt, Diane, 222n4
Wedgwood, Josiah, 139n8
Weedon, Chris, *Feminist Practice and Poststructuralist Theory*, 76–7
Weguelin, John R., 165n29
Wells, H. G., 189
wet-nursing, 30n19, 138
Wharton, Edith, 'Roman Fever', 11, 224–36

Which?, 7
Wilde, Oscar, *The Picture of Dorian Gray*, 91, 158
Wollstonecraft, Mary, 174
Woman, 78
Women: A Cultural Review, 78
Women's Studies, 16
Woolf, Virginia, 10–11, 188–202, 203–23
  'Byron and Mr Briggs', 200n3
  Jacob's Room, 200n4
  'The Lives of the Obscure', 203–4
  'Mr Bennett and Mrs Brown', 188–202, 208
  Mrs Dalloway, 10, 89–90, 191, 203–23
  'Modern Fiction', 198m 201n7, 209–10
  Orlando, 5
  'The Pastons and Chaucer', 221–2n4
  'Professions for Women', 175
  A Room of One's Own, 194, 198–9
  Three Guineas, 201n6
  To the Lighthouse, 220–1
  'An Unwritten Novel', 200n3
  The Waves, 175
Wordsworth, William, 46–7, 114

Yale University, 6

Zeitlin, Froma I., 163n12, 164n19
Zola, Émile, *Au Bonheur des Dames*, 6

EU representative:
Easy Access System Europe
Mustamäe tee 50, 10621 Tallinn, Estonia
Gpsr.requests@easproject.com

www.ingramcontent.com/pod-product-compliance
Lightning Source LLC
Chambersburg PA
CBHW051120160426
43195CB00014B/2280